Holistic Health

and

Biomedical Medicine

SUNY Series in the Political Economy of Health Care

Ray H. Elling, EDITOR

Holistic Health
and
Biomedical Medicine

A Countersystem Analysis

STEPHEN LYNG

State University of New York Press

Figure 1

"Hierarchy of Natural Systems."
American Journal of Psychiatry,
137:5, 537, 1980. Copyright 1980,
the American Psychiatric Association.
Reprinted by permission.

Published by
State University of New York Press, Albany

For information, address State University of New York
Press, State University Plaza, Albany, N.Y., 12246

Library of Congress Cataloging-in-Publication Data

Lyng. Stephen, 1950–
    Holistic health and biomedical medicine: a countersystem
analysis / Stephen Lyng.
        p.   cm. — (SUNY series in the political economy of health care)
    Bibliography: p.
    Includes index.
    ISBN 0-7914-0255-X. — ISBN 0-7914-0256-8 (pbk.)
    1. Social medicine—United States.   2. Dialectic.   3. Social
sciences—Research.   I. Title.   II. Series.
    RA418.3.U6L96   1990
    306.4'61—dc20   89-11531
                                                                                          CIP

10   9   8   7   6   5   4   3   2   1

FOR RUTHE

Contents

Acknowledgments   xi

Introduction   1

Part I: Dialectical Sociology and the Countersystem Method

Chapter One: The Dialectical Paradigm   9
     The Dialectical Paradigm—The Negation of Positivism   9
     The Philosophy of Internal Relations   14
         Historical Roots   14
         The Core Elements of the Philosophy of Internal
             Relations   15

Chapter Two: The Dialectical Theory of Society—Two
         Approaches   23
     The Scientific Dialectical Perspective   24
     The Praxis Dialectical Perspective   28

Chapter Three: Fundamental Relations of the Social Crystal   37
     The Human Being/Social Structure Relation   37
     Relations Between Elements of the Social System   40
     Relations Between Knowledge and Social Structure   42

Part II: A Countersystem Analysis of Medical Practice

Introduction to Part II   47

Chapter Four: The Medical Model of the Future: The Holistic
         Health Countersystem/Utopia   55

Principle of Organization   55
The Knowledge Dimension: Knowledge Content   64
    The Definition of Health   64
    The Role of Subjective Consciousness in Health
        Production   77
    The Source of Organic Disfunction   81
    Symptoms and Organic Disfunction   86
    Diagnosis of Organic Disfunction   87
    Treatment of Organic Disfunction   89
    Normative Elements   92
The Distribution of Medical Knowledge   93
The Social Structural Dimension   95
    Micro Structure: The Patient-Practitioner Relationship   95
    Macro Structure: The Structure of Medical Practice   96
Conclusions   98

Chapter Five: The Traditional Medical Model   99
The Medical Scientific Paradigm   100
    The Definition of Health   101
    The Role of Subjective Consciousness in Health
        Production   102
    The Nature of Organic Disfunction   104
    Diagnosis of Disease   112
    Response to Disease   113
    Treatment of Disease   115

Chapter Six: The Structural Relations of Health Production 119
The Distribution of Medical Knowledge   119
The Health Production Process   120
Interest Group Structure and the Traditional Medical Model   130
    Medical Practitioners   131
    The Owners of the Industrial Means of Production   135
    The Bureaucratic Imperative   140
Interrelations Between Interest Groups   146
The Principle of Organization   158

Chapter Seven: Diachronic Analysis of Medical Practice   163
The Evolution of Health Status   164
The Evolution of Medical Knowledge   173
    Domestic Medicine   174

The Transition to Heroic Medicine 175
The Revival of Domestic Principles: Thomsonian
    Medicine 179
The Challenge of Homeopathic Medicine 185
The Rise of the Medical Scientific Model 193
The Public Health Model: A New Form of Holism 196
The Historical Evolution of Medical Practice 203

Chapter Eight: Emerging Trends: Back to the Future 221
    Who Will Control the Health Care System of the Future? 231

Chapter Nine: Epilogue 241

Notes 247

References 255

Index 265

Acknowledgments

Although I can claim the ideas contained in this book as my own, they are actually the product of a collective effort by many people who have contributed either psychological or intellectual support to this project. I owe these people a great debt of gratitude for supporting my ambition to pursue critically-oriented scholarship. Intellectual edgework can be an intimidating business—one must have the support of people willing to applaud rather than ridicule the immodesty of such an undertaking if it is to succeed.

I wish to thank Jeff Ferrell and Ken Adams for helping me to formulate my initial ideas on the subject of dialectical sociology and for their contributions to my overall intellectual growth during an important period of my life. I also thank the members of my dissertation committee, David Warner, David Snow, and Joe Feagin, for their helpful criticisms of an earlier version of this study. Special thanks go to Walter Firey who served as the co-chair of my committee and a crucial member of the "Hegel Study Group" along with Anthony Orum, Lester Kurtz, and Nestor Rodriguez. The contributions that these individuals made in helping me to better understand Hegelian thought greatly influenced my thinking on the theoretical issues of concern in this volume. Les Kurtz also provided critical assistance for this project by arranging for financial aid during one phase of the work and by being a supportive colleague. Derek Gill, Kenneth Neubeck and Ray Elling provided insightful comments on several drafts of the manuscript as did several anonymous reviewers. Others who have contributed in various ways to the project include Kenneth Chambler, W. Boyd Littrell, David Franks, Diana Scully, Martha Huggins, Malcolm Willison, Rosalie Robertson, Christine Lynch, Patrick Miederhoff, and Jennifer Johnson. Their contributons are greatly appreciated.

Two individuals deserve special recognition, for without their help, this book would have never been completed. The first is Gideon Sjoberg, who has played many different roles in this project, from co-chair of my dissertation committee to personal counselor to me when my spirits flagged.

His substantive contributions to the conceptual content of this book are too extensive to document but his greatest contribution has been the example of his sociology. His long devotion to realizing the liberating potential of the sociological perspective has served as one of the primary inspiratons for this work.

The second person who has played a key role in this project is Ruth E. Wells Lyng. The many hours of assistance she has contributed to the various stages of the study would be reason enough for her to make some claim on the final product. But this is only a small part of the real contribution she has made. Without her love and her enthusiasm for my ideas, I would have never found the courage to undertake the project. In this sense, the book is as much hers as it is mine.

Introduction

The present volume is an attempt to describe and illustrate a theoretical/ methodological system of social scientific analysis. Although the central concepts of this system have been explicated in varying degrees of depth and clarity for several centuries, my goal is to present, in as clear a fashion as possible, this theoretical system as it looks at this point in the history of intellectual thought. Because of the unique character of this system, the manner in which it is described diverges somewhat from the usual format followed by theoretical treatises. This fact should not, however, distract the reader from the primary point of the book—the explication of the "dialectical" paradigm.

The dialectical approach is presented in its entirety in part I of the book. The first step in the description is a discussion of the philosophical basis of the dialectical perspective. This step is necessary because social theorists often base their models on implicit assumptions that later become the focus of criticism. Hence, for purposes of efficiency, I will discuss the core presuppositions of the dialectical paradigm before the theoretical model is presented. This section of the study relies on the insights of several thinkers who have worked within the tradition of "holism."

After the philosophical groundwork is laid for the dialectical paradigm, I examine an emerging body of work that endeavors to elaborate a form of sociological analysis based on this philosophical system. This body of work, which I designate as the "scientific dialectical" approach, represents an important step in the development of a viable alternative to traditional, positivist sociological analysis but, unfortunately, contains one fundamental flaw. A way of resolving this problem is proposed, and another version of dialectical analysis is elaborated—the "praxis dialectical" approach.

Finally, I conclude this section with an examination of the specific social relations that constitute the social system or "social crystal." The issues discussed include the problems of change and stability in the social realm,

1

the relationship between micro- and macro-level social phenomena, the place of human beings in the ontology and functioning of the social system, the nature of institutional networks, and the relationship between human consciousness and social structure. The main empirical referent for this discussion is modern postindustrial society, although I will have occasion to make references to primitive social organization as well. In general, what is presented in this section is a new scientific metaphor for social reality—the social crystal metaphor.

Because the theoretical/methodological system explicated in this volume rests on premises that differ substantially from the basic presuppositions of modern western culture, many of the ideas discussed here may strike the reader as "counterintuitive." In view of this problem, it seems especially important to provide an illustration of how a specific empirical domain can be analyzed according to the praxis dialectical approach. Part 2 of the study is dedicated to such an illustration. Beginning with chapter 4, I present a dialectical analysis of the U.S. health care system. The set of "relations" that make up the medical sector is examined in accordance with the methodological requirements of dialectical analysis. Each of the different dimensions of the medical sector is treated as a causally interdependent "facet" of the "whole" that is this institutional sector.

The unit of analysis of this study or, to state it in terms of the social crystal metaphor, the facet through which the medical institutional crystal will be examined is the medical knowledge dimension. In choosing to focus on this dimension, I have established as my central goal the task of describing the nature of the relationship between the system of theoretical knowledge we know as "anatomo-clinical theory" and the social structural arrangements that constitute the medical sector. Many different aspects of the health care system could be used as a starting point for the analysis. In accordance with the theoretical system outlined in part 1 of the study, the knowledge dimension is regarded as just one part of an integrated whole, a totality with a unique character that cannot be reduced to any one element, or level, or even to the sum of all of its constituent elements. While all dimensions of social reality determine the nature of the whole, however, the knowledge/social structure relations is regarded as a key "moment" of the social whole. This fact, along with several issues having to do with the substantive focus of the analysis, constitutes a justification for designating medical theory as the starting point for the analysis of the health care sector. These issues are discussed in some detail in the Introduction to part 2.

The structure of part 2 of the study reflects the decision to focus on the knowledge dimension of the medical sector. Because the analysis of the relationship between medical knowledge and structural arrangements in the medical sector involves some special problems, it has been necessary to adopt a unique methodological approach. The problems to which I refer involve the "core assumptions" (also termed "domain assumptions" and "incorrigible propositions") (Gasking 1955, 432) of knowledge systems that have been incorporated into or reflect common-sense knowledge. One of the most important characteristics of the culturally or historically specific assumptions that guide perception is their incorrigibility: those who carry them do not regard them as arbitrary assumptions but as "facts of nature."

This phenomenon makes the analysis of knowledge systems that dominate in one's own society a difficult task. Researchers who attempt to analyze a knowledge system current in their own culture find it difficult, if not impossible, to identify all of the core assumptions of that knowledge system precisely because these assumptions possess a taken-for-granted character. Thus, while analysts may be able to delineate many of the elements of the theory of reality being analyzed, internalization of the cultural *Weltanschauung* renders them incompetent to specify all of the assumptions of the theoretical system under examination.

The experience of ethnographers who study cultures other than their own suggests a method of analysis that may resolve this problem. When one is confronted with a world-view that is radically different from one's own, many of the core assumptions of both cosmologies become apparent. The essential feature of this experience is the clear contrast that it provides: the researcher is exposed to a view of reality that contradicts what s/he believes to be the facts of that reality. Moreover, s/he comes to realize that those who adhere to the alternative perspective regard their point of view to be just as "factual" as the analyst believes his/hers to be. Although cultural anthropologists have at times been ethnocentric in their attitudes toward the cosmologies they study, there has been a growing understanding that the confrontation between one's own world-view and a radically different world-view is not a matter of "factual knowledge" vs. "primitive belief system"; rather, it is merely the clashing of two different cosmologies. Thus, the confrontation of contrasting cosmologies provides an effective means for reassigning certain cosmological elements from the realm of factual knowledge to the realm of "culturally specific knowledge." An important consequence of this shift is that the assumptions upon which these notions are based cease to be "taken-for-granted" and instead become explicit.

In my attempt to identify all of the core assumptions of anatomo-clinical theory, I have adopted a methodological technique that relies on contrast as a way to bring into relief the taken-for-granted elements of this system. The methodological approach, which has been termed "countersystem analysis" (Sjoberg and Cain 1971), is distinctively dialectical in nature. The approach involves contrasting the system under study with a system that in certain respects represents its antithesis. The countersystem is "constructed" through a process of first negating certain features of the initial system and then elaborating a more extensive system on the basis of the negated elements. The countersystem may have no basis in empirical reality or it may correspond to a system that actually exists in empirical reality. In either case, once the researcher establishes a contrast between opposing systems, it is possible to ferret out the taken-for-granted features of the system under study.

In the first chapter of part 2 (chapter 4), I begin the dialectical analysis of the U.S. medical system by elaborating an analytical countersystem to traditional medical theory. This counter medical knowledge system is a constructed type—it is based on the medical perspective that has been developed and promoted by the "holistic health" movement. In accordance with the definition of countersystem, the holistic health paradigm is based on concepts and assumptions about health and illness that negate the anatomo-clinical conceptualizations. Chapter 4 consists of a delineation and explanation of each of these initial concepts and assumptions, as well as the set of related concepts that derive from the logical elaboration of this initial framework. This conceptual system will constitute a medical theoretical countersystem.

In the next chapter, the holistic health countersystem is used as a basis for identifying comparable concepts and assumptions (comparable in the sense that they address the same issues or problems) of the anatomo-clinical paradigm. Some of the elements identified by this method belong to the category of domain assumptions—they are assumptions that members of modern Western culture take as given in nature but which are actually only cosmological constructs used in the production of a culturally specific definition of reality. The delineation of these assumptions makes it possible to provide a detailed description of the anatomo-clinical paradigm, including not only its principal concepts but its philosophical basis as well. These aspects of the paradigm must be identified if we are to have a complete understanding of the interconnections between the medical knowledge system and social structural configurations of the health care system.

Equipped with this description of the anatomo-clinical paradigm, I attempt a dialectical analysis of the medical sector that starts with the knowledge dimension and then traces out its interrelations with other dimensions of the system. The dimensions I focus on include medical economy, bureaucratic organization, professional organization, and legal-legislative arrangements. Through this process of tracing out the various interrelations that constitute the health care system, a reproduction of the crystalline structure of the sector is accomplished. By the time this point is reached, however, the principal features of the crystalline structure as a whole have been identified as characteristics that are manifested in each of the individual facets of the crystal.

Chapter 8 consists of a discussion of some of the recently emerging trends within the medical sector examined in light of the countersystem perspective and the forgoing analysis of health production within the traditional medical model. Here I attempt to describe the various possibilities that exist for the further transformation of the health care system. Special emphasis is given to the possibilities for promoting the institutionalization of the utopian countersystem I describe in this volume.

Part I

Dialectical Sociology and the Countersystem Method

CHAPTER ONE

The Dialectical Paradigm

As I have indicated, the concerns of this study are neither strictly theoretical nor exclusively empirical in nature. Although my primary purpose is to pull together the various strands of an emerging theoretical perspective in the social sciences, I also wish to illustrate the value of this approach for empirical analysis. Thus, I will begin by presenting a systematic and detailed description of a theoretical and methodological approach I call the dialectical paradigm. This will be followed by an analysis of the U.S. health care system according to the principles of the dialectical method.

The dialectical paradigm as a whole is based on assumptions that are direct negations of certain positivist premises. This provides a convenient organizing strategy for presenting the main elements of the dialectical approach. In the process of analyzing the problems and shortcomings of an existing paradigm, an alternative approach is often crystallized, one that holds the promise of resolving the inherent problems of the existing approach by negating some of its basic assumptions. The discussion of the dialectical paradigm will be structured in accordance with this "critical method" of presentation.

THE DIALECTICAL PARADIGM—THE NEGATION OF POSITIVISM

The history of the discipline of sociology has as an overriding theme the constant struggle to shape itself in the image of the "hard sciences." Consequently, most sociological analysis is firmly rooted in an epistemological tradition that relies primarily on the rules of the "logico-deductive method" of positivist science. In the context of the present work, what is most important about this epistemological tradition is its distinctive approach to the process of analytical abstraction. Despite claims to the contrary (cf. Albrow 1974), all forms of scientific analysis (including the dialectical approach) make use of the process of abstraction. But while all analysis

9

depends on abstraction, epistemological traditions often employ very different assumptions about the nature of abstract theoretical categories. A central feature of the positivist epistemology is its reification of the products of the abstraction process (Ball 1979, 787).

Positivist epistemology maintains a clear separation between the world of mind and the world of matter but establishes the possibility for a science of nature by assuming that subjective categories can be made to correspond to elements of objective reality. As a direct consequence of this assumption, the objective world takes on the characteristics of the subjective world; if abstract theoretical entities exactly correspond to what exists in objective reality, then the "elements" of objective reality must possess the same qualities that abstract categories possess.

The assumption of correspondence between the subjective and objective domains creates some important problems. The first is defining the units of analysis: the method of systematic delineation and categorization allows one to produce strictly delimited analytical units; therefore, it is assumed that the objective world also consists of distinct, clearly specifiable units. Hence, an exact correspondence between the abstract, subjective "thing" and the concrete, objective thing can be established. Secondly, since a central goal of scientific analysis is to produce abstract theoretical categories that apply to all times and places, scientists tend to view the objective conditions to which theoretical concepts refer as being stable and unchanging as well. Universal concepts imply universal conditions. Among the few positivists that have been troubled by the obvious discrepancy between this position and the phenomenon of ubiquitous change in the natural and social order, a modified version of the same idea has gained currency—the notion that nothing ever stays the same but change always consists of the re-patterning of stable universal units (Albrow 1974, 184).

Positivist epistemology attempts to deal with more complex objective phenomena by creating equally complex conceptual systems. These are produced by using the rules of formal logic to integrate abstract categories for the production of entire conceptual systems. Like the elements of which they are composed, these conceptual systems are assumed to apply to all times and places, to be universal. Ideally, the system should also be logically closed—every logical implication of all combinations of propositions should be explicitly stated in some other propositions in the same system.

Again, the assumption of correspondence results in the characteristics of abstract conceptual systems being imposed on the objective phenomena to which they refer. Not only are natural systems assumed to be relatively changeless, it is also assumed that the relations between the units of objective reality conform only to the kind prescribed by formal logic—that is every entity must be either a cause or condition of every other entity. This latter assumption has been modified somewhat by "systems theory," which posits that objective entities always exist in a network of relationships with other entities and, therefore, determinant relations assume the form of "reciprocal causation" within systems. While the systems approach does free itself of the limitations associated with the assumption of unidirectional causation, systems theorists have, by and large, ignored the further implications of this modified conception of causation. The idea of "interrelation" (reciprocal causation) implies that the character of the thing or entity changes when its relations change. This idea clearly undermines the positivist assumption that objective reality consists of discrete, well-defined entities. Insofar as systems theory has remained squarely within the positivist camp, it has eschewed this latter notion.

Where the positivist approach becomes more problematic, however, is in dealing with features of objective reality that do not lend themselves to organization by subjective categories. Certain kinds of natural phenomena defy our efforts to impose subjective characteristics upon them. Hence, they often appear to the scientist as anomalies. During the last decade or so, several such anomalies have been identified within the social realm by sociologists attempting to demonstrate the shortcomings of the dominant paradigm in social science.

The most commonly discussed stumbling block for traditional sociological analysis is the phenomenon of social change. Most social scientists recognize the ubiquity of change in all social systems (recognizing also that some social systems undergo more change than others). Despite the widespread awareness of social change, most traditional sociological theories lack a logical basis for dealing with change. Traditional social scientists' efforts to account for "emergence, creation and novelty," and with "the determination of objects over time as they are formed and decay" yield what can best be described as "ad hoc explanations"—explanations that are tacked on to the theoretical system rather than following as a logical implication of the theory's basic premises (Albrow 1974, 185).

Social change is not only inconsistent with the logic of traditional social theories, it also challenges some of the most fundamental epistemological assumptions of these theories. Richard Ball (1979, 782) notes that the "law of identity," which is a principle of formal logic embraced by almost all existing social theories, does not accord with the observation that "an existing thing is never the same from one moment to the next." Theoretical categories are, by design and in their actual usage, much more enduring than the objective phenomena to which they refer. Moreover, the positivist assumption that theoretical concepts have universal applicability fails to take into account a form of social change that derives from scientific enterprise itself. One of the greatest contributions of the sociology of knowledge to general sociological theory is the insight that social scientific knowledge itself becomes an element of the very social system it attempts to explain (Friedrichs 1972, 266). Hence, in the act of generating universal propositions about the social system, scientists destroy any possibility of those propositions having universal applicability.

This phenomenon is at least partially responsible for some additional anomalies confronted by social science. First, there is the problem of prediction. While positivism emphasizes the importance of predictive accuracy, this goal has been rarely achieved in the social realm. Alluding to this problem, Martin Albrow (1974, 197) points to the further implications of Popper's contention that we cannot predict future history for we cannot know today that which we shall know tomorrow:

> This [contention] . . . has a wider set of ramifications than Popper allows and limits the possibility of producing the kind of sociological laws he favors. Any propositions which include reference to states of knowledge (and this does not mean simple scientific knowledge) must be limited in their relevance to just those states and with increments in knowledge cease to be relevant.

The contradiction between the changing nature of social reality and the rigidity of theoretical categories is not the only thing that accounts for the partial and distorted character of those categories. The reification of the units of analysis blinds us to the possibility that the qualities of an objective element change when there is a change in its spatial configuration. Traditional social scientific analysis has been persistently plagued by its inability to develop concepts that apply transituationally. Moreover, the effort to establish clear and distinct theoretical categories in a manner that follows from the either/or logic of the "law of the excluded middle" simply cannot be reconciled with the ambiguities of empirical contextual relationships (Ball 1979, 788). The notion that an empirical thing may reveal features that characterize its opposite in nonsensical if approached from a dualistic epistemological stance. Consequently, positivist social science cannot effectively deal with the phenomena of contradiction, opposition, negation, dilemma, and paradox within the social realm (Schneider 1971).

If the incompatibility of the Aristotelian-Cartesian method of abstraction with time and space variation in empirical content represents one class of phenomena that positivist social science has difficulty dealing with, a second broad category of anomalies derives from the positivist assumption of unidirectional causality. These kinds of anomalies often become most apparent in statistical analysis. For example, in quantitatively based social science (commonly recognized as the most rigorous form of social analysis), radically different theoretical explanations emerge from or are supported by the same set of "hard" quantitative data. This confusion derives, in part, from the feature of quantitative methodology that is widely recognized as one of its most serious limitations: while statistical manipulation can allow us to establish "correlations" between different factors, it cannot tell us anything about the direction of causation. As all introductory statistics texts note, determining the direction of causal arrows is usually a theoretical issue, not an empirical one. But this by no means resolves the issue. Regardless of one's choice of particular causal direction, there will always be empirical support for the opposite choice. This paradox may lead us to question the positivist assumption of unidirectional causation.

A related issue concerns the problem of ranking variables according to their explanatory importance. In quantitative analysis one can determine empirically which variables correlate most highly with the "dependent variable," but the problem of determining the factors that are most important for *explaining* variation in the dependent variable is always a theoretical matter. One has to decide whether "proximate" factors deserve more attention than "ultimate" ones, whether highly correlated independent variables can be regarded as conceptually distinct from the dependent variable or simply artifacts of measurement. Again, issues such as these can be approached in two different ways: they can be left to theoretical discourse and treated as problems that offer no hope of empirical resolution (the traditional approach), or they can be used as a basis for questioning the causal premises of positivist epistemology.

Finally, a third anomaly for positivist social science involves an issue closely associated with the statistical problems just discussed. In the attempt to determine the degree of causal influence of a set of independent variables upon a given dependent variable (through the technique of regression analysis, for example), social statisticians often confront the phenomenon of "interaction effects": several independent variables, when taken together, explain much more of the variation in the dependent variable than the sum of their independent influences. This effect resembles the phenomena that Karl Mannheim termed as principia media, the tendency of critical trends to come together in such a way as to create an entirely new subsystem that has an independent effect on the system as a whole. As Ball (1979, 794) notes, these phenomena indicate that ". . . change is not propelled by analytical variables taken one by one but rather by conjunctions of forces which form new and powerful configurations whose strength is largely a matter of interaction effects."

Such phenomena are problematic for positivist science because they contradict the reductionist premises of this approach. They belong to a class of empirical events that cannot be adequately explained by reducing them to their component parts. Component factors within a relational network constitute a "whole" with features that cannot be predicted by summing up the characteristics of the individual factors taken separately. Thus, the effort to analyze "systemic" or "holistic" phenomena by reducing them to their component parts and identifying the dominant causal influences is an approach that inevitably falls short of the goal of "complete" explanation.

In discussing these anomalies, my goal is not to provide an exhaustive review of problems confronted by the positivist approach, but rather to illustrate the general nature of these problems. I will now attempt to show that these problems disappear when social scientific analysis is structured in accordance with an alternative paradigm, one based on epistemological assumptions that negate some of the assumptions of the positivist paradigm. The following discussion of the philosophical system underlying the alternative paradigm, including a brief look at its historical roots, should lay the groundwork for advancing the primary agenda of this chapter—the description of dialectical social scientific paradigm.

THE PHILOSOPHY OF INTERNAL RELATIONS

Historical Roots

Throughout the history of thought, the development of positivism has been paralleled by the development of an epistemological system that, in many ways, can be regarded as its antithesis. This viewpoint, which has variously been called "holism" (Smuts 1926), "holism of content" (James 1984), and the "philosophy of internal relations" (Ollman 1976), has a history almost as long as that of positivism. The beginning of a philosophy of internal relations can be found in the work of the early Greek philosopher Promenades although it was not until the modern period that this perspective emerged in a systematic and comprehensive form. Spinoza's emphasis on unified nature (God) as the "single substance" of which all material entities, thoughts, social forms, are partial reflections, contrasted sharply with the more popular mechanistic view of each thing as possessing a logically independent character. Spinoza's conception of reality was scorned by his contemporaries and his contribution denigrated even by those who later elaborated these ideas (Russell 1945, 569), but his emphasis on "totality" served to introduce an important philosophical issue into the world of ideas.

Leibniz presented the issue in another form with his concept of the "monad." Although he differed from Spinoza in his preference for emphasizing the parts over the whole, he shared Spinoza's conception of things (monads) as being defined or determined by their relations to other things. Hence, both of these philosophers made a radical departure from existing conceptions of reality by suggesting that things are more than they appear to be. Through its relations to other entities, a thing consists of more than a collection of specific characteristics or qualities; it reflects the larger whole to which it is related.

Although the philosophy of internal relations existed in primordial form in the work of Spinoza and Leibniz, the first systematic examination of the issues raised by these two thinkers was undertaken by G. W. F. Hegel at the beginning of the nineteenth century. Many reformulations and substantive applications of this viewpoint would follow Hegel's initial effort, most notably the work of Marx and Engels, the late nineteenth century philosophers (Bradley, Taylor, McTaggart, Whitehead), the systems theorists and the Gestalt psychologists; but it was Hegel who first outlined a coherent and complete "theory of internal relations." Because of Hegel's central role in the development of this philosophical system, his work will serve as a starting point for the present description of its basic features, although the ideas of other scholars will be included wherever they are pertinent.

The Core Elements of the Philosophy of Internal Relations

A good starting point for a review of the philosophy of internal relations is to consider the conceptualization of the relationship between the whole and its parts within this system. Stated in the simplest terms possible, this approach holds that "the whole is more than the sum of its parts" (Phillips 1976, 6).

This idea finds expression in the Hegelian system in the form of statements about "organically articulated systems." Such systems incorporate many "notions" (or elements of the notion) whose connections with one another are intimate and "organic" in the sense that they are self-contained, their unity indissoluble. In the words of Hegel himself, "the organic being is, in undivided oneness and as a whole, the fundamental fact" (1966, 301). Hence, any attempt to reduce the whole to abstracted units or parts will produce distorted and partial knowledge:

> The essential nature of what is organic, since this is inherently something universal, lies altogether rather in having its moments equally universal in concrete reality, i.e., in having them as permeating processes, and not in giving a copy of the universal in an isolated thing." (Hegel 1966, 310)

In a particularly clear statement of this idea, Hegel writes:

[I]n relating the organic to the different facts of the inorganic, elements, zones, climates, so far as regards law and necessary connexion (sic), observation never gets further than the idea of "great influence." (1966, 327)

Hegel's conception of the whole presents us with an immediate problem however. If, as Hegel claims, the whole is the "fundamental fact," then how can we legitimately speak of "parts" in the first place? If the whole cannot be defined as the sum of its parts, then what can be said about the whole that broadens our understanding of it?

The relationship of the whole and its parts is described in several different ways within this philosophical system. As one scholar notes, the analytical technique of breaking the whole into its component parts ignores the importance to the system of the interrelations among parts (Weiss 1967, 802) and the way the "particular structure" of the whole influences our conception of the parts. A visual analogy can be helpful in developing an alternative conception of the relationship of the whole and its parts.

Representing the whole as a "hologram," is an alternative to the "parts and their interrelations" view of divisions within the whole. Careful examination of the hologram reveals a structure consisting of many distinct but related facets. The idea of facet differs from the notion of part in one important way: a facet can never be logically independent of the whole or the other units of the whole. Each facet is but one unique aspect or side of the whole; when one peers into a particular facet, the whole can be seen in its entirety, albeit a view of the whole that differs from the view seen from any other facet. Hence, the idea of removing a single facet from the whole is manifestly absurd because it is impossible to know where one facet ends and another begins. The structure of the hologram is such that we can always distinguish its individual facets but we can never separate them from the whole of which they are a part.

The hologram analogy helps to identify another feature of the relationship between a whole and its parts. While the whole is more than the sum of its parts, it is also true that "the whole determines the nature of the parts" (Phillips 1976, 6). In other words, each individual facet of a hologram reflects the whole in its totality. These ideas suggest a new conception of "identity." While an identity between two things is typically thought of in terms of mathematical equality $(1 = 1)$, relational equality involves a form of identity "where the entity in question is considered identical with the whole that is relationally expressed" (Ollman 1976, 32). Relational equality or identity between the whole and each of its parts has been one of the central theoretical concerns of many scholars working in the holist tradition. For example, Hegel's project has been described as an effort to analyze the abstract notions by which we make sense of organic reality, a plurality of categories that "form a system so organically connect that any one category involves all the others, and can be clearly interpreted only in light of the entire system. Each mirrors the whole system in itself" (Baille in Hegel 1966, 49).

Another scholar who embraced the holist orientation was Karl Marx. In his analysis of economy and society, Marx makes repeated reference to economic categories as "abstract, one-sided relation[s] of an already given concrete and living aggregate" (1904, 294). It was the Marxist philosopher, Joseph Dietzgen, however that presented the clearest statement of this idea, noting that the qualities by which we know a certain entity to exist are simply its relations to the other elements of the whole of which it is a part. In his own words, "any thing that is torn out of its contextual relations ceases to exist" (1928, 96). Hence, in order to understand the nature of any one part, we must also understand the nature of the whole.

One implication of the idea that the whole is reflected in each of the parts has become a core element of the holist tradition. An application of these ideas to the domain of "consciousness" suggests that mental constructs be treated as parts of the whole of social life. Despite Hegel's designation as an idealist, the logic of his system forces us to consider ideas as individual facets of the social whole. Consequently, one can find numerous references in his work to the "facet-like" character of theoretical concepts:

> For since *itself* maintains *itself* in relation to another, it is just that kind of natural existence in which *nature reflects itself into the notion,* and the moments of necessity separated out—a cause and effect, an active and a passive—are here brought together as combined into a single unity. (1966, 296, emphasis added)

As Hegel suggests, concepts are not *a priori* categories that can be applied to certain aspects of reality; they are not entities generated in a social vacuum to correspond to elements of an objective reality. Theoretical concepts and categories exist in an intimate relationship with the social conditions of their existence. They are components of the society itself, facets of the social whole that, by necessity, reflect the whole in its totality. As Marx notes in his analysis of the prevailing theories and belief systems of capitalist society, bourgeois categories and concepts are not simply devices for describing capitalist society; they constitute specific forms, manifestations or aspects of their own subject matter (1904, 294). In contrast to the scientist's belief in the nomothetic character of theoretical concepts, this perspective emphasizes the cultural and historical specificity of all concepts.

Following these ideas is a third element of the philosophy of internal relations—the notion that "the parts cannot be understood if considered in isolation from the whole" (Phillips 1976, 6). We have seen that the individual parts or facets of a whole reflect the whole in its entirety, assuming that the part is allowed to remain integrated within the whole. However, when a part is individuated from the whole through the process of analytical abstraction (or through the simple act of perception) the thing produced constitutes only a partial representation of the unabstracted part; the part abstracted cannot be equated to the part unabstracted. In Hegel's view, human cognition, by its very nature, involves the arbitrary abstraction of a part from its whole. Despite the indeterminate character of the organic whole, "observing consciousness" inevitably perceives it as "moments in the form of existence and duration" (1966, 300). We make sense of the world around us by breaking down "formless multiplicity" into distinct, but partial, categories and their causal connections. Consequently human cognition renders, at best, only partial knowledge about objective reality.

Each of the terms Hegel uses to represent the idea of abstracted parts, i.e., "determinations," "moments," "phenomena," etc., suggests something partial and unfinished. In the common-sense view, these things come to be seen as the elements of an objective system, which is nothing more than the total summation of these components. For this reason, the partial character of each moment goes unrecognized. The partiality of individuated things may contribute to the ambiguity that often arises about the direction of causation in a set of related factors or it may help explain the existence of residual categories in nominal systems. Hegel enjoins us to avoid accepting abstract categories uncritically and, in the words of his follower F. H. Bradley, to realize that conceptualization is "the violent abstraction of one aspect from the rest, and mere confinement of our attention to a single side of things, a fiction which . . . takes a ghost for solid reality" (1920, 14).

Hegel addresses a related issue by noting that any aspect of reality "can be selected equally right [or] equally wrong, to stand as representative of the entire other aspect; one as well as the other would merely 'represent' or stand for the essential reality (Wesen), but would not actually be the fact (Sache) itself" (1966, 321). This statement calls attention to the arbitrary nature of the determinations with which the human mind organizes objective reality. Hegel argues that the notions of difference and identity, of dichotomy and distinction, and the like, belong to the domain of human consciousness and are not inherent features of organic reality. "Organic existence is this absolutely fluid condition wherein determinations, which would only put it in relation to an other, is dissolved" (Hegel 1966, 293). The indeterminate and fluid character of organic reality is not captured by the categories of human consciousness.

As Bradley points out, such distinctions as "primary and secondary qualities," and "substantive and adjective features" arise and are assigned great importance only through the inevitable and necessary connection of the objective and subjective domains (1920, 16). Although human beings believe these distinctions to be given in objective reality, they actually exist as arbitrary determinations. Bradley posits that anything we take to be a primary quality or core feature of a particular phenomenon cannot be distinguished from a quality that is viewed as secondary (1920, 14). Moreover, he concludes that despite the central place of "facts" in scientific discourse, they are more ephemeral than usually supposed; the facts of every historical period are actually mere "appearances" (1920, 21).

The partial and arbitrary character of mental categories suggests the need for a more thorough examination of the relationship between subjective perception and objective reality. Determining the exact nature of this relationship has always been a concern of scholars working within this intellectual tradition. For example, Althusser (1965) deals with this problem by dispensing entirely with the "subject" as the ontological source of knowledge categories. Dietzgen, writing decades before Althusser, confronted a similar dilemma, an issue that has been called "the problem of individuation." This issue involves the following concerns: does the conception of reality as a unified whole preclude the existence of those separate structures or parts in which we see this unity? If not, how do we decide which units of the whole to treat as parts since the number of ways of dividing up the whole is endless (Dietzgen 1928, 103). Dietzgen answers these questions by positing the existence of "common qualities" or "like characteristics" among the elements of external reality. He believes that perceptual categories are relative and unstable but that within "sensual reality" we can identify broad similarities from which we can make generalizations (Dietzgen 1928, 119). Ollman (1976, 39) summarizes this position in the following way:

> If individuation is not an arbitrary act but one governed by broad similarities existing in nature itself, there is a necessary, if vague, correlation between such natural similarities and the structures conveyed by our concepts.

An objective reality, consisting of like characteristics, does exist but "conceptual activity of human thought is responsible for the precise forms in which we grasp the world" (Ollman 1976, 39).

Dietzgen's notion of common qualities in nature as a resolution of the problem of individuation is difficult to accept because the process of distinguishing like characteristics is not unlike the process of distinguishing parts of the social whole. Neither of the two concepts can be reconciled with the characterization of external reality as "formless multiplicity," relative, transient, and fluid. A different way of resolving this problem can perhaps be found in considering another holist proposition, the notion that "the parts are dynamically interdependent or interpenetrating" (Phillips 1976, 6). Central to this idea is the concept of *relation,* which may serve as a more useful conceptual device for capturing the essential nature of reality than the terms entities, things, or parts.

In considering the distinction between parts and their interrelations, one may ask, Where does one part end and another, to which it is related, begin? Moreover, is it possible that a change in the relations of a part means a change in the part itself? These empirical queries have prompted several scholars to suggest that we conceptualize a thing's "qualities" as its relations to other things. Dietzgen (1928, 96) was one of the first to argue that the existence of a particular thing is revealed by its qualities, which he defined as "its relations to other things." Perhaps the most explicit expression of this idea though is Bradley's conceptualization. Time and time again, he affirms that qualities cannot exist without relations: "Relations presupposes quality, and quality relation. Each can be something neither together with, nor apart from, the other; . . . Qualities are nothing without relations" (Bradley 1928, 21).

The equation of qualities and relations allows us to dispense completely with the term *thing* and explore the usefulness of conceiving of the basic units of reality in terms of Relations[1]. By taking this step, we can dispense with many of the problems associated with thinking of reality as an aggregate of things (which are defined by their qualities). While the notion of a thing involves the ideas of distinct boundaries, stability and endurance, the notion of a Relation suggests interconnectedness, instability, and dynamism. The former concept is most appropriate to the idea of system while the latter is essential to our conception of the whole or the crystal.

One of the best descriptions of the concept of Relation can be found in Bertell Ollman's (1976) analysis of the Marxian theory of alienation. Ollman defines a Relation as a given factor and its relations to other factors. Relations are viewed as "containing in themselves, as integral elements of what they are, those parts with which we tend to see them externally tied" (Ollman 1976, 14). In contrast to the systems approach, which assumes that system components are externally tied to one another, this perspective holds that relations are internal to each factor (hence, its designation as the theory of internal relations). External relations are contingent while internal relations are *necessary.*

The latter distinction is essential to our understanding of the philosophy of internal relations. Systems theory assumes that social wholes consist of components that exist in dynamic interrelation with one another, and while in actual practice separation of a given component from its relations to other elements may be impossible, "components" are not considered to be the same (logically speaking) as relations. Within the philosophy of internal relations, however, relations are ontological rather than logical; the interdependence of components is interior to each component itself (Ollman 1976, 26). In treating a Relation as the irreducible minimum of all units of our conception of social reality, the intention is not to reify the idea of "togetherness" or "connection"; rather, it is to show that this basic unit of analysis can be "extended to cover what is related, so that either term [thing and relation] may be taken to express both in their peculiar connection" (Ollman 1976, 26).

The notion of Relation can be used to deal with a number of paradoxical phenomena. First, it resolves much of the confusion over "causes" and "conditions." Instead of viewing both terms as opposing ends of a dichotomy (what is not a cause is a condition and vice versa), the relational view "finds as internally related parts of whatever is said to be the cause or determining agent everything that is said to be a condition, and vice verse" (Ollman 1976, 17). Thus, the concept of "internal relations" incorporates the form of causality suggested by the terms *mutual interaction* or *reciprocal effect*.

The idea of Relation can be applied to a second paradox, one that was of particular interest to Hegel. He variously noted the difficulty that traditional knowledge systems have with the phenomenon of the "interpenetration of opposites." Observation and the development of knowledge is continually confounded by one basic feature of organic reality—the fact that "what is determined must by its very nature get lost in its opposite" (Hegel 1966, 288). As long as organic wholes are broken down into stable and distinct categories, human observers will confront a world in which things possess characteristics that directly oppose the features that are taken as their "defining" characteristics. Despite common-sense beliefs to the contrary, entities never exist as "either one thing or another." As Hegel (1966, 311) states, organic reality involves "the relation of those opposites . . . and this relation is a pure process of transition."

While the relation of opposites challenges mechanistic assumptions about the nature of reality, this phenomenon is entirely consistent with the relational viewpoint. Conceptualization of a particular entity as existing in "internal relation" with other entities enjoins us to always treat the entity as an element in a network of identical and opposing elements (cf. Bradley 1928, 17). Hence, with the notion of Relation as our basic concept, the connection of opposites need not be seen as a paradox but as an inevitable feature of organic reality.

A final example of a paradox that disappears when interpreted in terms of a Relation is the "transformation of quality into quantity." A Relation can be thought of as a network of *continua* between several subjectively defined terms. If we focus exclusively on the terms and ignore the continuous nature of the Relation, then the network will be manifested as two or more nexus of similar and/or different qualities. If, by contrast, we break the Relation down into arbitrarily defined categories specified according to quantitative additions or subtractions along the continuum, then what we initially regarded as a qualitative distinction becomes transformed into incremental changes in quantity. This relationship, which can be expressed as the law of transformation of quality into quantity, is specifically addressed by Hegel (1966, 305):

> But when . . . they [two terms] are also set down as different, qua existent and for thought, as they might be if made aspects of the law, then they appear quantitatively distinct. Their peculiar qualitative opposition thus passes into quantity.

While I have touched on only a few of the main elements of the philosophy of internal relations, the preceding discussion provides a general introduction to the epistemological system that undergirds the dialectical paradigm. This epistemological framework is "anti-positivist" in the literal sense of the word: its central premises directly negate the basic premises of the positivist framework. The tactic of negating these positivist assumptions reflects a desire to provide an effective way of dealing with the anomalies that confront traditional social science. Having reviewed the philosophy of internal relations, I now wish to discuss ways of elaborating theoretical and methodological principles of sociological analysis based on this epistemological position. In the section that follows, I describe two such theoretical/methodological systems.

CHAPTER TWO

The Dialectical Theory of Society—Two Approaches

A review of existing literature on the subject of "dialectical sociology" reveals two distinct theoretical frameworks—both firmly rooted in the philosophy of internal relations. To date, the only scholar who has made explicit reference to these two separate lines of thought has been Richard Appelbaum (1978). He argues that the recent attempt by American sociologists to elaborate a dialectical framework has been, for the most part, a misguided enterprise. Starting from the premise that Marxian theory constitutes a systematic and complete dialectical theory of society, he maintains that these sociologists have abstracted from the Marxian framework only those elements that can be used to "correct" the obvious deficiencies of functionalist theory and have left untouched Marxian concepts that challenge the basic assumptions of functionalism. Appelbaum regards this trend as particularly unfortunate because he sees these latter concepts as the more important features of dialectical theory—they constitute the "heart" of the dialectical sociological method of analysis.

Appelbaum thus designates two dialectical approaches: the "formalist" and Marxian frameworks. The former emphasizes the "heuristic principles" of holism, conflict, and dynamic equilibrium while the most salient feature of the second approach is the fact that it "attempts to straddle the methodological schism between the idiographic and nomothetic approaches to social phenomena" (Appelbaum 1978, 74). He chooses not to distinguish between this latter system as a general dialectical framework and its more specific expression in the form of Marxian theory. In his view, nothing can be gained from abstracting any of the more general dialectical principles from the Marxian system, whether they be the principles that the formalists find useful or those that they choose to ignore.

Appelbaum's characterization of the past work in this area serves as a useful starting point for the present description of the dialectical sociological paradigm. Following this analysis, I will discuss both of the dialectical traditions Appelbaum distinguishes although I will characterize each tradition in a somewhat different way than he does. The divergence from Appelbaum's approach reflects two basic concerns. First, I believe that both approaches should be described in formal terms for reasons that are discussed below. Secondly, while it is possible to distinguish between the two approaches in terms of Appelbaum's criteria, I believe that they *must* be integrated if we are to have a complete and comprehensive dialectical theory of society. Again, the reasons for this claim will be made clear as the discussion proceeds.

THE SCIENTIFIC DIALECTICAL PERSPECTIVE

Directing attention to Appelbaum's formalist perspective, we must first dispense with the term *formalist* as a label for this perspective. Because I have elected to express both dialectical viewpoints in "formal" terms, this category cannot be used in distinguishing the two approaches. Thus, I have chosen for the first line of thought the term *scientific dialectics,* which, for reasons that will become apparent, clearly distinguishes it from its counterpart, the "praxis" orientation.

One of the important insights of the scientific dialectical approach is the essential similarity it finds in the categories of positivist social science and those of common-sense knowledge (Ball 1979, 787). This similarity derives from the fact that the methods of analysis used in positivist social science are, in some ways, indistinguishable from the methods by which common-sense knowledge is generated. In the common-sense understanding of reality, a thing is what it is called; it can be nothing else (Berger and Luckman 1966). In other words, common-sense actors implicitly assume that the subjective terms used to talk about reality are exactly identical to the objective elements that constitute that reality. Moreover, this assumed identity between subjective and objective reality leads to the related assumption that these two dimensions share the same basic qualities: both consist of clearly definable "units," which exhibit the characteristics of stability and persistence. The phylogenetic relevance of this latter assumption is not difficult to appreciate. For a species that relies on rational decision-making in dealing with its environment, it is crucially important that the environment exhibit the stability needed for the effective use of strategies that rely on a means/end kind of logic; the establishment of goals and the selection of the appropriate means for achieving those goals can occur only in an environment in which the things one deals with lend themselves to unambiguous definition and do not change from moment to moment.

As indicated in a previous section, the positivist approach to sociological analysis is also rooted in the presupposition that the subjective categories and objective elements can be made to exactly correspond. Thus, while social scientists tend to see a basic distinction between their explanations and those of common-sense actors, both forms of knowledge rest on a dualistic conception of the subject/object relationship and, therefore, are subject to the same kind of criticism. As Albrow (1974, 187) notes, sociology's preoccupation with stability does not result, in the first instance, from the dominance of a conservatively oriented functionalism; rather, it follows from the dualistic assumptions inherent in a "natural science of society." Consequently, the assumed stability of the objective social world is the basis of a "vital parallelism between scientific and common sensical views of the world" (Albrow 1974, 187).

This insight concerning the relationship between common-sense knowledge and social science has a number of important implications. If the fundamental similarity between these two kinds of knowledge can be attributed to their common method of abstraction, then the only way that social scientists can hope to produce more advanced forms of knowledge is to develop distinctively scientific methods of analysis. The new methodology should consist of techniques that allow researchers to transcend the dialectical opposition between subjective conceptualization and objective conditions. The analysis must employ a method of subjective conceptualization that captures the organic, indeterminant nature of objective social reality.

The development of this new methodology is the primary focus of the orientation identified here as the "scientific dialectical" perspective. In search of new paradigmatic principles, scholars working within this tradition have looked to the philosophy of internal relations for alternative epistemological assumptions upon which to base this new approach. As demonstrated in the first part of this chapter, the principle methodological implication of the philosophy of internal relations is the notion that the irreducible unit of analysis must be the Relation rather than the "entity" or the part. Scientific dialecticians have organized their new methodology around this basic idea.

Analyzing social phenomena in terms of Relations is no simple matter. Consequently, most of the work that falls into the category of "scientific dialectical sociology" has consisted of studies that deal with a limited range of problems. Moreover, not every scholar who has contributed to the development of this approach has been consciously committed to elaborating a relational methodology. The initial efforts in this area were primarily concerned with correcting the deficiencies of functional analysis and, therefore, borrowed elements of the relational approach to resolve theoretical problems. For example, in one of the first systematic attempts to establish the sociological relevance of the dialectic, Schneider (1971) focused only on the aspects of this notion that bear on the issues of irrationality, disequilibrium, conflict, and change—phenomena that have presented problems for functionalist analysis.

More recent work in this area has been more explicitly oriented toward methodological issues. Here we find a growing interest in developing a method of conceptualization that takes into account the ubiquity of change in the social realm. Albrow argues that sociologists should shift their attention from the search for the permanent units of the social system to phenomena such as "emergence, creation and novelty" or "the determination of objects over time as they are formed and decay" (1974, 195, 193). Such a shift requires a methodological approach that "carries within itself the constant search for renewal and also, necessarily, the destruction of language [and] of theory" (1974, 195). Obviously, this kind of approach cannot conform exclusively to either nomothetic or idiographic principles but must be a combination of both kinds of analysis (Albrow 1974, 198).

In a much more comprehensive and detailed treatment of the scientific dialectical position, Ball (1979) elaborates these ideas in some new directions. He suggests that one of the most fundamental features of dialectical sociology is the theoretical/methodological principle of "expression." The principle of expression contrasts with the taxonomic mode of logic (characteristic of both causal and logical analysis) by emphasizing the need for a holistic form of analysis (1979, 787). All analysis requires that parts be distinguished, but the principle of expression proposes that this be done in a way that reveals how each part expresses the whole to which it belongs. Such an approach to the parts/whole relationship has further implications for how one conceptualizes the relationship between parts. Consistent with the earlier discussion of Relations, Ball suggests that we think of the elements of a social system as "expressing" one another rather than existing in some causal relationship (1979, 789). This conception serves as a logical justification for some alternative methodological strategies. For example, if one accepts that all elements of a social system or subsystem constitute mutually constitutive expressions of the whole, then one's methodological task is ". . . to find the principle by which the various aspects are arranged" (Ball 1979, 789). On a micro-sociological level, the verification of relationships in which one has affirmed the opposite or reversed subjects and predicates may yield important insights (Ball, 1979, 788). Such strategies can serve to illustrate empirically the dialectical notion of "the relational identity of elements."

This brief outline of the "scientific dialectical method" should indicate the basic nature of the approach. The method strives for a "transcendent" logic or grammar (Friedrichs 1972; Ball 1979) that allows researchers to deal with the indeterminant nature of objective social reality. The elaboration of this perspective seems to create a new opportunity for social scientists to achieve the traditional goal of "scientifically valid" knowledge. If this orientation is subjected to more careful scrutiny, however, we find that the optimism is not entirely justified. The basic flaw in this line of reasoning involves, once again, the issue of the relation between subject and object. Initially, a dialectical conception of this relationship served as a basis for rejecting the epistemological claims of traditional social science: because the subjective and objective dimensions are inherently opposed, exact correspondence of the two realms is logically impossible. The very nature of subjective perception and conceptualization, it was argued, insures that the totality of objective existence can never be captured with our subjective categories; and considering the nature of objective reality, an understanding of the "totality" is crucial for understanding any one aspect of that social whole.

While the dialectical conception of the subject/object relationship occupies center stage in the critique of positivist social science, it recedes from view in discussions of the potential that resides in the dialectical method for achieving scientific ideals. A modified approach to the subject/object relation emerges when scientific dialecticians assess the promise of their own method. What was initially conceived as a fundamental opposition between two poles of a dialectical relation now becomes an opposition that is manifested only when certain kinds of subjective conceptualization are undertaken. The "opposed and necessary" quality of the relationship is not something that applies to the subject/object relation in general—it is specific to the common sensical and positivist social scientific methods of conceptualization. Adherents to the scientific dialectical approach posit that when a "transcendent" method of conceptualization is adopted, the opposed character of the subject/object relation disappears, exact correspondence between the two realms becomes a real possibility, and, most importantly, social science has a rightful claim to the exalted status of "valid" knowledge.

The contradiction in this approach is clearly revealed: the perspective cannot support its claims to scientific status (as science is traditionally defined) and also maintain a consistent conception of the subject/object relation. When scientific dialecticians shift the focus of their analysis from entities or elements to Relations, they continue to conduct their analyses in terms of spatially and temporally delimited units: conceptualizing the social world in terms of Relations does not free one of the need to arbitrarily cut off various connections between the unit of analysis and other facets of the broader interrelated structure. This process of delimitation clearly violates the organic character of the objective conditions under analysis. Precisely this kind of violation was the basis of the dialectical critique of traditional social scientific methods.

While scientific dialecticians have succeeded in developing a truly unique method of analysis, their attempt to reorganize social science in accordance with the scientific dialectical orientation does not constitute a satisfactory resolution of the epistemological problem discussed at the beginning of this section. In their zeal to protect the special status of social scientific knowledge, dialecticians have created an approach that suffers from the same basic shortcomings as the system they criticize. The failure of the scientific dialectical perspective to resolve this problem forces us to consider another theoretical/methodological alternative. The praxis dialectical perspective is the approach that I believe holds the greatest promise for addressing these difficulties.

THE PRAXIS DIALECTICAL PERSPECTIVE

The scientific dialectical approach criticizes traditional social science on epistemological grounds by rejecting the positivist presuppositions that make it possible to claim that social scientific knowledge is valid knowledge. In contrast to this approach, the praxis orientation moves beyond the epistemological dimensions to consider these issues from a sociology of knowledge perspective. According to this viewpoint, the epistemological and/or methodological problems of social scientific analysis are much less important than identifying the social functions or consequences of social scientific research (both in its present form and in terms of future possibilities).

At the level of basic premises, the praxis dialectical perspective is indistinguishable from the scientific perspective. Both orientations begin by considering the implications of the dialectical conception of the subject/object relation for social science research methods. Beyond this common concern, however, the two dialectical perspectives diverge. In contrast to the scientific dialectical approach, the praxis orientation holds that the opposition between subject and object cannot be transcended by simply making use of alternative methods of abstraction. An exact correspondence between the subjective and objective realms simply cannot be accomplished under *any* set of methodological standards. Consequently praxis dialecticians seek to apply the dialectical conception of the subject/object relation consistently: as a fundamental assumption of the praxis perspective, this conception is not to be compromised for any reason, not even to protect the legitimacy of the idea of a "science of society." In adopting this position, the dialectician's critical focus is pushed past methodological issues to a consideration of a more basic issue—the problem of the proper role of social scientific inquiry in modern society. The detailed critique of traditional social science in terms of the functions it fulfills is the starting point for elaborating the praxis perspective.

In discussing the scientific dialectical orientation, we saw that the recognition of a fundamental similarity between traditional social science and common-sense knowledge—the fact that social scientists and common-sense actors make use of the same method of abstraction—constituted a crucial step in the development of this viewpoint. Likewise, an important step in the development of the praxis orientation is the recognition of another basic similarity between traditional social science and common-sense knowledge, a similarity in some of the social functions fulfilled by each type of knowledge.

The nature of these functions can be discovered by considering, once again, the phylogenetic relevance of the dialectical relationship between the realm of subjective conceptualization and objective social conditions. Human survival strategies based on "rational action" require that the environment be cognitively stabilized. One mechanism that fulfills this function is the process of "typification" (Schutz 1962). The human species possesses a unique ability to cognitively organize reality into "typical" categories, categories of phenomena that share certain basic qualities. An especially important aspect of this ability is the tendency to treat typifications as clearly delimited things. In doing so, it become possible to deal with these things in a rational manner: ends and means can be clearly defined and relations between them easily established.

An equally important function of the typification process is the part it plays in creating the possibility of meaningful interaction between social actors. People interact with one another on the basis of a shared understanding of the environment (a common definition of the situation), and this common understanding can be achieved only if the environment can be assumed to remain relatively stable. If people responded to the constant change in the objective conditions by continually re-establishing the meaning of existing terms or by creating new terms to correspond to new conditions, then communication and collective action would become difficult if not impossible. The practice of dissecting objective reality into typical categories and treating these categories of things as clearly defined, stable entities greatly simplifies the communication process.

This phylogenetic explanation of the typification process can be easily extrapolated to explain the function of common-sense knowledge systems viewed at the macro level. If typification is viewed as a process that imbues objective reality with the stability needed for rational action and effective communication in micro-social settings, then it follows that complex systems of typifications (i.e., conceptual systems) function to "give form" to all aspects of a complex objective reality. Moreover, considering the basic similarity between common-sense knowledge and social science with respect to ontological assumptions and methods of abstraction, we may also conclude that social science fulfills essentially the same function as common-sense knowledge—that is, to lend subjective form to *existing* social conditions (or, more correctly, previously existing conditions). This is not a claim that there are no differences in the nature of the subjective formulations in social science as opposed to common-sense knowledge. Without question, the greater logical and methodological rigor of social science leads to subjective formulations that manifest a much higher degree of "validity" than common-sense formulations. However, since complete validity can never be accomplished in subjective formulation, this difference cannot become the basis of a difference in the basic function of the two forms of knowing.

Understanding the function of social science in these terms allows us to consider further some of the social consequences of this process. As the sociology of knowledge teaches, a focus on explaining the existing order leads to the incorporation of certain taken-for-granted assumptions about the nature of human nature and of social reality into one's explanatory framework. Typically, these assumptions reflect the analyst's location within a historically specific interest structure. Just as some interests dominate over others within the social order, some ideologically based assumptions about human nature and the nature of social reality dominate over other possible assumptions. This means that many of the common-sense taken-for-granted assumptions that social scientists uncritically accept are assumptions that support the interests of dominant social groups. The classic example of this phenomenon can be found in Marx's treatment of "commodity fetishism" (1938) in which he demonstrates how historically and ideologically specific common-sense assumptions about the value of material objects became incorporated into classical economic theory. This exemplifies the more general tendency of social scientists to explain social phenomena in terms that do not challenge the existing interest structure. In providing subjective expression to existing conditions, traditional social science functions to lend scientific legitimacy to the dominance of ruling groups in society.

This consequence can also be examined in terms of the inevitable partiality of social scientific knowledge. Because objective social reality is constantly changing, every effort to conceptualize this changing reality will yield, at best, partial knowledge: the moment we conceptualize a set of objective conditions, those conditions change, if only because our knowledge of the conditions immediately becomes an element of the very system we are analyzing. A social science exclusively dedicated to explaining "what is" in actual fact does not explain existing conditions at all; rather, it explains what has already taken place.

The partial character of social scientific explanation leads to a further consequence. Insofar as social scientific formulations influence the thinking and action of social actors seeking to solve problems (both inside and outside of the policy arena), the partial nature of these formulations typically gives rise to nonrational strategies. The reductionist thrust of social scientific explanations tends to draw attention away from the many different factors that are causally important within the social whole and ultimately works to delimit the social actor's strategic alternatives for exercising control over his or her social environment. Moreover, the process of assigning "causal primacy" to a particular set of factors often carries ideological implications. For instance, the emphasis on the "controlling" character of values within the Parsonian theoretical system can be criticized not only because it leads to a neglect of other causally important factors but more importantly because it tends to disguise economic determination as value-consensus. This criticism, of course, cannot in any way justify the equally reductionist analytical approach of assigning causal primacy to economic factors.

In short, the praxis orientation embodies the same set of initial assumptions that undergird the scientific dialectical approach—in particular, the belief that traditional social scientific knowledge is inherently "partial" in nature, both in a diachronic and synchronic sense. While the scientific orientation views this partiality as an epistemological problem that can be corrected, the praxis orientation views it as inevitable and unresolvable (not only for social science, but for all forms of knowledge). Nonetheless, the praxis and scientific viewpoints do share a basic commitment to reorganizing the social scientific enterprise, although for entirely different reasons. As dictated by its sociology of knowledge focus, the praxis orientation points to the negative social consequences that result from the uncritical acceptance of common-sense assumptions. This practice serves to lend scientific legitimacy to partial knowledge systems that are ideologically slanted to favor the interests of dominant social groups. Consonant with the specific focus of its critical analysis, the praxis viewpoint seeks to reorganize social science *not* by altering its methodological principles, but by redefining its ultimate goals.

The goals of the social scientific enterprise, as defined by the praxis paradigm, differ considerably from the formal goals defined by positivist social science. While claiming a formal commitment to developing propositions that apply to all times and places, positivists have in actual practice generated conceptual frameworks that constitute subjective expressions of historically and culturally specific social conditions. The praxis orientation proposes to remove this discrepancy by establishing formal goals that accord with what social science is capable of achieving—partial explanations but ones that serve to enhance the possibilities for progressive social change. Whereas traditional social science produces explanatory frameworks that, because of their dependence on common-sense assumptions, function to legitimize existing conditions, the praxis orientation seeks to delegitimize existing conditions by employing assumptions that clearly contradict common-sense presuppositions.

In more specific terms, the praxis approach uses two distinct knowledge-producing strategies, which correspond to the two kinds of "partiality" that characterize all forms of subjective conceptualization. The first strategy relates to the problem of "diachronic partiality"—the fact that efforts to analyze existing conditions inevitably result in the production of conceptual systems that are immediately outdated. One way of dealing with this problem is to shift the focus from explaining "what is" to articulating "what can be." By developing conceptual systems that can serve as blueprints for the society of the future, the problem of the diachronic partiality of our subjective formulations is minimized. The future-oriented nature of this approach makes possible the generation of conceptual systems that possess an ideological content supportive of "emerging interests" rather than the production of social scientific legitimations of the existing interest structure as provided by positivist social science. Of course, the identification of emerging interests is a normative undertaking: one focuses on interests that one would like to see supported. Regardless of which interests serve as the ideological basis of conceptual elaboration, the act of conscious "interest advocacy" insures that social scientists will not implicitly legitimize the dominant interests of the existing structure in the name of "value-neutral" social science.

A second strategy for producing knowledge that delegitimizes existing social conditions involves the other form of conceptual partiality, "synchronic partiality." A factor that contributes significantly to the persistence of a given set of social structural arrangements (in particular, a given interest structure) is the empirical verifiability of reductive "theories of reality": when the structuring effects of many different factors are reduced to one or two categories that can be empirically verified as "causally dominant," then features of the social system that, if consciously identified, could become the focal point of widespread social protest are often obfuscated. For example, accounting for the existence of current patterns of medical practice in the United States in terms of certain value orientations in effect draws attention away from the structuring influences of such things as professional autonomy, economy, and bureaucracy. An explanation of this pattern in terms of commonly accepted cultural values is much less likely to lead to a general questioning of its legitimacy than an explanation that emphasizes the medical profession's autonomy. As a general rule, the more we know about the many factors that impinge on a given set of social conditions, the greater our ability to assess the desirability of these social arrangements and, in turn, the greater the possibility of constructive social change.

This second analytical strategy attempts to transcend the tendency toward reductive explanation by making use of the analytical principles introduced in discussing the scientific dialectical perspective. The basic thrust of the approach is to analyze a particular social pattern or phenomenon as a facet of a broader social whole that reflects its connection with a multitude of different factors. This is achieved by focusing on Relations rather than entities as the irreducible unit of analysis.

Although relational analysis occupies a central place in both the praxis orientation and the scientific dialectical perspective, it is important to note the different way in which each perspective makes use of this form of analysis. The scientific dialectical perspective proposes to remove the opposition between the subjective and objective dimensions, which would presumably allow social scientists to establish an exact correspondence between their subjective categories and the elements of an objective social reality. In contrast, the praxis orientation embraces relational analysis not for these epistemological reasons but for practical purposes. Adherents to the praxis perspective regard the goal of universally valid knowledge as unattainable and therefore eschew any commitment to the search for such knowledge. While the relational method cannot be expected to yield sociological "truth," it can be used as a tool for broadening our knowledge of the social environment, as a method by which we can increase our understanding of the complex of elements that make up the environment. Hence, the praxis approach makes use of relational analysis for this more modest purpose.

Having described the general character of diachronic and synchronic relational analysis, I now wish to outline the broader analytical scheme under which both of these strategies can be subsumed. At the highest level of abstraction, both approaches appear to converge on the fundamental concept of Relation. By tracing in a more detailed fashion the logical steps that lead to this convergence, I will describe a framework that incorporates the various techniques discussed above.

Aspects of diachronic relational analysis discussed here have several important implications. If the principle goal of dialectical analysis is to develop conceptual frameworks that can serve as blueprints for the social system of the future, then what does this mean for our analyses of the present and the past? Should we abandon completely these forms of research and concentrate solely on future-oriented research? The answer to this question can be found in the dialectical conception of "the determination of social objects across time." While it seems quite natural to make clear distinctions between past, present, and future within our common-sense frame of reference (and, for that matter, within the positivist social scientific paradigm), these distinctions are regarded as only arbitrary within the dialectical paradigm. From the dialectical standpoint, crucial aspects of what a thing is at any given moment are what it has been in the past and what it will be in the future. This approach placed primary emphasis on the immanent character of social objects. As Hegel expressed so eloquently, the change in an object across time involves the process of that which is implicit in the object gradually becoming explicit. Hence, it may by possible to make analytical distinctions between past, present, and future, but these distinctions are, by no means, given in objective reality.

Past, present, and future social conditions are always related; therefore the effort to generate conceptual frameworks that describe future social conditions creates some additional analytical tasks. Simple elaboration of a vision of the future that is rooted in a set of alternative (i.e., contrary to common sense) assumptions about social reality and the nature of human nature is not enough. One must also demonstrate how these future social arrangements relate to past and present conditions. Any reasonable account of the society of the future must include an analysis of the present and the past in terms that are consistent with the basic assumptions of one's future-oriented conceptual system. The present and past must be redefined in terms that accord with one's hopes for the future.

Although this kind of analysis would appear to be entirely unique, it is not without precedent. For example, one could properly designate the Marxian approach as a form of future-oriented research. Although contemporary dialectical thinkers persistently refer to Marxian theory to illustrate various dialectical principles, few have made explicit reference to what may be the most fundamental link between the Marxian system and current dialectical thinking. One could properly argue that Marx's starting point is neither the historical analysis of the material basis of human society nor the analysis of capitalism but, rather, the elaboration of an utopian vision of future social conditions—the social system that Marx designated as "communism." As a first step in his analysis, Marx established a set of new principles upon which to base society, principles that accorded with his humanist philosophical stance. Only after accomplishing this task was he able to transcend the prevailing ideology of his time and see the past and present from a new perspective. In Marxian theory, we have a clear case of an approach that analyzes the past and present in terms that accord with particular vision of the future.

Marx's system not only illustrates the general character of future-oriented research, it also exemplifies a specific variation of this form of analysis. Inspite of his analytical orientation to the society of the future, it cannot be overlooked that Marx actually dedicated very few pages to describing his communist utopia. The bulk of his analysis focuses on the society of the present—that is, social life under capitalism. What makes Marx's approach distinctive is the fact that his vision of the future provides the necessary assumptions by which he analyzes both the present and the past—his vision of the future had to be established prior to his analysis of any other time dimension. Thus, Marxian theory demonstrates that one can engage in analyses of past or present social conditions and still fit within the broad category of future-oriented research. Indeed, linking analyses of the present to analyses of the past and explorations of future possibilities is absolutely essential. The common thread in all of this research, however, is the fact that each form of analysis has as its starting point some distinct vision of the ideal society of the future.

One problem we confront in the effort to develop a future-oriented research agenda involves the phenomenon of synchronic partiality. I noted earlier that the verifiability of any number of competing frameworks points to the holistic character of objective social reality, which, in turn, indicates the need for the second analytical strategy within the praxis perspective, "synchronic relational analysis." While this analytical strategy cannot yield theoretical categories that capture the totality of objective existence, it allows us to produce concepts that reflect the interrelated character of this reality.

Future-oriented research assigns as much importance to this latter concern as it does to the goal of generating categories that are rooted in some utopian vision of the future. Within the praxis perspective, these two strategies are not mutually exclusive but, rather, are capable of being integrated; they are, in fact, most effective when used together. The analyst must examine past and present conditions in terms of their multifaceted, multidimensional character in order to maximize the possibility of institutional change toward the ideal future society. To engage in this kind of analysis is to embark on a reflexive exercise: The analysis starts with the development of a utopian system, which because it is an ideal system can be described only in crude terms. This system, in turn, supplies a set of assumptions about social reality that can serve as the basis of an alternative perspective on past or present conditions. With the completion of a multidimensional analysis of past and present relations, the analyst now possesses information needed for a revision of the initial ideal system, a revision that will make the system a more realizable alternative for the future. At this point, the cycle begins anew, with the researcher returning to the analysis of past and present conditions but now equipped with a set of modified future-oriented assumptions. Obviously, there can be no end-point for this kind of analysis. Our conception of the ideal system must constantly be revised in light of continuing research on past and present conditions. Ongoing change in existing conditions means that dialectical analysis must be a never-ending process.

In short, we cannot hope to adequately understand the determination of a social structure across time without also understanding the relation between it and other social structures (or the relations between elements of a social system) across space. The most effective form of praxis dialectical research combines the two basic analytical strategies described earlier—the analysis of the social unit in terms of both its diachronic and synchronic relations. This is the sense in which the two analytical strategies can be said to converge and make possible a more general form of "relational analysis."

To complete the description of the praxis approach I will next discuss the set of Relations that this perspective defines as fundamental facets of the social whole.

CHAPTER THREE

Fundamental Relations of the Social Crystal

One of the central goals of the relational method of analysis is to identify the various Relations that make up society and describe their basic nature. Some of the more important connections within the social domain that can be treated as fundamental units of analysis are: (1) the relations between human beings and social structure; (2) the relations of different social structures to one another within the social system or social whole; and (3) the relations between theoretical and common-sense concepts and categories and other elements of the social whole (the connection between human consciousness and social reality). I will now explore each of these relations in more detail.

THE HUMAN BEING/SOCIAL STRUCTURE RELATION

Consonant with the holistic conception of reality as ever changing and indeterminate, the dialectical perspective is rooted in the idea of "process." Social patterns are not fixed and enduring; they are constantly being created and recreated by the action of individuals. Social arrangements emerge from the interaction of individuals as they attend to socially defined tasks. People adopt specific roles and form relationships with other role-takers in the performance of these tasks. Some forms of interaction become somewhat routinized so that they receive the special designation of "institutional behavior." Even interaction of this kind, however, is subject to continuous modification.

The fluid character of social patterns derives from the continuous circulation of different individuals (or different value/belief orientations within the same individuals) in various social roles. As people confront and respond to new structural contingencies and evolving social and economic forces, the nature of the interaction patterns, institutions, and structures change. This relation between human actors and social forms means that the "social world is in a continuous state of becoming" (Benson 1977, 3).

37

Despite the mutable character of social reality, other forces work to constrain human behavior and limit social change. For instance, every social system possesses a particular "interest structure" in which the interests of some groups are favored over the interests of others. The group or groups whose interests are favored by certain economic, social, and ideological arrangements possess the resources to insure that existing social arrangements will be reproduced. While such forces act to constrain the development of new social forms, they can never completely impede the forces that give rise to social change.

A second constraining influence involves "adaptations that, once made, inhibit more effective ones" (Schneider 1971, 667). Regardless of whether selected interest groups take steps to limit social change, the existence of established ways of doing things (social structures fulfilling specific functional requirements) tends to preclude the development of alternative patterns. Innovating new strategies for achieving individual and institutional goals requires a significant energy expenditure and always involves a certain risk of failure. Consequently, institutions and social actors often conform to established structural patterns in order to conserve energy and minimize the possibilities of failure. The efforts of powerful interests to hide, through ideological manipulation, the dysfunctions of established social structures serve to enhance this tendency.

The discussion of the individual/social structure Relation in terms of the spontaneous and constraining forces within the social domain raises an issue that has been perhaps the single most important problem confronted by advocates of holistic theory and methodology within the social sciences. In an important study of the longstanding debate between the "individualist" and "holist" social scientific perspectives, Susan James (1984) describes the epistemological and normative dimensions of the conflict between the two theoretical/methodological approaches to social scientific explanation. Her study is particularly timely in light of the recent emergence within sociology of the same basic problem in the form of the "micro-macro" debate (Alexander, et al 1987; Coleman 1986; Knorr-Cetina and Cicourel 1981; Maines 1982). The latter expression of the individualist-holist conflict is even closer to the essential problem we confront in the present analysis—the problem of finding a place among the various "causal forces" emphasized by the present holistic framework for individual (micro) level features that may serve as determinant forces within the social domain.

As James convincingly demonstrates, neither of the two approaches can effectively dismiss the other as a valid and useful form of social explanation. For a variety of reasons having to do with fundamental epistemological concerns, advocates of the individualist position have failed in their effort to demonstrate that holist theories can be reduced to individualist categories. At the same time, the "absolute holism" that is advocated by such scholars as Althusser (1965, 1970) and Poulantzas (1975a, 1975b) also fails to stand up to a critical reading from those who assume that subject acts as causal force in society and is not simply an illusory category. What James is able to discern about this conflict is that the disagreement devolves *not* so much on practical, epistemological matters (i.e., the issue of reductionism) but rather reflects two distinct normative orientations:

> (Individualism and holism) are more fundamentally divided by their disparate conceptions of the human individual—a fact which lies at the heart of their views of explanation. Crucial to individualism is the conviction that people are agents who determine the course of events both by choosing between existing options, and by creating the options themselves. Good explanations must accordingly respect this vision by giving pride of place to the individual beliefs and purposes which shape the social world. Holists, on the contrary, are concerned to understand the ways in which individuals are constrained by their social environments and argue that the best explanations are informed by this standpoint. The main difference between the two approaches is thus their commitment to discrete ranges of causal factors—to the beliefs, actions and intentions of individuals on the one hand, to the constraining properties of social wholes on the other (1984, 176).

Once it is understood that the dispute between individualists and holists is rooted in normative as well as pragmatic considerations, advocates of both approaches are forced to consider the value implications of their respective frameworks. I have already discussed the interest orientation that lies behind my adoption of a holistic analytical framework. It is necessary at this point to also reconcile the form of holistic analysis used in this study with my commitment to the "individualist" vision of human beings as agents who possess the *potential* for determining the course of events. In this effort, I follow James's lead in advocating that analysis be conducted in terms of a "concessive holism" (James 1984, chap. 6) that can accommodate both the individual and structural, micro and macro dimensions.

Several frameworks qualify as abstract sociological theories that fit within the concessive holist tradition: in addition to the Annales school of historical analysis, which James uses to illustrate this form of analysis, one could point to the Frankfurt school's synthesis of the Marxian and Freudian systems (cf. Marcuse 1955) and the newly emerging Marx-Mead synthesis (Litchman 1970; Blake 1976; Goff 1980; Batuik and Sacks 1981; Joas 1981; Schwalbe 1986) as examples of concessive holist approaches. While space could be devoted to describing these frameworks, the goals of the present study are best served by eschewing an abstract description of specific social relations in favor of an illustration of the concessive holist methodology employed in the analysis of empirical data. The empirical "sociology of knowledge" analysis of medical practice to be presented in subsequent chapters will serve this function.

RELATIONS BETWEEN ELEMENTS OF THE SOCIAL SYSTEM

A second kind of Relation emphasized by the dialectical paradigm is the relation between specific components of the social order. As noted in the discussion of the philosophy of internal relations, wholes are constituted of many different elements or facets existing in internal relation with one another. The exploration of these multiple interconnections forms a central concern of holistic analysis.

Structural interconnections with social reality evolve as a by-product of social construction process. Since the forces that give rise to new structural arrangements operate within an already established social order, relations between social forms are constantly being crystallized and re-crystallized. In discussing this process, one typically speaks of the crystallization of elements, components, etc., in order to facilitate discourse, but what actually takes place is the crystallization of Relations, those ambiguous forms in which separate components can never be clearly distinguished. In fact, the phrase *the social production of Relations* expresses more precisely than any other terminology the importance of the social context for the social construction process. New social structures do not emerge in a vacuum. As evolving facets of the social whole, each new structure reflects within itself the entire social system. In this sense the existing social order can be said to "shape" or "determine" the nature of newly produced social structures.

Among the various interconnections that make up the social whole, one variety of Relation is especially important. The term *contradiction* refers to a relational structure that has received a great deal of attention from dialecticians because of the important role it plays in social change. Contradictions are "ruptures, inconsistencies, and incompatibilities in the fabric of social life" (Benson 1977, 4). They are Relations whose polar ends stand in direct opposition to one another, the "emergent" product of the two ends of a continuum that, taken separately, appear as direct antitheses of one another. Hegel's notion of the "interpenetrating of opposites" refers to this type of Relation. Within the Marxian framework, the contradiction between the interests of the capitalists and the proletarian classes (which is just one Relation among many constituting the capitalist system) plays a crucial role in the evolution of this system.

The Marxist treatment of contradictions illustrates how this concept is used within the praxis dialectical perspective. The concept of contradiction figures prominently in the Marxian perspective on social change and is the basis of the two laws of social development—the laws of "development through contradiction" and "spiral form of development." The former law focuses on one way in which the development of a component of the social system is influenced by the particular network of components in which it is embedded. In some cases, developing components contradict one another— one component cannot develop freely in a certain direction because of the transformation of another component in the opposite direction. The resolution or "working out" of such contradictions often determines the nature of the development of the system as a whole. The existence of such retarding effects in social evolution lead to a spiral rather than a linear form of development—the "law of spiral development."

From the dialectical perspective, contradictions are viewed as Relations that shape social development through their effects on social production. Benson (1977, 5) lists these effects as follows:

> (1) They may occasion dislocations and crises which activate the search for alternative social arrangements; (2) they may combine in ways which facilitate or in ways which thwart social mobilization; (3) they may define the limits of change within a given system. Consciousness of these limits may permit the ultimate negation of the limits; but in the interim the contradictions may be quite constraining.

In accordance with the way connection is conceived within the holistic framework, the relationship between contradictions and social production can be understood as causally reciprocal: contradictions effect social production and social production creates contradictions. This latter connection is manifested in two distinct ways: the social production of both "diachronic contradictions" and "synchronic contradictions."

Diachronic contradictions arise from the confrontation between existing social arrangements and new social forms that continuously evolve. Every social entity possesses temporal relations: included in its component parts are its ties to what it was in the past and what it will be in the future. Very often tension develops between these components, creating a state of affairs that has important consequences for subsequent change.

Synchronic contradictions refer to the tension between social structures that emerges in differentiated social wholes. In addition to their temporal relations, elements of the social system exist in some spatial relationship with one another; at any given point in time, every component of the social whole occupies a place in a particular configuration of components; each element is internally related to every other element. Although interconnection or interpenetration characterizes this system, coherence or coordination between system elements does not always exist. In short, social formations that develop in different social spaces sometimes stand in opposition to one another.

RELATIONS BETWEEN KNOWLEDGE AND SOCIAL STRUCTURE

A third fundamental Relation emphasized by the dialectical paradigm involves the relationship between social structure and the products of human consciousness. This Relation serves as the primary unit of analysis for the empirical study of medical practice, which is the focus of the remaining chapters of this volume. As we have seen, the relational view posits that the products of consciousness exist in internal relation with all other components of the social system; all knowledge systems emerge as facets of the social whole and therefore reflect the whole in its totality.

This Relation has been a special concern in the present volume because, as we have seen, it can serve as a reference point for differentiating common-sense perception and traditional scientific theorizing from dialectical thinking. I have addressed this issue in considerable detail already; therefore, I will simply underscore the central themes of the earlier discussion. Although consciousness of the internal relations between mental constructs and other components of the social system pervades dialectical thinking, these ties go unrecognized in everyday human perception and positivist scientific analysis. We find Marx criticizing the common-sense perspectives and social scientific theories of his day for focusing only on directly observable facts and abstracting these "appearances" from the social context that gives them meaning. Such appearances and abstractions are reified by scientists and nonscientists alike. Reification reaches a maximum degree when, according to Ollman (1976, 228),

> these appearances are given concepts which link them to whatever they superficially resemble in other places and times. Well suited for the work of classifications and the search for analogies, these concepts do not and cannot permit an adequate comprehension of their subject matter.

In contrast, awareness of the intimate relationship that exists between scientific (and nonscientific) theories and the social order forces us to abandon long-cherished beliefs about the nature of scientific theorizing. Despite the tendency to treat the idea of "objective science" as sacrosanct, no form of scientific research is free from the influence of social values. Our values determine what problems we choose to address; they shape our decisions about the relevancy of specific empirical observations; they even structure our perception of empirical reality. Moreover, this perspective undermines the central positivist premise that facts have an existence independent of "theories." Facts are constituted through the imposition of subjective categories on an indeterminant external reality. Consequently, if facts are organized by theories, and theories, in turn, are shaped by values, then facts and values are internally related. This connection between social values and scientific knowledge constitutes one of the more important aspects of the knowledge/social structure Relation.

Part II

A Countersystem Analysis of Medical Practice

Introduction to Part II

In the first part of this volume, I described a new paradigm for sociological analysis that has emerged in recent years. My primary concerns in presenting this new system have been first, to provide a comprehensive description of the elements that make up the system; second, to indicate logical contradictions and other problems that exist with the various versions of this form of analysis; and third, to suggest a new version of the dialectical approach that resolves these problems. In the second part of this study, I provide an empirical illustration of the ideas presented thus far by undertaking a dialectical analysis of an actual empirical domain.

The analysis in this section focuses on the network of relations involved in the practice of medicine, in particular, the mode of medical practice that predominates in contemporary American society. Attention will be directed to analyzing the multifaceted character of the medical sector as a whole, as well as aspects of the larger social environment in which the medical sector is embedded. The broad scope of the analysis reflects the fundamental concern in this type of study for understanding how various social structural elements interrelate to form the health care subsystem.

While the study seeks primarily to explain the character of contemporary medical practice, this does not mean that strict time boundaries can be established for the analysis. As I argued in part 1, the dialectical analysis of a contemporary social form requires that it be examined in terms of its relations with both past and future forms. The study will focus on both the synchronic and diachronic relations of medical practice; therefore, establishing strict empirical boundaries for the analysis is pointless.

While it is inappropriate to strictly define the empirical domain in dialectical analysis, we do find a parallel in this type of analysis to that other essential step within the traditional paradigm—the need to establish a basic unit of analysis. We have seen that no form of analysis allows one to examine the totality of a multifaceted social sector. In dialectical analysis, as in all social scientific analysis, one must establish a starting point for the relational approach.

This requirement is fulfilled in the present study by drawing on a metaphor for social reality that contrasts sharply with the metaphor implicit in more traditional analyses. While social scientific studies typically employ mechanistic or system metaphors, the present study makes use of the "social crystal" metaphor. Instead of conceptualizing the unit of analysis as an autonomous, independent entity consisting of either the sum of a set of well-defined component entities or a distinct element in a large system of elements, the unit of analysis in this study is conceptualized as a facet of the crystalline structure that we know as the "medical sector." The unit of analysis can be seen to "reflect" the totality of the whole to which it belongs; it can serve as a "window" on the whole that the analyst endeavors to understand.

When the unit of analysis is conceived in this way, the task of selecting the analytical unit for an actual empirical study takes on added importance. While all facets, aspects, or dimensions of a social crystal reflect the whole of which they are a part, some aspects of the crystalline structure reflect more directly the logic of the whole than do other aspects. In accordance with the earlier discussion of "reflection," this statement can be taken to mean that some aspects contribute more than others to defining the organizing principle of the whole. Therefore, the unit of analysis should be an aspect or facet that the analyst believes most directly reflects the organizing logic.

In the present study, the unit of analysis (the facet through which the system of medical practice will be examined) is the knowledge dimension— in particular, the realm of "formal medical theory." The centrality of this facet in the structure of medical practice has been long recognized by analysts of the medical sector. Stephen Toulmin (1976, 41) echoes the sentiments of many others (Parsons 1951; Friedson 1970; Foucault 1973; Zaner 1976) when he states that "epistemologically speaking . . . the status of medical knowledge is an historical fact about the practice of medicine at the time in question. The nature and goals of medical understanding as currently perceived both determine and reflect the spirit in which patients are currently treated." Medical knowledge is such an integral part of the practice of medicine that any adequate analysis of this activity cannot fail to take account of existing theories of medical practice. In dialectical terms, medical knowledge can be expected to reflect very directly the organizing principle of the medical sector.

The decision to treat the medical knowledge dimension as the basic unit of analysis means that the present effort is best regarded as an empirical study in the sociology of knowledge. This type of study examines the connections

between a particular knowledge system and a particular set of social
arrangements, revealing the way in which a specific knowledge system
determines and is determined by the socio-historical context in which it
exists. This approach to analyzing the relationship between medical
knowledge and contemporary medical practice is somewhat unique.
Although the medical knowledge/medical practice relationship has been the
subject of much scholarship, it has been traditionally analyzed from an
epistemological standpoint; the principle concern has been to establish which
of a variety of different kinds of knowledge are most relevant to the practice
of medicine (Toulmin 1976). This effort has informed our understanding of
medical practice, but it has failed to take account of one important fact: at
every historical juncture, one kind of knowledge, one way of conceiving
health and illness, usually predominates over all other possible conceptions.
In this respect, the contemporary system of medical practice is no exception.
Many different forms of knowledge may be appropriate to the healing of the
sick but contemporary medical practice relies on a single, exclusive body of
knowledge—a system of thought that has been designated as anatomo-
clinical theory (Foucault 1973). What is needed at this point is an analysis
that can account for the hegemony of this medical perspective by answering
the following two questions: (1) what social structural factors in modern
American society have influenced the evolution and maintenance of the
prevailing mode of medical knowledge? and (2) how has this system of
thought also influenced existing social structural arrangements within the
medical sector? Providing answers to these questions will tell us a great deal
about the nature of modern medical practice.

With the unit of analysis established, the formal research format
described in part 1 now must be translated into a methodological strategy
appropriate to the analysis of the empirical case. The first step in the research
format is the identification of a specific utopian system which will serve the
dual functions of allowing us to examine the "future Relations" of the
empirical domain under analysis and, more importantly, to provide an
analytical reference point for the study. The sociology of knowledge focus of
the study gives added importance to this step. Following Karl Mannheim's
proposals for empirical analyses in the sociology of knowledge, the study
will be broken down into two separate kinds of analysis—"philosophical
analysis" and "social structural analysis" (Mannheim 1952). One difficulty
that confronts researchers employing the former kind of analysis is the
problem of dealing with "cultural bias": in the effort to specify the
fundamental presuppositions of a knowledge system belonging to our own
Weltanschauung, basic cultural presuppositions or domain assumptions
(Gouldner 1970, 31) go unrecognized because of their taken-for-granted

character. The several techniques Mannheim recommends for dealing with this problem have one common characteristic: they all involve the use of a contrasting perspective that can be compared to the system under analysis point by point, thereby forcing the analyst to identify internalized cultural presuppositions.

This sociology of knowledge approach involving the technique of "analysis through contrast" (see also Feyerabend 1978) is part of a more general methodological strategy known as countersystem analysis (Sjoberg and Cain 1971). This method calls for an analysis of a social system or sector by contrasting it with a different system or "countersystem" that meets some criteria for being the "negation" of the first system. By adopting this approach, one may more easily recognize the taken-for-grated features of the system under analysis. For the purposes of the present study, the concept of countersystem can be regarded as functionally equivalent to the utopian system employed by the praxis dialectical approach.

A utopian countersystem appropriate for the present analysis of the medical sector must, therefore, include a set of contrasting social relations, as well as a contrasting medical perspective. Identifying such a medical system is no easy task. To be of any use in the analysis of the existing system of medical care, the countersystem must be structurally comparable to the system under analysis: it must incorporate a comprehensive system of medical theory that also reflects the social relations of the utopian system. In addition, the knowledge system, along with the social structural factors to which it is related, must express a specific organizing logic, a "principle of organization" consistent with a moral/ethical position identified by the analyst. To invent such a system from scratch would obviously pose some significant problems; consequently, it may be prudent to consider the possibilities for building on an already existing system of alternative medical concepts and practices.

Fortunately, a number of developments in recent years have made it possible to adopt such a strategy. Within the United States (and in some other Western countries) during the last decade or so, a social movement has crystallized around a new definition of health and illness, one that differs in a fundamental way from the conception of health and illness that has prevailed in these countries during most of the twentieth century. Like most social movements in the initial stages of development, the "holistic health movement" has not rigorously defined the boundaries of its domain of interest and its central political concerns. From the viewpoint of some members of the movement, this constitutes one of the major strengths of the movement because the scope of the critique it offers and the discussion of alternative structures is very broad. Holistic health adherents have used their new definition of health and illness as a basis for elaborating an alternative medical paradigm, an alternative set of social arrangements for medical practice, and an alternative form of patient-practitioner relationship. Although the diffuse character of the movement has given rise to some problems, it is comprehensive enough to serve as an appropriate template for the analytical utopia to be used in the present study.

In adopting the perspective of the holistic health movement as a template for the countersystem, I am not seeking to provide a sociological analysis of the holistic health movement or even to offer an exhaustive account of the major ideas proposed by members of this movement. Such an account is probably not possible in light of the ill-defined nature of the movement. The empirical evidence collected on the holistic health movement has been used strictly for the purposes of elaborating the utopian countersystem. Moreover, since the holistic health perspective only approximates the medical system that represents the author's "ideal," some important differences exist between the movement perspective and the medical countersystem explicated here.

The principle point of divergence involves the explicit effort to root the analysis within the neo-Marxian paradigm. The present study belongs to a growing tradition of Marxian analyses of American medicine (Krause 1977; Navarro 1977; Brown 1979) but represents a version of this type of analysis not attempted before. In addition to emphasizing the Marxian method (countersystem analysis) and avoiding the traditional overreliance on the reified political economic conceptualizations of classical Marxism, the study makes explicit use of Marx's philosophical/ethical principles in establishing the central precepts of the medical countersystem. In particular, the countersystem definition of health is an elaboration of the definition employed by the holistic health movement that has been altered to reflect Marxian assumptions about the nature of human nature. This modification is made possible by the fact that the movement's definition of "health" is logically consistent with Marx's conceptualization of "species being" within his communist utopia. By integrating these two concepts, a dimension will hopefully be added to the countersystem model that is currently missing in the medical model advocated by the movement. This new dimension involves health-determining structures at the "macro-structural" level.

The countersystem also diverges from the medical perspective advocated by the holistic health movement by incorporating elements of some other alternative medical models that have been largely overlooked by progenitors of the movement perspective. Concepts and assumptions taken from the "public health" and the "psychiatric/biopsychosocial" medical models have been integrated into the countersystem where they can appropriately fill gaps that currently exist in the holistic health paradigm. In numerous places I have found it necessary to expand or alter holistic health conceptualizations in order to make the countersystem more comprehensive or rigorous. In short, the countersystem model is designed with specific analytical and practical goals in mind and therefore may resemble the movement perspective only in the most general terms.

Another issue that requires attention before initiating the countersystem analysis of medical practice concerns some of the details of the organizing scheme used in the study. The present analysis is a study in the empirical sociology of knowledge; a large part of the study, therefore, involves the task of distinguishing between the social structural and knowledge dimensions and describing the basic features of both. The main body of the study consists of four broad subsections—a description of each of the two medical models (the traditional and the utopian systems) in terms of both their knowledge and structural dimensions. An additional goal of the study is to demonstrate the way in which the knowledge/social structure Relation reflects the whole to which it belongs, to specify the fundamental principle or principles of organization that structure or undergird the system under analysis and that, therefore, receive expression in every facet of that system. One must do more than simple demonstrate the existence of "relational identity" between the various facets of the social sector; one must also specify the basis of that relational identity by locating the specific logic or principle of organization underlying the system.

A few caveats about the principle of organization are necessary at this point. First, it should be noted that the dialectical perspective always locates the principle of organization in the relationship between the major interest groups/social statuses involved in the sector under analysis. Within the Marxist framework, for example, the principle of organization of capitalist society can be found in the relationship between the capitalist and the worker, the two major interest groups in this type of society. Marx's analysis of capital is rooted in a description of the nature of this relationship, which he saw as the basis of the "logic of capitalism," a logic that is reflected in all aspects (read facets) of capitalist society.

Closely related to this is a second important point. The postulate that the principle of organization resides in the relationship between social groups does not mean that the dialectical perspective is properly defined as a social determinist approach. To say that the knowledge dimension reflects or expresses a logic that is defined by the relationship between two or more social groups is not to claim that social structural conditions determine ideas. As Richard Ball (1979, 789) notes, "A dialectical method insists that the material and ideal are mutually constitutive expressions of a whole. The principle by which the various aspects are arranged is the style or spirit of the whole."

Accordingly, the description of the two medical models will involve an identification of their respective principles of organization, which are found in relationship between the two major interest groups within each system of medical practice—the relationship between patients and practitioners. Viewing this relationship as the locus of the organizing logic of the medical sector is not unprecedented: a well-known analyst of medical practice has stated that "In every medical action, there are always two parties involved, the physician and the patient, or in a broader sense the medical corps and society. Medicine is nothing else than the manifold relations between these groups" (Sigerist 1943). In the language of the dialectic, this statement suggests that the patient-practitioner relationship defines the "spirit of the whole" in medical practice, a spirit or principle of organization that permeates all facets of the medical sector.

The way in which the organizing principle of each system is treated will, of course, reflect the significance of the two systems as defined by the broader methodological strategy adopted in this study. In the case of the countersystem, the main goal will be to describe an ideal form of patient-practitioner relationship, one that accords with the author's moral/ethical position. In the case of the traditional medical system, the chief concern is to analyze this relationship as it presently exists, which will entail using the ideal form of this relationship as a contrast to the existing form (analysis through contrast). Hence, the different way each principle of organization is approached corresponds to the different purposes involved in discussing the two medical models: In the case of the utopian countersystem, my efforts are synthetic in nature while my treatment of the traditional medical model is analytic. In dialectical analysis, the analytic and synthetic must be combined.

The countersystem methodology requires, of course, that the order in which the various parts of the study are presented diverge from the format used most often in traditional empirical studies. Following the traditional convention for the temporal analysis of an empirical domain, the analyst would begin with the past, proceed to the present, and end with the future. However, the dual function of the countersystem creates an dilemma. When the future (i.e., the utopian countersystem) is *also* treated as an analytical reference point, this system must be elaborated *before* one attempts to analyze either the past or present. In accordance with the priorities established by dialectical theory, the latter function is regarded as the more important of the two. Therefore, contrary to the traditional conventions of diachronic analysis, the study begins with a description of the "future of medical practice" (the utopian countersystem) followed by an examination of the traditional system described in terms of its present and past Relations.

In summary, I will describe two opposing models of medical practice beginning with an elaboration of a utopian medical model to be followed by an analytical description of the traditional medical model within modern American society. The descriptions of both of these models will consist of three basic dimensions: (1) the principle of organization underlying each system, (2) the medical paradigm (the mode of medical conceptualization) that predominates within each model, and (3) their respective social structural configurations.

Having explained the details of the organizing framework, we can now begin the first phase of the empirical analysis by describing the utopian countersystem—the holistic health medical model.

CHAPTER FOUR

The Medical Model of the Future: The Holistic Health Countersystem/Utopia

PRINCIPLE OF ORGANIZATION

As states in the introduction to this part of the study, the principle of organization of a social system, which can also be termed the "spirit" or *Zeitgeist* of that social whole, is an entity that must always be defined in terms of the relationship between the major status groups within that system. At the highest level of abstraction, we can identify two major status categories in any system of health care: patients and providers. These two statuses are represented not only at the micro level, but at the macro-level as well. The micro categories of "patient" and "practitioner" correspond to the macro categories of the "lay public" and the "medical corps." One of the goals of this analysis is to describe how the "logic" of the micro-level relationship between patient and practitioner is expressed at the macro-level, and in turn how macro-level relations reciprocally effect micro-level relations.

The effort in this section is primarily synthetic in nature; therefore, the present task involves creating an ideal form of relationship between patient and provider. The relationship is ideal in the sense that it accords with the author's political/ethical stance, which now can be explicitly identified.

The two general perspectives I have relied on to construct a medical countersystem—the perspective of the American holistic health movement and the general system of philosophical and socio-economic analysis developed by Karl Marx—are logically connected in a fundamental way. Although the empirical foci of these two perspectives are very different, both are rooted in a common conception of the nature of human nature, which, in turn, implies a common political/ethical orientation. This political/ethical stance is a much-discussed dimension of Marxian theory, but it has, so far, remained an implicit dimension of the holistic health perspective.

Consequently, the place to begin the discussion of political/ethical concerns is the view of human nature shared by holistic health and Marxian theory.

A recurring theme in the holistic health literature is the idea of human transformation, renewal, and evolution. Moreover, a principle preoccupation of almost all of the different "modalities" that make up the holistic health paradigm is a concern for the development of techniques that will allow one to control the direction of change in one's Gestalt. In the holistic health perspective, change is viewed as endemic to human existence and, therefore, a central parameter of human nature. In contrast to a static conceptualization of human nature that would apply to people in all times and places, this perspective appears to call for a more diachronic or historical approach to human nature.

Such an approach to human nature can be found in classical Marxian theory. The key concepts that Marx employs in his view of human nature are the Hegelian notions of "estrangement" and "supersession." Hegel conceived of estrangement (which he also refers to a negation, alienation, or externalization) as the process by which the individual's species being, or human nature, is expressed in the form of objective entities. Supersession, by contrast, is the process of reappropriating this objective expression of human essence. What human beings, in their traditional (non-Hegelian) modes of thinking, see as "objective" reality is to them "alien." In contrast to this view, Hegel posits that the human being and the objective world are identical.

Thus, Hegel provides a conception of human nature that directly opposes the static, psychobiological conception. For him, human nature is best understood as a socio-cultural and historical phenomenon. Human nature is revealed in the cultural products of human labor (mental labor, to be sure) and these cultural products have a history. Human nature is a potential that is being realized and transformed through time. A central concern for those who would wish to understand human nature, then, is to identify not only what it is (through historical analysis) but what it *can be* as well.

Following Hegel, Marx sees human nature as a historical phenomenon— the product of an ongoing unfolding of human potential as the human species evolves through various dialectically related stages of human history. Hegel, however, had viewed supersession as involving the systematic critique of philosophical systems, while Marx specifies as the "real appropriation of man's objective essence" (i.e., supersession) the annihilation of the estranged mode of his social being (1964, 187). He leaves no doubt about the exact meaning of this statement when he goes on to define practical humanism: "Communism, as the supersession of private property, is the supersession of *real human life* as man's possession and thus the advent of practical humanism" (Marx 1964, 187, emphasis added).

In short, Marx sees human nature as that which is revealed in the social life of individuals participating in historically specific modes of production. Existing only as an unrealized "potential" in the earliest stages of human civilization, human nature has become increasingly externalized in the course of human history, to reach its full flowering in the communist mode of production. Perhaps the most important of Marx's statements on human nature, then, is his conception of "communist man." Regrettably, Marx's description of his communist utopia was somewhat vague but one often-quoted passage helps to identify his view of fully realized human potential under communism:

> (A)s long . . . as activity is not voluntarily, but naturally, divided, man's own deed becomes an alien power opposed to him, which enslaves him instead of being controlled by him. For as soon as the division of labour comes into being, each man has a particular, exclusive sphere of activity, which is forced upon him and from which he cannot escape. He is a hunter, a fisherman, a shepherd, or a critical critic, and must remain so if he does not want to lose his means of livelihood; whereas in communist society, where nobody has one exclusive sphere of activity but each can become accomplished in any branch he wishes, society regulates the general production and thus makes it possible for me to do one thing today and another tomorrow, to hunt in the morning, fish in the afternoon, rear cattle in the evening, criticise after dinner, just as I have a mind, without ever becoming hunter, fisherman, shepherd or critic (Marx and Engels 1976, 53).

This passage reveals a utopian or countersystem view of human nature that emphasizes the development and use of the entire repertoire of human capabilities that an individual may possess. For Marx, the externalization of species being is not only an issue of concern to social philosophers who wish to understand the nature of human nature but also the concern of every individual engaged in a private search for the meaning of the life experience. He believed that the ethical life involved the personal quest to discover what it means to be a human being, a goal that can be achieved only through the full development of human powers. When individuals are afforded an opportunity to develop and experience all that they are capable of and use this experience as empirical base for reflecting on their humanity, they achieve the full potential of human existence.

In articulating this unique conception of human nature and elaborating a vision of the ethical life based on this conception, Marx emphasizes the importance of the socio-economic determination of human possibilities. The

✓ full development of human powers is possible only under specific structural conditions—those that define communist society. Moreover, communism is simply the last step in a long evolutionary sequence in which men and women have periodically thrown off the shackles of oppressive social systems to make way for new social orders that offer new possibilities for human growth. Marx is particularly concerned to define a political and epistemological agenda that accords with his view of human nature and his philosophical/ethical stance. This effort is rooted in two basic premises: First, Marx proposes that the possibility for the further development of human potential depends on the revolutionary activity of oppressed peoples. Second, he asserts that the discussion of the nature and course of human behavior is not the subject matter of a value-free social science but is the battle ground of competing ideologies. Therefore, one logical extension of Marx's ideas about human nature is a definite social change agenda, one that is supported by a praxis-oriented social science and a revolutionary working class.

It must be acknowledged that certain elements of this theoretical/ philosophical system are particularly troublesome to anyone seeking conceptual building blocks for the development of viable countersystems. For instance, one may question whether Marx's vision of communist man is actually being realized within the type of societies that have historically adopted the banner of communism. There is little evidence that the communist mode of production, in the forms it has taken in the world today, offers the structural conditions required for the "full development of human powers." While this and other problems (a discussion of which is beyond the scope of the present analysis) have led to a great deal of valid criticism of the Marxist system as a theory of history and society, the system does offer an explicit framework for defining a utopian view of human existence. This framework is rooted in the same epistemological tradition as the holistic health paradigm and shares the latter's ethical emphasis on the exploration of human potential. For these reasons, the decision to elaborate a medical countersystem that links the Marxian view of human nature with elements of the holistic health perspective is both logically sound and ethically desirable. Such a synthesis accomplishes two basic goals. First, it serves to extend the Marxian perspective into the study of health care in a way that has not been attempted before. Secondly, it provides a critical edge to the holistic health perspective that is currently absent.

Having identified the ethical/political framework for the medical countersystem, it is now possible to describe the basic nature of the ideal patient-practitioner relationship. The effort to describe these roles must begin with an identification of those elements of the patient-practitioner relationship that transcend the culturally and historically specific forms in which it has existed. A theoretical, abstract definition of the relationship is required, one that can be used as a basis for elaborating the more substantive ideal. This abstract definition should be rooted in the assumptive framework just described, in particular, the assumptions about the nature of human nature that undergird the Marxian system. The most important concern is to adopt a definition that reflects a "processual" view of human nature rather than the more traditional static view.

The abstract, theoretical model of the patient/practitioner relationship that accords with these requirements is conceptualized here in terms of the "health production process." Patients are defined as individuals seeking a state of being we know as health, this being something that is always culturally defined. Practitioners, by contrast, are individuals who possess one essential input required for the production of health—medical knowledge. Practitioners possess knowledge of the essential nature of some health-related aspect of human existence, knowledge that allows for the control of those aspects of human existence. As these two definitions indicate, the basis of the relationship between patients and practitioners is their joint commitment to the goal of "producing health."

Conceptualizing patient and practitioner in terms of the health production process provides a theoretical foundation for elaborating a type of patient-practitioner relationship that accords with the ethical orientation described above. At this point, substantive details can be added to translate this abstract definition into a more practical form of relationship. However, in pursuing this goal, we immediately confront a serious contradiction.

A central issue in elaborating an alternative model of the health production process is the problem of who *controls* this process. Using traditional Marxian economic theory as a guide, we may regard the health production process as analogous to the process of commodity production. Marx's analysis of the capitalist mode of production and his discussion of the communist alternative both reveal his belief in the desirability of worker control over the productive process. In capitalism, workers and owners vie for control over the process but workers are at a structural disadvantage in this struggle and therefore must toil under terms dictated by their employers. This leads to the conditions of alienation and exploitation that Marx emphasizes as a central theme in his analysis of capitalism. In the communist alternative, by contrast, control over production rests in the hands of workers themselves or their representatives, which allows workers to organize the productive process in accordance with their own interests.

Just as worker control over material production represents the ideal in Marx's communist utopia, patient control over health production is the ideal in the holistic health countersystem. In the medical countersystem, individuals have absolute control over all domains relevant to their health-seeking efforts. Here an important contradiction arises, however. The very notion of a patient-practitioner relationship itself, defined either empirically or theoretically, contradicts the principle of patient control. To the extent that a practitioner has any input at all in the patient's effort to produce health, the patient is denied his or her right to self-determination. Thus, the only utopian health care system that would be completely consistent with the countersystem principles is one in which the social role of practitioner does not exist; in other words, a system of self-healing.

While it is possible to conceive of a health care system based on the practice of self-healing as a theoretical possibility, we must ask if such a system is a practical possibility. There are several reasons for questioning the viability of a self-care system. First, one form of health production involves dealing with illnesses or injuries so physically or mentally incapacitating that the individual cannot initiate the process themselves. Most people have experienced at one time or another an illness episode that leaves them immobilized and incapable of helping themselves. In the case of incapacitating illness, some other person or persons must undertake a course of health-seeking action on the patient's behalf.

A second factor that works against the practical viability of a system of self-healing emerges when we consider the nature of health and health production. According to the abstract conceptualization of health production, individuals create a healthful state by making changes in some part of their physical/psychological/social existence: they make alterations in various dimensions of the human system that accord with knowledge of the laws that govern those subsystems. Without knowledge of this type, the individual could never hope to make changes that would achieve the desired results.

When the role of knowledge in health production is considered in conjunction with a conception of health as a multidimensional phenomenon, it is clear that the knowledge needed to make effective changes in all of the dimensions of an individual's existence is overwhelming. Consequently, it would be impossible for every member of society to internalize this knowledge in the course of normal socialization. For that matter, it would be impossible for even a "medical knowledge specialist" to acquire all of this knowledge (a point that will be important for the critique of the traditional medical model in a later section). Thus, the social category of practitioner appears to be a necessary element in any system of health production (except in the most primitive societies).

The practitioner role is a functionally necessary element in health production; therefore, the patient-practitioner relationship is an inevitable feature of any system of health production. In light of this fact, the goal of elaborating a health production approach that is completely consistent with the principle of patient control must be abandoned in favor of a system that does only minimal violence to this principle. The goal should be to establish a form of patient-practitioner relationship that approximates the self-care ideal.

If the knowledge required to assess the patient's health needs and establish a course of action to fulfill those needs must be supplied, in some instances, by a practitioner, then what kind of practitioner role would fulfill this function while not seriously compromising the patient's control over health production? This question is best answered by focusing on the problem of diagnostic decision-making. A caveat of medical reasoning is that a particular set of empirical facts can be explained in a number of different ways: a particular set of "symptoms" can suggest several different diagnoses. Consequently, the most important aspect of "making a diagnosis" is the selection of one explanation or diagnosis over all other possibilities. The significance of this event in the subsequent actions of everyone involved means that the individual who makes these decisions is the dominant party in the relationship. The individual who defines the health care goals (which also involves defining "health problems") and establishes an appropriate strategy for achieving those goals has the power to control the course of events.

In the ideal system, the patient would possess as much of this decision-making power as possible. This, of course, means that the practitioner's decision-making power would have to be limited, so that in the course of "supplying knowledge," the practitioner does not threaten the patient's ability to make the ultimate diagnostic and treatment decisions. The only kind of practitioner role that would fulfill these requirements is one in which the practitioner acts as "educator" and "advisor." The primary task of practitioners would be to impart as much of their medical knowledge to their patients as possible, to provide their patients with medical categories and concepts that they can use to establish health goals and/or deal with health problems. A crucial part of educating patients would be to make them aware of all of the possible diagnosis/explanations that are relevant to a given health goal or health problem. This task defines the boundaries of the practitioner's professional role. Having received this type of advice from the practitioner, the patient would assume the responsibility for selecting a diagnosis and treatment regimen from among the various alternatives presented. In doing so, patients exercise their power to control what happens to them; their right to self-determination is protected.

With health education as its primary component, the practitioner role would be virtually indistinguishable from the role of other educators within the human sciences. The only difference is that medical educators would focus on more "practical" concerns (although when this kind of practitioner role is compared with the roles of more praxis-oriented psychologists, sociologists, etc., this difference disappears). Absent from the educator role (including both the nonmedical and medical educator) is any right to impose a particular explanation/diagnosis upon the individual seeking knowledge. The educator never goes beyond merely "presenting a perspective" (or perspectives) that embodies an explanation (or explanations) of specific empirical phenomena, which, in turn, suggests a particular course of action that will achieve the desired goal.

In summary, this way of conceiving of the practitioner role suggests a form of patient-practitioner relationship in which the patient, rather than the practitioner, ultimately controls the patient's destiny. The practitioner role does not incorporate an expectation that patients will turn over control of their body/mind/lifestyles to practitioners who then make decisions and take actions that "are in the patient's best interest." A key assumption of the countersystem perspective is that if given a range of alternative diagnoses and/or treatment regimens, patients are competent to choose the alternative that is most appropriate to their health needs (which contrasts, of course, with the traditional medical paradigm's assumption of patient incompetence in this regard; cf. Katz 1978). Later analysis will reveal that this is just one of several features of the knowledge and social structure of the utopian system that simultaneously determines and reflects the ideal patient/ practitioner relationship.

Viewed in terms of "power," the ideal patient-practitioner relationship can be seen to involve a clear-cut differential. Again, in contrast to the traditional medical model, the ideal patient-practitioner relationship is distinguished by the dominance of patients over practitioners. To the extent that the practitioner establishes the range of diagnostic alternatives from which the patient makes a final selection s/he does exercise some control over the way that the patient's health goals/problems are defined, but the patient's control over the process of choosing a final diagnosis places most of the power in the hands of patients.

By conceiving of the patient-practitioner relationship in terms of this power differential, an abstract representation of the Relation that serves as the organizing principle of the utopian medical model has been established. In accordance with the societal metaphor of the "social crystal," it will be shown that this patient-dominated power differential is reflected in all aspects or facets of the utopian medical model. The rest of this chapter will be dedicated to completing the task of tracing the organizing principle, as I have defined it, through the various facets of the system.

Before concluding this section, however, one more issue requires attention. Although the organizing principle for the utopian system (defined in terms of the patient-practitioner relationship) has been specified, deficiencies exist within the present conceptualization of this principle. For example, one could argue that despite the claims made for it, this conception is not completely consistent with the ethical stance that informs it. Practitioners, it was stated, have limited power in their relations with patients because they do not exercise control over the diagnostic selection process; their job is to simply provide patients with the entire range of possible diagnoses from which the latter can make their own choices. One can legitimately ask, "How can any practitioner hope to be knowledgeable of all of the possible diagnoses that can be applied to a specific empirical condition?" Since no one person could possibly possess this range of knowledge, the practitioner will inevitably exercise some control over the selection of a diagnosis. This control derives from the practitioner's perspectival or paradigmatic delimitation of the set of possible diagnostic alternatives.

By the same token, when practitioners exercise their right or duty to distinguish between valid and invalid diagnoses, we again find them exercising control over the diagnostic selection process through their delimitation of the range of possible alternatives. Although there may be some debate over the validity or usefulness of a particular diagnostic framework (or treatment regimen), the practitioner has the discretionary power to either arbitrarily include or exclude the diagnosis/explanation as an alternative presented to the patient. This form of practitioner power is, in a sense, unavoidable because it would be unreasonable to expect practitioners to make use of diagnostic categories or treatment regimens that they sincerely believe are not valid.

While these are legitimate criticisms of the ideal patient-practitioner relationship in its present formulation, it will be shown that these problems disappear when this relationship is viewed within the context of the utopian system as a whole. Up to now, patient and practitioner roles and the nature of the relationship between the two have been discussed at the micro-level only. However, the categories of patients and practitioners refer not only to individual statuses but to collectivities as well. (In Western-industrial societies, the terms "health consumers" and "health providers" are often used to refer to patients and practitioners at the collective level). Consequently, the patient-practitioner relationship must be described as a collective or macro-level phenomenon also. In doing so, we will move toward a more complete understanding of the patient/practitioner relationship as a micro-level phenomenon, and in the process, also resolve many of the problems discussed in the preceding paragraphs. Within the dialectical framework, one can never hope to fully understand micro Relations without also taking into account macro Relations and vice versa.

Having described the patient-practitioner relationship within the medical countersystem, we will next turn to the macro-level structures of this system, beginning with the structure of knowledge within the holistic health model.

THE KNOWLEDGE DIMENSION: KNOWLEDGE CONTENT

The Definition of Health

The most fundamental element in any medical paradigm is a specific definition of health that serves as the conceptual and normative lynch-pin of the system. While health may be highly valued in many societies, there certainly has been no cultural or historical consensus about what constitutes a healthy state. To the extent that medical categories are necessary inputs in the production of health goals and a particular definition of health establishes the parameters of these goals, the way health is defined within a given medical paradigm becomes the core presupposition underlying all of the medical categories that make up that paradigm. The definition of health advanced by the utopian holistic health paradigm consists of two fundamental concepts. First health is viewed not as a particular "state of being" but rather as a process. Accordingly, three basic activities define the health production process: (1) action directed toward maintaining existing human capabilities; (2) action directed toward developing new human capabilities; and (3) action directed toward maintaining balance between the elements of the human system in an environment that changes constantly. The second "core" concept is the notion that health is a multidimensional process. This way of defining health represents a logical elaboration of the central presuppositions of the ethical/political framework discussed previously. In particular, it qualifies as a Marxian definition of health, insofar as it is rooted in Marx's conception of "fully developed human nature" (species being).

As noted above, the Marxian view of human nature, as it is expressed under the utopian conditions of the communist mode of production, emphasizes the full development and use of human capabilities. The hallmark of Marx's countersystem is the absence of structural arrangements that contribute to "alienation from species being." The economic and social structure of this society promotes rather than inhibits the realization and exploration of all those species capacities that constitute "human genetic potential." People can explore the full range of social, psychological, and physical experience and develop their human powers to the greatest extent possible.

In accordance with these ideas, the countersystem definition of health ✔ emphasizes the development and maintenance of human capacities. Moreover, this definition incorporates a processual view of health. Individuals actively pursue health by making use of the potential for directing change in the different dimensions of their existence. Thus, health is not a static condition, a state of affairs in which individuals are free of the requirement of engaging in health producing action. Within the holistic health system, health is something that can only be "sought after" but never completely achieved. In this sense we define health as a process rather than a state of being.

Having established the processual nature of health, the problem of identifying the basic parameters of the "health process" can now be addressed. Three basic forms of action make up the health process, the first being "action directed toward maintaining human capabilities."

One of the most fundamental presuppositions of the holistic health system is the idea of the inevitability of change—more specifically, the inevitability of change in the human Gestalt. The holistic health perspective recognizes four basic kinds of change: (1) change that is directed or controlled by the individual; (2) change that is determined by "external forces;" (3) change that takes the form of growth and development; and (4) change that takes the form of decay and decline. An important milestone in every individual's development is reaching that stage of the life cycle we know as maturity. Although people tend to believe that development stops at this point, it clearly does not: the continued growth and development of some facet of the human Gestalt is possible throughout the entire life cycle. While reaching maturity does not signal the end of the growth process, it does mark an important stage in the developmental sequence. Maturity signals the point at which an individual has acquired the minimum number of capacities required for survival as a relatively autonomous member of a particular biosocial environment. Before maturity is reached, a powerful impetus exists for individuals to exercise their capacities (i.e., to develop them). In the mature phases of the life cycle, however, this impetus is greatly reduced. Consequently, if the biosocial environment does not call for the use of a particular capacity by "mature" individuals, then it is unlikely that they will continue to exercise this capacity (take for example, the fact that most mature members of modern industrial societies do not make use of their capacity for physical exertion because fewer and fewer social roles within this kind of society are focused on physically demanding tasks).

In summary, every mature member of society confronts two alternative approaches to life. Those adopting the "passive" approach allow the external social environment to determine which of their developed capacities will remain vital and accept the inevitable decline of other "socially irrelevant" capacities. Those that take the "active" approach seek to control of their existence to insure the vitality of all existing capacities, through the use of specific "maintenance techniques" (which I will say more about in a later section). Within the holistic health system, the latter approach is preferred, and, thus, "maintenance" activity is defined as one of the three kinds of action that constitutes the "health production process."

Another fundamental element of the health production process is a category of action that is similar to "maintenance activity." Implicit in the holistic health proscription to maintain the vitality of previously developed "species" capacities is the belief that the more capabilities an individual possesses, the better. When this normative stance is conjoined with an understanding of the nature of growth and development in the human species, i.e., the fact that development is possible in some facet of the human Gestalt throughout the entire life cycle, it suggests the need to continually develop new species capabilities. The creation of a broad array of species capabilities can be accomplished through a twofold strategy: first, the loss of capacities can be minimized by relying on "maintenance activity," and, secondly, new capacities can be added through "growth activity." Both kinds of action are advocated by the holistic health approach, and both are viewed as essential facets of the health production process.

The third category of action included in the health production process is action directed toward maintaining "balance" between the different facets of the human Gestalt. Balancing activity is a form of action that has certain essential characteristics in common with the other two health activities; it is an ongoing process with no final endpoint, and it ultimately contributes to the development of internal rather than external control of change in the human Gestalt. In order to fully understand the concept of balance, however, we must first explore another central idea within the holistic health system—the notion of multidimensionality.

The concept of multidimensionality is, perhaps, the most fundamental idea within the medical countersystem because it is the common link between all three of the existing medical paradigms used to construct the alternative system. The multidimensionality of human existence is clearly a central element of the public health perspective. Insofar as the latter perspective focuses attention on the social and ecological determinants of human health, it presupposes that human biological function is influenced by factors operating at several different levels. This perspective incorporates the simple insight that the action of molecules and microbes takes place and can be examined within several different frames of reference: one important frame of reference is that defined by the human body, but equally important frames include the systems defined by ecological and population parameters. The character of these latter frames of reference and their relevance to human health will be discussed in more detail below.

An even more explicit statement of the importance of multidimensionality to human health can be found in the psychiatric/biopsychosocial medical model. Where the public health perspective emphasizes the systemic connections between ecological factors and the human body, the biopsychosocial model calls for equal attention to a dimension that, in some sense, intervenes between the body and ecological systems—the human psychosocial system. Unlike the perspective the holistic health movement, which has borrowed the concept of multidimensionality from medical traditions outside of allopathic, professional medicine (traditions like homeopathy, traditional Chinese medicine, etc.), the impetus for the development of the biopsychosocial model has come from within professional medicine itself.

The biopsychosocial model first appeared within modern professional medicine in the form of the "psychiatric" perspective. This perspective initially emerged in response to a growing belief within medicine that effective medical care could not be provided without attention to the role of psychosocial factors in the etiology of disease. In the earliest stages of this movement, the primary goal was "the integration of psychosocial factors into the fabric of all medical education" (Weiss 1980, 124). Weiss notes, however, that this goal was soon abandoned as psychiatry was increasingly drawn in the direction of a specialty branch of medicine. Lured by the higher status accorded members of specialty disciplines, psychiatrists began to narrow their concerns to the treatment of specific problems rather than focusing on the more general problem of treating all disease within a biopsychosocial framework. This movement in the direction of specialization resulted not only in the collapse of the psychiatric challenge to the biomedical model; it also led to a triumph of the biomedical model *even* within the field of psychiatry as more and more psychiatrists restricted their activities to the biomedical treatment of psychiatric illness.

Despite the failure of this initial movement to incorporate a multidimensional emphasis into medicine, the concern for this problem has remained, and a new challenge to the biomedical model has arisen within the ranks of professional medicine. This latest challenge has taken the form of an explicit advocacy of a "biopsychosocial medical model." Emerging primarily through the pioneering work of George Engel (1977, 1980), this model incorporates the systems perspective developed in biology by Weiss (1969) and Bertalanffy (1968), which posits that nature is ordered in terms of

FIGURE 1. Hierarchy of Natural Systems

SYSTEMS HIERARCHY
(LEVELS OF ORGANIZATION)

BIOSPHERE
↕
SOCIETY-NATION
↕
CULTURE-SUBCULTURE
↕
COMMUNITY
↕
FAMILY
↕
TWO-PERSON
↕

PERSON
(experience & behavior)

↕
NERVOUS SYSTEM
↕
ORGANS/ORGANS SYSTEMS
↕
TISSUES
↕
CELLS
↕
ORGANELLES
↕
MOLECULES
↕
ATOMS
↕
SUBATOMIC PARTICLES

the hierarchically arranged continuum illustrated in figure 1. In addition to demonstrating the relevance of this model to medical theory, Engel shows how it can be used as a framework for analyzing actual empirical medical events, such as a case of coronary artery occlusion (Engel 1980). He makes a persuasive case for the need to incorporate evidence from the more emergent psychological and social dimensions of the human system in order to develop an adequate understanding of the specific course of events in typical medical occurrence. While biomedically trained physicians make decisions that impact upon patients' interpersonal and social lives with a minimum of information about these people's psychological and social experiences, this is not true for the biopsychosocially oriented physician. The latter recognizes that to best serve the patient, higher-system-level occurrences must be approached with the same rigor and critical scrutiny that are applied to systems lower in the hierarchy. This means that the physician identifies and evaluates the stabilizing and destabilizing potential of events and relationships in the patient's social environment, not neglecting how the destabilizing effects of the patient's illness on others may feed back as a further destabilizing influence on the patient (Engel 1980, 543).

The principle strength of Engel's biopsychosocial model is the emphasis it places on combining a holistic approach to biological/medical reality with an uncompromising concern for scientific rigor. Unfortunately, the scientific underpinnings of the model have led to restrictions in scope that have prevented the full incorporation of all of the factors and types of relationships possessing practical and theoretical relevance to human health. Despite Engel's criticism of biomedical reductionism and mind/body dualism, he still roots his model squarely within the positivist scientific tradition. He relies on the systems theory version of holism that adopts many of the assumptions criticized in the first chapter of this volume, i.e., that elements of the system are distinct entities given in an objective reality and observable through common sense perception; that systems have clear cut boundaries; and that they tend toward equilibrium. Moreover, the dimensions included in his model are defined by the traditional disciplinary boundaries—biology, psychology, and sociology. In order to effectively serve its methodological purposes, our countersystem must be more inclusive and adopt alternative scientific assumptions about the nature of causality, and the relationship between parts and wholes. To address these concerns, we must look to a third medical perspective for concepts that can be used to construct the countersystem—the perspective of the holistic health movement.

Perhaps the most common theme to be found in the holistic health literature is the idea of the holistic nature of reality; in particular, the holistic nature of health reality. References to the "relations between body/ mind/spirit" are ubiquitous in discussions and publications associated with the holistic health movement. In accordance with the philosophical system discussed in chapter 1, this perspective places primary emphasis on the whole or the "totality" in its approach to human health.[1] Human beings are regarded as holistic entities that can be analytically dissected into many different interrelated dimensions. Tiller (1978), for example, establishes a scheme for dividing up the human organism that distinguishes between (a) the instinctive, intellectual (rational), and the spiritual levels, and (b) the "physical" and "etheric" dimensions (the former involving electrical energy, "positive" energy, and positive mass and the latter involving magnetic energy, "negative" energy, and negative mass).[2] He goes on to speculate about a broad hierarchy of interrelated dimensions beyond anatomical/ physiological structure: underlying anatomy and physiology is chemistry, which, in turn is rooted in conventional energy fields, which derive from the "frame of spirit," which is, finally, rooted in "the devine."[3]

This way of dividing up the human Gestalt is an elaboration of a more common scheme adopted by holistic health advocates. Much of the holistic health literature deals with a distinction between the physical and "psychic" dimensions. These two most fundamental levels of the organism are viewed as existing in a dualistic relationship: every structure in the physical plane has its counterpart in the psychic plane.[4] Just as the physical dimension can be divided into additional subdimensions, so can the psychic level. An individual's psychic structure involves three subdimensions or, more correctly, three "subtle bodies": the "astral plane" (involving emotions), the "etheric plane" (involving vital energy), and the mental plane or consciousness.[5] As with other dimensions of the human organism specified by various organizing schemata, these three "planes" of an individual's psyche exist in a co-determinant relationship; the three subtle bodies are interpenetrating entities.[6]

Although most of the efforts to identify the various interpenetrating dimensions of the human system have focused on the organism as the subject of analysis, another thread within holistic health thinking emphasizes the notion of the organism as a part of a larger whole or wholes. To insure complete logical consistency with the philosophical system that underlies the holistic health paradigm, the focus must be broadened beyond those relations internal to the human organism to include the relations between the organism and "external" factors. For example, holistic health advocates point to one aspect of traditional Chinese medicine that qualifies it as a truly holistic system—its emphasis on the role of environmental factors in health and disease. Such things as wind, cold, heat, wetness, dryness, etc., are regarded by Chinese medicine as crucial elements in the etiology of disease.[7] This approach accords with the proposition that the human being, as an element of some larger system, always reflects the whole of which s/he is a part, in this case, the whole of a complex climatological environment. But this is not the only macro-system to which human beings belong. Because human beings occupy many different environments—social, cultural, spiritual, etc.—a large number of "external relations" are involved in human health. Consequently, many of the individual medical perspectives found under the holistic health umbrella have been included precisely because they focus on one or more of these external relations.

A crucial element of the holistic definition of health, then, is its emphasis on the human Gestalt. The human species possesses a complex physiological/anatomical system, a system that can serve as an empirical referent for one's health producing efforts. However, the human system consists of much more than anatomy and physiology. At the same time that we are a functioning biological organism, we are also a "self-conscious" entity. In turn, our capacity for consciousness and "symbolic communication" allows us to participate as members of various social (interactional) units. Membership in these interactional networks is necessarily associated with membership in broader social, cultural, economic, and population systems. In short, the thing that most distinguishes the human species is the breadth of our multilayered, multidimensional essence, or species being.

The problem of developing a scheme for dividing up the human Gestalt is the subject of much debate in holistic health circles. For present purposes, we will rely on the set of categories that appear most often in the literature. Human existence consists of the following aspects: the anatomo- physiological dimension (the body), the energetic dimension (vital energy field), the mental dimension (the mind), the social dimension (lifestyle as structured by society), and the spiritual dimension (the soul). These categories are properly regarded as heuristic devices: they provide a way of discussing the different dimensions of the human whole but should not be reified as objective categories.

Perhaps the best way to understand how the different dimensions of human existence relate to one another is to think of the human Gestalt in terms of a set of "wholes within wholes." That is, each dimension exists as a distinct whole that includes itself and all of the more reduced levels below it. Hence, the most reduced whole is the body (that includes as facets all of the different anatomical and physiological systems), followed by the whole of the body/energy field, the whole of the body/energy/mind, the whole of the body/energy/mind/society and finally culminating in the most emergent whole of the body/energy/mind/society/spirit. This way of conceptualizing the human Gestalt forces us to recognize that while every dimension is related to every other (each is a facet of the larger whole of human existence), units within this larger whole act as distinct wholes in and of themselves; i.e., they have properties that are uniquely their own. The notion of wholes within wholes is the basis of several important holistic health concepts, as we will see in later sections.

Having established the basic idea of the holistic nature of human existence (both in the synchronic and diachronic sense), it is possible to move on to a related aspect of the holistic health paradigm—the problem of specifying the principle characteristics of wholes in general and the human whole in particular. One of the most important of these characteristics involves the problem of causal determination within wholes.

A holistic conception of causality can be derived from various propositions associated with the philosophy of internal relations (see chap. 1). These include the notions that "every part or facet of a whole both determines and is determined by every other part"; "the whole is more than the sum of the parts"; and "the whole is reflected in each of its parts." These ideas lead to a concept that occupies a central place in the holistic health paradigm. If every whole in the human Gestalt is also a part of some larger whole and if the whole determines the nature of the parts, then it follows that the "more emergent" wholes determine the nature of the "less emergent" wholes. A "hierarchy of causal factors" exists within the human whole, with the more emergent levels having causal primacy over the less emergent levels.

This notion has led many holistic health advocates to emphasize the whole rather than the part in their health producing activities. Balancing techniques and techniques for managing and/or treating disfunction usually deal with the ultimate rather than the proximate causes of the disfunction. In general, the holistic health approach calls for all health-oriented action to be focused on the most emergent levels of human Gestalt, although it is acknowledged that this cannot always be done.

These considerations have important implications for the countersystem definition of health. In view of the multidimensional nature of human species being, the three forms of health action can be seen to involve a wide range of human experiences. For example, to prevent the deterioration of existing human capabilities, one's maintenance actions must not only deal with many different physical capacities, such as a person's ability to run, walk, leap, dance, etc., but with a whole host of emotional, psychological, social, and spiritual capacities as well. The failure to exercise certain emotions periodically will have the same effect on emotional capacity as the failure to exercise one's body has on physical capacity—both capacities atrophy if not used. The countersystem definition of health must, therefore, emphasize the multidimensional character of maintenance activity. Travis points the direction for this kind of definition with his conception of "high level wellness," which is defined as "giving care to the physical self, using the mind constructively, channeling stress energies positively, expressing emotions effectively, becoming creatively involved with others, and staying in touch with the environment."[8]

The concept of multidimensionality is also relevant to the second category of health activities. In fact, many holistic health advocates identify "the development of new human capabilities" as the central feature of the health production process. In accordance with its existentialist philosophical roots, the holistic health perspective assumes that the tremendous flexibility and range of our species capabilities coexists with an equally extensive "needs structure." We have the *capacity* to express or manifest our species being in a number of unique ways; therefore, we *need* to do so if we are to feel satisfied, self-actualized, or, in holistic health terminology, whole. The process of developing new species capabilities represents, in some sense, an extension of process of maintaining existing capabilities. Both processes are essential for maximizing species expression which, in turn, provides the sense of wholeness that is the basis of the holistic conception of health.

In yet another statement of the holistic definition of health, the notion of developing new species capabilities receives special emphasis. Many holistic health advocates subscribe to the yoga conceptualization of health as "the ability to move freely with consciousness from an inner focus to an outer one, to move with consciousness from a rational to a nonrational and emotive mode, to move with consciousness from a focus of material values to oneness with the metaphysical values of the higher self."[9] This definition points to an important aspect of the process of developing new species capacities—the need to broaden the existential base of conscious reflection beyond those domains that are emphasized by the culture to which one belongs. As members of Western culture, we are not encouraged to focus on the nonrational, emotive, or metaphysical domains (although some scholars have posited that a shift toward these domains may now be occurring in Western societies; see Turner 1976). For many of us, the development of new species capacities would require the exploration of these latter planes of human experience. To the extent that all of the capabilities we develop represent expressions of our species being, our conscious reflection on these actions informs us about what it means to be a human being: the more capabilities we develop, the richer the existential base for conscious reflection and the more we learn about our humanity. Consequently, holistic health advocates argue that species capacity development is most useful when it is accompanied by systematic reflective awareness.

Finally, the notion of human multidimensionality can be related to the third and last health producing activity—action directed toward maintaining equilibrium or balance in an environment that constantly changes. We have seen that when the holist approach to causality is applied to the human Gestalt, a model emerges in which all of the different dimensions of an individual's existence—the biological, psychological, social, and spiritual— exist in an interpenetrating network. In other words, the character of any one of these realms is a product of its relations to *all* of the other realms of human existence. Extract one of these dimensions and all the others will cease to be what they were before.

A closer examination of the relations between elements within the human Gestalt reveals two basic kinds of interpenetration: interrelations can be either "harmonious" or "disharmonious." Two or more facets of the human system are harmoniously related if there is not conflict, tension, or contradiction between them—as, for example, when an individual's life goals are consistent with the opportunity structures of the society in which s/he lives. Disharmonious relations, in contrast, involve facets of the system that are fundamentally opposed. This is exemplified by the dialectical opposition between the human need for companionship and the need for solitude—to the extent that one of these needs is satisfied, the opposing need is left unsatisfied and vice versa.

Although both kinds of interpenetration exist within the Gestalt of every human being, the holistic health perspective posits that the principle driving force of all organic life is the tendency toward equilibrium or balance. According to the inherency theory, the resolution of imbalance or disharmony through the operation of homeostatic mechanism is endemic to all organic life.[10] This integrative process is believed to be so fundamental to life that it is often referred to as the "vital force."[11] Consonant with this assumption, the holistic health perspective establishes a basic identity between health and "equilibrium"[12] (although a particular *kind* of equilibrium as we will see later), and identifies the integrative force as a self-healing mechanism of the human Gestalt.[13]

Because homeostasis is a complex phenomenon, various aspects of this mechanism are discussed at length in the holistic health literature. One issue that unfortunately does not arise in this discussion is the apparent contradiction between the idea of "health as equilibrium" and the idea of "health as process." If health is equated with "balance between the various facets of the human whole," then how can this be reconciled with the claim that health is a process rather than a state of being? The answer lies in the consideration of another fundamental feature of human existence—the fact that *change* is ubiquitous within the human Gestalt. Although the homeostatic mechanism moves the system toward equilibrium, which, by definition, is a stable state, all actual human systems constantly undergo change: the very moment that readjustment to earlier changes has been completed, new changes necessitate further readjustment. Consequently, balancing the system is a process that has no end-point; true equilibrium is an ideal state that can never be attained in an actual human system.

These considerations indicate the true character of balancing action as a component of the health production process. Although health cannot be equated with a "balanced state," it can be equated with "movement toward balance." When the holistic health conceptual system is expanded to include the notion of "conscious control of the human system" (a concept that will be discussed later), it becomes possible to equate health with "the search for or active pursuit of balance." This latter equation is embodied in the yoga proposition that the process by which the various aspects of the self are integrated is, most fundamentally, a process of transformation.[14]

The identity between health and the active pursuit of balance has led holistic health advocates to focus on various techniques for achieving harmony, integration or balance. For example, Hatha Yoga has been placed under the holistic health banner, in part, because it provides a set of specific techniques for integrating body, mind, and spirit.[15] Similarly, other holistic health modalities embody balancing techniques that focus on many different facets of the human system: a central goal of naturopathic treatment is to increase spiritual harmony by means of meditation, breathing exercises, prayer, or progressive relaxation[16]; "autogenic training" is a specific relaxation technique that functions to stimulate the body's natural homeostatic balancing mechanism[17]; "polarity therapy" attempts to balance vital energy through love, thought, attitude, manipulation, exercise, and diet.[18] Each modality deals with a different facet of the human Gestalt, but they all contribute to a movement toward balance.

One category of balancing techniques that receives special attention in the holistic health literature is the group of techniques designed to deal with inherent disharmonies or contradictions in the human system. A fundamental tenet of the holistic health world-view is the hermetic principle that everything in the universe has its complement.[19] In accordance with this principle, elements of the human Gestalt are often conceptualized in terms of "dialectical opposition." For example, yoga practitioners rely on the dialectical notion of "yin/yang" in conceptualizing the human body: organ systems that fulfill "internal functions" are yin while those that fulfill "external functions" are yang.[20] Within this conceptualization, the two dimensions are viewed as *both* contradictory *and* complementary. Although any two organ systems may oppose or contradict one another, one system cannot function without the other. The vitality of each system (and the larger whole to which these two systems belong) can be insured only by attending to the maintenance requirements of both, which is accomplished by oscillating back and forth between them.[21] This oscillation between complementary poles represents another form of balance, a form that is believed to be the basis of the body's vital energy.[22]

The dialectical relationship between various organ systems is just one of many different types of polarities that concern holistic health practitioners. Techniques for balancing dialectically opposed processes often differ depending on the specific disharmony one confronts. Reichian therapy focuses on the polarity between the sympathetic and parasympathetic nervous systems. This approach posits that the two systems exert opposing and complementary influences on one another and that oscillation between these two poles (expansion and contraction) is necessary for good health.[23] Yoga also deals with the polarity between body and mind. One technique by which it mediates this polarity is through the use of posture, which functions as "a dynamic position, in which the practitioner is perfectly poised between activity and non-activity, between 'doing' and 'being done by' the posture."[24] Similarly the concept of "samadhi" refers to the unification of the meditator and the object of meditation.[25] In short, the notion of balance involves not only the process of integrating elements of the human system but also the process of mediating polarities, and both of these activities are properly defined as health producing action.

Before we leave the subject of balance, one more issue requires attention. A theme that recurs in the holistic health literature is the notion that people possess specific powers of control over their own existence, powers that are largely left untapped in contemporary Western culture. In theoretical terms, this idea can be expressed in the following way. In any organic whole, the individual facets that make up the whole both determine and are determined by that whole. Applying this conceptualization of the parts/whole relationship to that part of the human Gestalt that we know as "individual will" and the whole of human existence suggests a way to assess the degree and nature of the control that individual egos exercise over their existence. Just as the individual will (and all other aspects of human existence) is shaped by the broader totality to which it belongs, the individual will can also influence the more emergent levels of the human Gestalt.[26] Every individual is a reflection of the biosocial world in which s/he lives, but s/he also has the power to alter that world. As stated in hermeticism's ninth principle, individuals create their worlds, their health, and their feelings; learning to control this ability (through attitude and concentration exercises) is essential.[27] This ancient idea finds expression in contemporary scientific research as well: as Levins notes, the notion that humans have self-directing, self-healing powers is increasingly supported by research in the biological sciences.[28] In the holistic health system, the determinant nature of individual will is incorporated into the concept of balance.

The homeostatic mechanism is an inherent feature of all organic life, but balance is *not* synonymous with homeostasis. The homeostatic mechanism can, and often does, lead to a state characterized by disfunction. For example, individuals inhabiting social environments that place great demands on them often experience psychological discomfort (anxiety, stress, etc.), which can result in physiological disfunction (ulcers, heart disease, etc.). In this case, the homeostatic mechanisms of the body compensate for the disruption of equilibrium, but the end result is a state that threatens the integrity of the body. Individuals who experience such physiological disfunctions can, however, alter this state through a number of approaches. They may choose to deal with the ultimate (as opposed to proximate) causes of the problem and endeavor to make basic changes in lifestyle;[29] (lifestyle is not *the* ultimate cause[30]; it is a more proximate cause than "social structure"); or they may wish to mediate between a demanding social environment and a negative psychological response by practicing various stress reduction or balancing techniques (such as biofeedback, autogenic training, meditation, etc.).[31] Both approaches represent ways in which individual will can alter the system of which it is a part and, in doing so, create a positive equilibrium state (or, at least, a movement toward such a state).[32]

In summary, a definition of health has been provided in this section that will serve as the central concept of the medical countersystem. Rooted in the Marxian perspective on the nature of human nature, this perspective emphasizes the flexibility, range, and emergent character of our species being or species nature (biogram). This flexibility accounts, in part, for the multidimensional or holistic character of human existence. In the ideal state, the individual attends to all of the different facets or dimensions of his or her existence. Simply stated, health is the *process* of investing conscious attention and energy into as many of the different dimensions of human existence as possible. This energy investment takes the form of maintenance, growth and development, and balance.[33]

The Role of Subjective Consciousness in Health Production

The notion of the multidimensional character of human existence is a central element of the holistic health paradigm, but multidimensionality is only one of several basic themes found in this body of thought. A concern that is no less important than the holistic character of the human system (and not unrelated to this idea) is the problem of the role of consciousness in the health production process.[34]

The emphasis on consciousness reflects a basic concern of the philosophical system that undergirds the holistic health paradigm. One of the core issues of the philosophy of internal relations (see chap. 1) is determining the nature of the relationship between the conscious subject and the external object. This philosophical system offers a unique resolution of this problem by positing a mutually determinant (dialectical) relation between these two realms. In this system, the "conscious subject" is a fundamental force in the dynamic of nature because it is a necessary while, at the same time, an *opposing* part of everything we define as external reality.

This way of conceptualizing the relationship between consciousness and objective reality has important implications for the medical sphere. If this concept is applied to the human Gestalt, all of the various parts or facets of this whole belong to one pole or moment of a dialectical Relation; the other moment of this Relation is, of course, the conscious subject or ego. All of the different dimensions of the human Gestalt distinguished above can be assigned to the same basic category—they are the objects of conscious reflection. The individual's body, energy field, lifestyle, society, etc., all represent external reference points for human consciousness. In a sense, every individual subject inhabits this multidimensional environment; or, more correctly, the subject exists in *opposition* to this environment.

Among the various Relations that make up the human system, the one that is unquestionably the most important is the mind/body (or psyche/soma) Relation.[35] Almost all of the perspectives included in the holistic health system embrace as a central concept the dialectical conception of the mind/body relationship—the notion that the "psychic anatomy" is relationally identical to the "physical anatomy."[36] This conception is particularly applicable to the phenomenon of organic disfunction. For example, Rolfing theory posits that disfunction in one sphere is always either a "reflection of" or "reflected in" the other sphere: "muscular tension and emotion are two aspects of the same organic pattern."[37] Similarly, the Reichian approach, which explains disfunction in terms of the "armoring process," argues that "muscular armoring" and "character armoring" represent the physical and psychical aspects of a total defense system.[38] As these statements suggest, no "bodily condition" can exist apart from an associated "condition of the mind." Any effort to distinguish bodily diseases and mental diseases as two separate realms of reality is a fruitless endeavor. The mind and body are absolutely opposed to one another, but they are parts of the same continuum.

The central place of the dialectical conceptualization of the relationship between subject and object or mind and body within the holistic health system is reflected in the fact that much of the holistic health literature deals with the process of investing "conscious attention" into the various dimensions of one's existence. Many of the modalities affiliated with the perspective consist of specific techniques for increasing awareness of some aspect of the human Gestalt. Examples of such techniques include the Bates eye method,[39] breathwork,[40] sensitive message,[41] biofeedback,[42] Reichian Therapy,[43] autogenic training,[44] dreamwork,[45] hypnosis,[46] meditative discipline,[47] T'ai Chi,[48] witnessing,[49] and dance therapy.[50]

Holistic health advocates believe that the therapeutic potential of these awareness techniques lies in their effectiveness for tapping into the healing mechanism, which is viewed as a counterpart to the processes that give rise to certain kinds of bodily disfunction. This perspective posits that the origin point of many forms of bodily disease is the psyche or mind.[51] Some forms of bodily disfunction are viewed as the concrete manifestations of a negative condition existing in the mental sphere. In most cases, the mental production of bodily disease occurs unconsciously, leading the individual to assume that the illness derives from other, nonpsychic sources. A major concern of holistic health practitioners is to make people aware of the mental origins of their illnesses and, further, to encourage the use of "conscious attention" as a means to either prevent disfunction or to eliminate illness once it appears.

There are two separate ways in which conscious attention can promote health. First, by simply being more aware of body functions, one can acquire the knowledge needed to make informed choices about daily routines that will allow one to avoid disfunction and/or enhance the body's self-healing mechanisms. For example, by becoming aware of the effect of certain foods or emotional states on one's digestive system, an individual can regulate food intake and the emotional climate during meals so as to prevent digestive problems. The yoga perspective advocates the use of postures (asanas) as a means to increase the individual's awareness of body strengths and weaknesses, which can then lead to a more healthful lifestyle.[53] Breath awareness can allow one to learn about and alter neuromuscular conditions such as chronic tension, nervousness, and unhealthy habitual breathing patterns.[54] These forms of conscious attention yield valuable information ✓ about the unique constitution of one's body, information that can be used in the effort to exercise a greater degree of control over this system.

The second health promoting function of conscious attention involves a more direct method of controlling bodily processes. As the technique of "biofeedback" illustrates, most people possess the capacity to "mentally direct" physiological processes. In biofeedback, an individual can manipulate many of the "autonomic" processes by simply making mental contact with these processes and "willing" the desired change.[55] Autogenic training works in much the same way as biofeedback, although it uses a different set of techniques to control various autonomic mechanisms.[56] The most important use of this mental control capacity, however, is to influence the body's self-healing processes. Advocates of "meditative contemplation" posit that by sustaining an idea in the mind, we establish contact with the healing forces of the body: "we are symbolic creatures; our bodies react to ideas."[57] Similarly, hermeticism embraces the notion that healing primarily consists of "paying attention" to body functions.[58] Actual techniques for mentally enhancing healing mechanisms include the "organ specific formula" associated with the autogenic method[59] and the technique of "creative visualization."[60] The latter

> is a method of visualizing the disease process, for use with malignancies
> . . . The cancer patient is taught to relax and is then guided through a

meditation in which the tumor is visualized. The treatment (chemotherapy, surgery, radiation, etc.) is then visualized, and the tumor is seen to slowly weaken, shrink, and finally disappear altogether. The mediation instructions may be taped for home use, four times a day. This technique may prove useful in the treatment of other diseases as well, even where there is no suspected psychogenic component as there is in cancer.[61]

The primary significance of both forms of conscious attention is that they allow the individual to control health maintenance and the process by which disfunction is eliminated. The holistic health perspective posits that in many instances individuals themselves unwittingly create their diseases and therefore only they have the capacity to "heal" themselves. Those who claim the capacity to heal others can, in actuality, only help patients to heal themselves, usually by convincing them that a particular agent or technique has curative power.[62] A major goal of holistic health is to promote an understanding of the *true* nature of disfunction (its appearance and elimination) so that control over healing can be shifted from health providers to individual laypersons.

As a part of the effort to encourage the development and use of awareness techniques, holistic health advocates have emphasized several different modes of conscious attention. The predominance of rationalistic methods of apprehending reality in modern Western society suggests that the potential of other methods may not have been adequately explored.[63] Consequently, a central concern of holistic health is to create a complementary blending of the intellectual (logico-deductive) and the sensuous (intuitive) forms of knowing. For example, one goal of meditation is to develop intuitive abilities to a point where the individual can acquire comprehensive, "ineffable" or "noetic" knowledge. This is believed to allow for a more continuous, holistic apprehension of reality.[64] Many holistic health modalities place special emphasis on the use of intuitive knowledge, including naturopathy,[65] iridology,[66] Reichian therapy,[67] and Chinese medicine.[68]

An example of a technique for generating intuitive knowledge is dream analysis. This method, which has had a long history (particularly within Chinese medicine[69]), is rooted in the belief that an intimate relationship exists between dreams, mental activity, and physiological processes. Consequently, one can discover a great deal of important information about bodily activity in one's dreams.[70] Another repository of information hidden from normal waking consciousness is the "psychic event." Entelechial therapy relies on "altered states of consciousness" (which can be produced by a number of techniques) to reveal information about how specific beliefs and attitudes affect a person both physiologically and emotionally.[71] In general, "psychic diagnosis" (diagnosis based on information yielded in altered states of consciousness) is viewed as one of the principle methods of developing a greater awareness of bodily function.

Closely associated with the development and use of intuition as a method for increasing people's awareness of their multidimensional existence are the techniques mentioned earlier in discussing mental control of bodily processes. In addition to the practices of autogenic training, biofeedback, and visualization, the technique of "passive concentration" can function as an effective method for exercising control over autonomic processes. A point often expressed in the holistic health literature is the idea that autonomic functions cannot be controlled by the will alone.[72] Overt efforts to affect change sometimes lead to the opposite of the desired outcome.[73] Consequently, mental control of autonomic processes can sometimes be achieved only by adopting a "passive attitude" toward the changes that are desired. The "not-doing" approach[74] allows one to initiate changes through a method of "non-exertion."[75] Through a number of practical techniques (including meditation, breathwork, T'ai Chi, dance therapy, polarity, etc.) one can "stop the internal dialogue"[76], which is correlated with an important mental shift—the shift from logical thought (located in the left hemisphere of the brain) to intuitive thought (located in the right hemisphere).[77] Only after one has succeeded in reaching the intuitive mode can the subjective will be realized within the objective domain of the body.

The emphasis on "increased awareness" is not focused on the body exclusively. The multitherapeutic thrust of the holistic health system means that psychological/emotional awareness, social awareness, and spiritual awareness are considered to be no less important than the bodily awareness. Just as increased awareness of the body results in a greater level of control over this dimension of the human system, an investment of conscious attention into the more emergent dimensions contributes to greater control over these domains as well. This perspective advocates a way of life characterized by a high degree of personal introspection, social awareness and activism, and spiritual reflection.

The Source of Organic Disfunction

The holistic health system, like any medical paradigm, must confront the problem of specifying an "essential" spatial plane in which to locate bodily disfunction. Many different dimensions or systems within the whole of the body could be a potential locus for bodily disfunction: organ systems, tissue systems, and biochemical systems. However, the holistic health approach to causality within the human Gestalt—the proposition that every whole subsumes the less emergent wholes below it—is inconsistent with any effort to locate organic disfunction in only one part of the body whole. To the extent that each part of the body exists in an interpenetrating relationship with every other part, what affects one aspect of the system will affect all other aspects as well. Disfunction in one organ or tissue affects the functioning of all other organs and tissues.[78] When we speak of organic (as opposed to metaorganic) disfunction, we are dealing with a condition of the body as a whole and never the condition of a part taken separately.

The holistic health perspective applies the same basic logic to the problem of identifying the sources of bodily disfunction. In view of the holistic nature of human existence, it makes little sense to search for a single cause of a given disorder. Within the holist epistemological system, the notion of cause and effect is discarded in favor of the idea of the "coexistence and interaction" of all the elements that make up the human system. For example, the naturopathic approach embraces the idea that a particular bodily disfunction must always be traced to the simultaneous interaction of many different factors rather than a single "disease agent."[79] Different holistic health modalities focus on different aspects of the human system (because it would be impossible for any one modality to deal with every aspect of the human Gestalt), but all of the modalities share a common belief in the multifactorial nature of bodily disfunction.

The fact that everything is causally related to everything else within the human Gestalt does *not* mean that we cannot make categorical distinctions within this system: making these is not only possible but necessary. Accordingly, the causal factors involved in bodily disfunction are distinguished at the most abstract level as belonging to two planes—the time and space planes. Within the latter plane, one finds further categorical distinctions—the various wholes within wholes discussed earlier. These distinctions are relevant to practical, therapeutic matters because there is a rough correspondence between the different categories of causal factors and the various modalities that make up the holistic health system. Each modality tends to emphasize one category of causal factors rather than another in dealing with bodily disfunction.

Within the spatial plane, bodily disfunction is regarded as a manifestation of some form of imbalance at one of the metaorganic levels. In particular, bodily disfunction is the result of a homeostatic response to imbalance in some other dimension of the human Gestalt.[80] As Tiller notes, an asymmetric mechanical stress applied to the bodily will result in the development of bone girders in a direction to support that stress. Other forms of stress or imbalance (vital energy, mental, social, or spiritual imbalance) have an analogous effect on the organic system (the whole of the body).[81] The equilibrating mechanism of the body produces alternations in body structure to offset a state of imbalance in some portion of the body's environment.

The most immediate (most proximate) environment to which the body's homeostatic mechanism must respond is the individual's "extended energy field."[82] Several holistic health modalities locate the source of bodily disfunction within this dimension. These perspectives posit that bodily disfunction "is not within the cells, per se, but is rather a perversion of the vital energy pattern that animates them."[83] Homeopathy, for example, is distinguished by its techniques for locating (and treating) the cause of bodily disfunction on a dynamic, energetic level rather than on the physical or chemical level.[84] The Reichian perspective posits that pent up sexual energy (termed *sexual stasis*) takes the form of blocked vital energy currents that, in turn, give rise to both psychological and physical disfunction.[85] Although most of the perspectives that emphasize the energetic realm acknowledge the possible influence of "more emergent" causal factors associated with vital energy imbalance, they hold that the energetic dimension is often the best access point for the treatment of bodily disfunction.

Another form of imbalance that can ultimately lead to bodily disfunction is imbalance in the mental plane. Just as the body's homeostatic mechanism produces alterations in organic structure to compensate for asymmetric mechanical forces or blocked vital energy, it also produces alterations in response to psychological imbalance.[86] A variety of mental states can be correlated with organic disfunction. Perhaps the most well-known and well researched disfunction-producing mental state is stress. Some have suggested that many of the epidemic diseases of modern Western culture, including coronary artery disease, hypertension, and cancer, are ultimately linked to the high levels of stress endemic to modern social life.[87] Although the possibility of a link between mental stress and organic disfunction is a new and controversial notion for Western medicine, this idea has been systematized in Chinese medicine for thousands of years. In fact, this latter perspective (which has been formally embraced by the holistic health system) has succeeded in correlating specific kinds of stress with specific kinds of physical disorders: excessive anger is associated with liver disfunction; excessive fear with kidney disfunction; excessive longing with spleen disfunction.[88] Other disfunction-producing mental imbalances mentioned in the holistic health literature include "frustrated expectations,"[89] "failure to love oneself,"[90] and "worry."[91]

The next level of the human Gestalt that can harbor disfunction-producing conditions is the ecological environment. The kind of imbalances in this realm that relate most directly to organic functioning consist of conditions effecting exchange between the organism and the environment. A great deal of organic disfunction is associated with either excessive or deficient exchange between the organism and the environment. An individual who ingests, absorbs, or inhales either too much or too little of certain substances will experience physical distress. Socio-ecological conditions that structure or effect nutrition and substance abuse are crucial causal factors in the phenomenon of organic disfunction. Equally important are socio-ecological factors that relate to the prevalence of environmental toxins. Air, water, and soil pollution are causal factors in many of the diseases that characterize modern society (particularly the cancers). The holistic health approach views imbalances in this realm as particularly important precursors of organic disfunction.

One aspect of the ecological environment that deserves special attention is the category of organisms that we know as "pathogens." As with the other diseases discussed thus far, the holistic health system conceptualizes the phenomenon of pathogen-produced disfunction in terms of the relationship between the attack of the pathogen and the response of the body's homeostatic mechanism. Two things are stressed by this approach: First, pathogens exist in great variety and numbers, and they continually evolve over time, which means that they can never be eliminated from the environment. Second, the body is under constant attack by pathogens, and it effectively defends itself most of the time. We become aware of the attack of a pathogen only when our body defenses break down or reach a level where we begin to experience symptomatic responses (fever, aches, etc.). This suggests that in pathogen-produced disfunction, a "susceptible organism" is as important a factor in the etiology of disease as the pathogen itself. The disease does not result from the pathogen attack alone; it results from the *interaction* of the pathogen and a susceptible organism.[92]

In articulating these ideas, holistic health advocates move into the principle domain of a medical perspective with a long history and a permanent place in the pantheon of medical knowledge systems. The public health perspective, which has remained a viable medical perspective even as the biomedical model has risen to a position of preeminence during the twentieth century, has recently received support from a newly emerging body of evidence. Some of this evidence can be found in Thomas McKeown's (1979) study of causal factors in the "demographic transition" of the eighteenth, nineteenth, and twentieth centuries. It has been widely accepted that the decline in the mortality rate and general improvement in health during this period was due to spectacular advances in the realm of personal medical services. However, McKeown demonstrates through his analysis of mortality and morbidity statistics for England and Wales that personal services had very little to do with the improvement. In the case of most of the infectious diseases that threatened the population, the decline in mortality began *before* the introduction of practice-based medical scientific procedures to treat the diseases. This leads

McKeown to conclude that other factors played a more important role in bringing about the decline.

In his effort to identify the critical causal factors, McKeown directs the focus to the social and ecological environmental variables that impinge upon human biological function—the ultimate causal factors emphasized by holistic health. He argues that four factors account for the decline in the death rate during this period: (1) the improvement in nutrition that resulted from advances in agricultural techniques; (2) the institutionalization of environmental sanitation measures in the late nineteenth century; (3) control over reproduction that kept the population from exceeding the carrying capacity of the environment; and (4) immunization and vaccination practices that improved resistance to disease. McKeown embraces the holistic health position in proposing that the principle effect of these four changes at the metaorganic levels of society and the ecological environment was to decrease susceptibility to the attack of pathogens. Other researchers adopting the public health perspective have produced evidence similar to McKeown's, lending further support to this proposition.[93]

In summary, the holistic health system views bodily disfunction as the organic manifestation or reflection of a state of imbalance at some higher (metaorganic) level of the human Gestalt. In addition, any given disease condition is believed to result from the interaction of the particular array of elements that make up an individual's Gestalt at a given point in time—elements located in the plane of the body as well as elements outside of this organic whole. While organic disfunction can be conceived in terms of coexistence and interaction of many elements (as opposed to the single cause and effect conceptualization), this phenomenon occurs in the broader framework of the wholes within wholes that make up the human Gestalt. In dealing with the problem of "locating the source of organic disfunction," the holistic health perspective adopts a twin strategy: on one hand, it pursues a multifactorial approach, specifying as many different causal elements as possible; but, at the same time, it places special emphasis on the ultimate causes of disfunction, which, by definition, are the conditions that exist at the most emergent levels of human existence.[94]

In the search for the ultimate sources of imbalance, priority must be assigned to the social dimension. The way in which individuals structure their daily reality (which is, of course, a reflection of the kind of society in which they live) has a powerful impact on their mental (psychological/emotional), energetic, and physical existence. Numerous references are made in the holistic health literature to the effect of lifestyle on the vital energy field.[95] Similarly, there can be no question of the intimate link between one's mental state, one's lifestyle, and the society to which one belongs.[96] All of the mental states correlated with organic disfunction—i.e., stress, the way in which individuals view themselves, their expectations, values, etc.,—are shaped by the social structural environment (which includes the phenomena of social-ization, interaction, and the way one acquires one's means of subsistence). Social structure also has a powerful influence on the ecological factors that were identified as causal factors in organic disfunction. This is clearly dem-onstrated by intra- and intersocietal variations in nutrition, substance abuse, and levels of environmental toxins.[97] Even the distribution of pathogens is structured by social interactional patterns, as the discipline of social epide-miology has clearly shown. In short, holistic health's commitment to empha-sizing the ultimate sources of organic disfunction over the proximate sources gives this perspective a decidedly sociological bent, suggesting that organic disfunction is best understood as a reflection of the structure of society. As we will see later, this notion has some important implications.

All of the causal factors discussed thus far belong to the spatial plane. This represents just one of two basic categories of causal factors, the other one being the time plane. In addition to emphasizing the relations between organic disfunction and imbalance in the metaorganic realms, the holistic health ap-proach argues that a disease condition must be understood in terms of its relations to past physical or mental traumas.[98] Consonant with this notion, several different modalities (naturopathy and homeopathy, in particular)[99] embrace the "law of cure." This law states that as the body becomes nour-ished and cleansed, symptoms of old illnesses appear in reverse chronological order.[100] Similarly, the Reichian and Rolfing perspectives point out that body tissue manipulation is often accompanied by the spontaneous appearance of pain and emotional release associated with past traumatic events.[101] These phenomena suggest that the distinctions we make between one incidence of disfunction and another are rather arbitrary. Just as organic disfunction is continuous across space, it is continuous across time as well.

Symptoms and Organic Disfunction

In the previous section, organic disfunction was defined as a reflection of imbalance at some metaorganic level of the human Gestalt. Hence, the countersystem perspective views organic disfunction as a sign or signal of a condition existing in a spatial plane outside of the whole of the body. This exterior spatial plane (or planes) constitutes the locus of most of the conditions that give rise to disfunction.

This way of conceiving organic disfunction points to an important problem. If organic disfunction is a physical sign of a metaorganic condition, then how are we to conceptualize that category of phenomena termed as "symptoms" in Western culture? This question can be answered by returning to the relationship between metaorganic imbalance and the body's homeostatic mechanism. As noted earlier, a condition of imbalance within any of the metaorganic dimensions leads to an immediate compensatory response by the body's homeostatic mechanism, a response that can ultimately produce an alteration in organic structure. Prior to any tissue alteration, however, the body undergoes a set of changes that can be classified as "defensive measures"—efforts by the body's natural reactive mechanism to rid itself of toxicosis (which is the material manifestation of imbalance within the metaorganic realm).[102] These defensive measures constitute what we know of as symptoms: vomiting works to rid the body of gastrointestinal poisons; fever works to burn up toxins.

Both symptoms and organic disfunction are viewed as reflections of metaorganic imbalance, and the two terms refer to the same general phenomenon—both are physical signs of metaorganic conditions. The difference between these two categories has to do with their respective positions in the causal sequence. In contrast to the medical scientific assumption that symptoms indicate the existence of pathological tissue, the holistic health approach posits that symptoms can precede the appearance of pathological tissue.[103] A disturbance in the vital force (or any other form of metaorganic imbalance) is manifested in the organic realm as toxicosis, which activates the body's defensive mechanisms and a specific symptomatic reaction. If appropriate treatment follows the onset of symptoms, the appearance of pathological tissue can often be prevented.[104]

Diagnosis of Organic Disfunction

In light of the unique way in which bodily disfunction is conceptualized in the holistic health system, one would expect a correspondingly unique approach to the diagnosis of disfunction. The location of the sources of organic disfunction in domains outside of the body dictates that diagnostic perception must also be directed to these metaorganic realms. However, as Tiller points out, one cannot hope to adequately perceive new dimensions of reality unless one is equipped with a system of appropriate cognitive categories.[105] In modern Western culture, we have access to an extensive and systematic set of cognitive categories for perceiving the *organic* aspect of the disease process, but we possess few categories that are appropriate to the metaorganic realms. Consequently, holistic health advocates have suggested the need for a new system of diagnostic terms that can be appended to the existing system. These diagnostic terms, which may include such concepts as "loneliness," "guilt," "powerlessness," etc., would refer to the nonphysical aspects of the disease process.[106]

In addition to altering the spatial focus of diagnostic perception, the holistic health approach reorients the diagnostic process to a new time frame. The process by which metaorganic imbalance is translated into alterations in organic structure does not occur instantaneously. It involves a set of specific events in a particular time sequence: imbalance leads to toxicosis, which, in turn, leads to a symptomatic defensive response. Depending on the outcome of this defensive response, tissue damage may or may not follow. The existence of this lag period between the development of metaorganic imbalance and the appearance of tissue disfunction creates an opportunity for effective medical intervention. If one attends to the various signs of imbalance that appear before the onset of tissue disfunction, then an appropriate treatment regimen can be adopted and tissue damage can be avoided.

This treatment approach focuses on a category of signs that develop prior not only to tissue disfunction but to symptoms as well. In the section dealing with the nature of the body whole, it was stated that every element or aspect of this system exists in an interpenetrating relationship with every other element; hence, each part is a reflection of its relations to every other part. This implies that certain of the more accessible parts of the body reflect changes that occur in less accessible parts. Since the homeostatic response to imbalance precedes the appearance of symptoms, one can detect imbalance long before symptoms emerge by looking for the signals of these homeostatic changes in certain key body parts. Different holistic health modalities emphasize different "access points." Chinese medicine focuses on the radial pulse, which is believed to reflect changes in the meridians, the bowels, and other key organs (with twenty-seven separate pulse indications).[107] Iridology singles out the eye as the most useful access point, positing that the eye is connected to every organ, the nervous system and the circulatory system,[108] and reflects the "emergent character" of interacting body parts.[109] Several modalities (Yoga, Reichian therapy, etc.) focus on the respiratory system and suggest that "breathing patterns" reveal many different kinds of organic changes.[110] The polarity approach posits that all the body can be seen in the head, neck, feet, and hands; therefore, it focuses its attention on these body parts in diagnosis.[111]

By using these different access points as a basis for diagnosis, the holistic health approach, in effect, shifts the time frame of the diagnostic process. Organic disfunction is diagnosed as it actually unfolds rather than *after* tissue damage has already occurred. Of course, this kind of diagnosis is effective in preventing tissue damage only if it is practiced as a form of maintenance activity. The various diagnostic access points must be examined on a regular basis and not simply because a problem is suspected.

Response to Organic Disfunction

The holistic definition of health as action leading to the maintenance and development of human capabilities and the pursuit of balance, is distinguished not only by the unique goals and action that it advocates but also by what it *doesn't* advocate. In contrast to definitions of health that have prevailed in other historical periods, this perspective does not designate "the elimination of organic disfunction" as a health-producing activity. In this system, an individual can experience organic disfunction and still be considered as healthy. Organic disfunction is not the opposite of health.[112]

If the elimination of organic disfunction is not a part of health production, then what is the proper response to this phenomenon? The answer to this question lies in the conceptualization or organic disfunction. Representing a sign or signal of a state of imbalance within one or more of the metaorganic dimensions, organic disfunction can be treated as a "feedback message."[113] Rather than treat disfunction as something to be eliminated, this perspective views the experience of disfunction as an opportunity to learn about oneself.[114] More specifically, it can be used to set a direction for balancing efforts (which is one component of the overall health production effort). Symptoms, which also signal tissue disfunction, can also be regarded as feedback messages.[115] Both phenomena indicate the presence of a specific form of imbalance, which then allows one to choose the balancing techniques that are most appropriate to one's needs.

These considerations point to additional aspects of the conceptual approach to disfunction within this system. Implicit in the notion of organic disfunction as a feedback message is the idea that disfunction can be properly designated as "biological deviance," i.e., a departure from a particular standard of biological normality. While disfunction is regarded as deviance in the biological sense, it is not treated as "social deviance"—something that, because of its biologically abnormal status, is considered as undesirable. Organic disfunction is merely information that can be useful for organizing one's health producing efforts, not something to be eliminated at all costs.[116] This approach to disfunction allows the holistic health system to avoid what its advocates believe are the iatrogenic consequences of a disease elimination approach:

> [a] system that constantly focuses on what's wrong, on what needs to be treated/cured, is a system which will inadvertently create more of what it is designed to alleviate, i.e., more illnesses to treat/cure.[117]

Treatment of Organic Disfunction

The holistic health system adopts a truly unique approach to health and organic disfunction: A commitment to a health production agenda that includes the pursuit of maintenance, growth and development, and balance is assumed to make action directed toward eliminating disfunction unnecessary. The body's self-healing properties are so enhanced by this kind of health production approach that the need for medical treatment is minimized.

This orientation notwithstanding, holistic health advocates acknowledge that on occasion, even the most healthy of individuals experience organic disfunction that must be treated. The problem, of course, is to specify the precise circumstances under which one ceases to regard organic disfunction as a feedback message and instead endeavors to treat or eliminate it. Two kinds of circumstances justify this shift in orientation. Obviously, when disfunction becomes life-threatening or when individuals are so incapacitated by disfunction that they can no longer engage in health production action, then treatment efforts must be undertaken.

Under either of these circumstances, treatment of a special kind is required. In general, organic disfunction is properly dealt with by taking steps to aid the self-healing mechanisms of the human Gestalt. The concept of the "healing power of nature" is the foundation of many holistic health modalities, including such approaches as naturopathy,[118] homeopathy,[119] Chinese medicine,[120] and polarity.[121] Natural healing avoids the use of symptomatic, palliative treatment[122] and, instead, involves only techniques that act in harmony with the self-healing processes of the human system.[123] A variety of distinct techniques serve this function, but all of them can be grouped into either one or two basic categories: (1) mental techniques that involve the use of mental awareness/control of physiological processes, and (2) physical techniques, which consist of various physical and/or biochemical manipulations.

A number of the mental healing techniques have been discussed in the section dealing with the concept of consciousness and awareness control. A technique like creative visualization involves the use of mental imagery to enhance the healing process: one may create a metaphorical mental picture of the illness and a defensive response to that illness, or imagine the dissolution of energy blocks and the free flow of vital energy through the body.[124] In addition, several mental techniques exist for eliciting a relaxation response that is believed to be of great therapeutic value.[125] For example, the Bates eye method posits that most vision problems result from a stress-related muscle tension, which can be dissolved through relaxation.[126] Lomi and autogenic training are two similar techniques for eliciting a therapeutic relaxation response.[127] Finally, one even finds some modalities emphasizing love (love of oneself and love of others) as a healing force that can be mentally stimulated.[128]

Even more numerous are the different physical techniques for aiding self-healing processes, which involve two subcategories. The first refers to the ingestion of substances that are believed to enhance the body's efforts to rid itself of disease. In accordance with the conception of symptoms as the manifestation of the body's defense against toxicosis, several modalities attempt to augment this defensive effort by administering "natural agents" that work in the same direction as the symptoms.[129] Another form of biochemical manipulation, adopted by such modalities and perspectives as Chinese medicine and hermeticism, is nutritional therapy. Chinese medicine regards food as medicine and posits that certain foods either aggravate or help specific ailments.[130] Other approaches advocate nutritional manipulation for disorders ranging from vision problems to radiation sickness.[131]

The second subcategory of physical techniques consists of various forms of anatomical manipulation. Here, the principal goal is to release blockages in vital energy, which are believed to be the proximate metaorganic sources of body disfunction. Acupuncture is perhaps the most well-known technique for accomplishing this goal. This ancient practice, which involves injecting needles into key locations in the body, results in the stimulation or dispersal of the flow of energy, which, in turn, allows for the regulation of bodily functions supported by that energy.[132] The balancing of vital energy also serves as a key concern of polarity therapy and the chiropractic, both of which employ techniques for manipulating the patient's body.[133] Finally, the technique of T'ai Chi attempts to balance vital energy through the use of coordinated, dance-like movements.[134]

Another unique aspect of treatment within the holistic health model involves the individualized approach to disease categorization. Recall that disease is conceived within this system not as the pathogen but rather as the interaction between the pathogen and the body. The uniqueness of every organism means that the *relation* between the organism and the pathogen is also unique. Consequently, no logical foundation exists for a treatment approach that emphasizes "standard diseases." All treatment must ultimately be focused on "unique individuals experiencing disfunction." Homeopathic therapy offers, perhaps, the best illustration of this principle: Homeopaths do not prescribe medicine according to the name of a disease but rather prescribe for the patient's unique configuration of symptoms.[135] In a similar way, acupuncture treatments are always modified according to the practitioner's awareness of the distinctively individual needs of each person.[136]

Other unique aspects of holistic health treatment are closely associated with this latter feature. The unique character of every patient mandates that treatment be focused on the whole of the body and not just its separate subsystems.[137] The most reliable indicators of the nature of the organic disfunction are the individual's own subjective feelings.[138] By accepting all patient complaints as legitimate symptoms of disfunction, one can orient treatment to patients rather than the patient's medical tests.[139] Treatment that is directed to the whole of the body also deals with that aspect of infectious disease usually ignored by more traditional treatment approaches—the susceptibility of the organism. As suggested earlier, infectious disease consists of two opposing moments: (1) the virulence of the disease agent, and (2) the resistance of the body to disease. Traditional treatment approaches neutralize virulence by attending to only one side of this relation. The holistic health approach tries to redress this imbalance by attempting to make systemic changes in the body that decrease susceptibility.[140]

This completes the description of the various presuppositions and concepts that make up the medical paradigm of our utopian medical model. Having outlined the cognitive dimension of the alternative medical model, I will now describe some of the key normative elements.

Normative Elements

As with all medical models, the system of beliefs about the nature of health and disease outlined in this chapter implies a set of normative principles that govern the process of health production. The core value of the holistic health system is the notion that individuals should assume responsibility for their health and the management of their illnesses to the greatest extent possible. The conception of health advanced by this perspective implies that only individuals themselves are capable of producing their own health. Conceptualized in terms of a health production process, health involves a commitment by the individual to a particular kind of lifestyle—one characterized by an ongoing effort to maintain and develop species capabilities and to maintain balance. The idea that someone can provide health for someone else (the kind of relationship that is implied by the terms "health provide" and "health consumer") is inconceivable in this system. One can acquire health only by taking the responsibility to make the necessary alterations in lifestyle required of a healthy individual.

The same basic value orientation is applied to the problem of managing organic disfunction. This approach sees some forms of disfunction arising from an unconscious choice to be ill (by virtue of the individual's acceptance of imbalance within the socio-ecological realm, and the tendency to harbor negative attitudes about oneself and others.) The individual and collective creation of illness implies another possibility—that people possess the power to heal disfunction as well. In some health care systems, the self-healing processes of the body are manipulated not by the individual experiencing illness but by another individual who fulfills a healer role (leading to the erroneous belief that the latter possesses the power to heal disfunction). In the holistic health system, by contrast, individuals experiencing illness are encouraged to assume an active stance towards the healing process—to learn to activate the self-healing mechanism themselves rather than relying on the suggestive power of omnipotent healers. In general, holistic health attempts to instill within the lay public a commitment to developing our ability to control our bodies (an ability that is largely untapped in Western culture) as one part of a more general commitment to actualizing all of our species capabilities to the maximum extent possible.

To assume the value of personal responsibility for health is not to ignore the fact that under some conditions, one must relinquish the responsibility for dealing with disfunction to someone else. Insofar as some forms of disfunction are associated with high levels of incapacitation, one may be forced to allow others to assume responsibility for treatment decisions and/or actions. By the same token, this approach does not assume that a practitioner role is an unnecessary part of a viable health care system. Medical knowledge and skill are still regarded as unequally distributed resources in the population— no single person can be expected to internalize all of the knowledge needed to deal with all of the health problems that s/he will confront in a lifetime. As we will see later, the goal of individual responsibility for health can be reconciled with these problems through the institutionalization of a particular set of social structural arrangements. The goal of individual responsibility cannot always be realized, but an alternative health care system can be envisioned in which this notion serves as a normative ideal.

THE DISTRIBUTION OF MEDICAL KNOWLEDGE

In addition to dealing with the problem of knowledge content, a sociology of knowledge approach must also take account of the distribution of knowledge in the social system under analysis. Hence, a crucial concern of the present study is the issue of how medical knowledge is distributed in both the utopian and traditional models. This section provides a description of the pattern of knowledge distribution within the holistic health system.

In order to synthesize a knowledge distribution structure that accords with the medical paradigm described above, we must first return to some of the key presuppositions of the holistic health approach. A central element of this perspective is the idea of the multidimensional nature of human existence (and the concept of the human Gestalt). A good portion of our discussion of the holistic health perspective involved examining the part that this feature plays in the phenomena of health and illness. One issue remaining to be addressed is the problem of relating the multidimensional conception of health and illness to the development of a systematically organized body of applied knowledge for dealing with these phenomena. In other words, we must determine what kind of medical knowledge system is required to deal with every possible facet of health reality, particularly if concepts that are appropriate to some dimensions cannot be logically integrated with concepts that are appropriate to other dimensions (for example, spiritual concepts versus anatomo-physiological concepts).

This problem can be addressed by considering some implications of the preceding discussion of the countersystem medical paradigm. Throughout this discussion, repeated references have been made to the various modalities and perspectives found under the holistic health umbrella. The core concepts discussed above serve as a metaconceptual framework for all of these holistic health modalities. While the separate modalities are rooted in a common set of presuppositions, they each focus on different dimensions of the human Gestalt: iridology is concerned exclusively with the eyes; T'ai Chi with body movement; acupuncture with the vital energy field. In addition, different modalities dealing with the same realm of the Gestalt often use different conceptual categories for organizing that realm. For example, both the autogenic approach and the meditation perspective emphasize the various physiological mechanisms associated with the relaxation response, but each modality conceptualizes this phenomenon differently.

What distinguishes the holistic health model, then, is its eclectic approach to medical thinking and practice. A basic tenet of holistic health thinking is that no one body of medical knowledge can take into account all aspects of health reality, and, therefore, all medical perspectives are inherently partial. Consequently, the only way to deal with all of the different facets of health reality is to adopt a multitherapeutic approach, which, in turn, demands a multiperspectival system. As David Hayes-Bautista notes,

> an illness . . . can have any number of causes, most of which are interrelated; the causes can be organic, but they also can be economic, social, political, cultural, ecological, psychological, etc. They cannot be treated in isolation. If then there are multiple causes to any illness, there is a need for multiple interventions, and these multiple interventions can occur at several different levels.

The unique feature of knowledge distribution this system is *not* the fact that one finds a variety of distinct medical perspectives existing side by side within the same social context. Historical and cross-cultural examination reveals that this feature is common to many societies (and certainly characteristic of contemporary Western culture). This distribution of knowledge is unique in this system because all of the separate perspectives included in the holistic health framework are granted equal legitimacy. Unlike the situation in other medical systems, adherents of different approaches do not compete with one another to establish their knowledge system as the only valid one for understanding the nature of health and illness. Every perspective is viewed as a potentially legitimate approach within its particular domain of interest. As a matter of policy, the holistic health approach promotes a system of health care that is both comprehensive in scope and responsive to the unique needs of individual health producers by encouraging the development and use of many different medical perspectives.

THE SOCIAL STRUCTURAL DIMENSION

Having completed the description of the knowledge dimension of the medical countersystem, we can now consider the social structural implications of this alternative model for conceptualizing health reality. In the language of holism, the task ahead consists of tracing Relations from the knowledge dimension into the social structural dimension (assuming the existence of a relational identity between these two realms). We will begin with the central social Relation of all systems of medical practice, the relationship between patient and practitioner.

Micro Structure: The Patient-Practitioner Relationship

In the holistic health system, the role of patient is defined as an individual who is committed to a specific course of health production activity. Patients may also seek to deal with organic disfunction in a way that defines the direction of their health production activity (by indicating the nature of some source of imbalance). Although patients often do establish a relationship with a practitioner in an effort to deal with disfunction, the defining criterion of the patient role in this system is the commitment to health production. Thus, one does not have to be ill in order to enter into a patient-practitioner relationship.

One important factor that structures the patient role is the norm of personal responsibility for health. In the holistic health system, a patient does not assume a passive stance towards health. People and the institutions they maintain create health and disfunction; therefore, a patient is expected to take full responsibility for all health-related matters. This activist stance applies not only to the individual's use of specific health production and treatment techniques but to the socio-political realm as well. Beyond the organic and psychological causes of disfunction are the social, cultural, economic, and political factors that impinge on the health of every member of society. The norm of personal responsibility is particularly relevant to these domains.

The relational counterpart of the role of patient is, of course, the practitioner role. Just as the patient role is consistent with (relationally identical with) certain cognitive/normative elements of the holistic health system, so is the practitioner role. The holistic health emphasis on patient control of all action directed toward health production and the management of disfunction would seem to eliminate the need for the practitioner, but, in fact, the practitioner fulfills an important function in this system. The patient is expected to take responsibility for all health matters, which is possible only if one possesses the knowledge needed to make one's health-related actions effective. Given the tremendous complexity of health reality and the knowledge systems that refer to various aspects of that reality, no individual patient could possibly acquire all of the knowledge needed to guide his or her actions. Therefore, individuals who are trained in specific medical disciplines must provide the patient with the required information. This important function of disseminating information is the central focus of the practitioner role.[141]

In order to maximize the degree of control exercised by the patient over health production and disease elimination, the practitioner assumes the role of teacher or facilitator.[142] The practitioner is expected to help patients reach their health care goals rather than act as a healer. This approach is consistent with the holistic health notion that all healing is self-healing. The practitioner's role is to encourage patients to be fully aware of the direct connections between the various facets of their existence (mind, society, etc.) and the functioning of their bodies. Rather than making use of the power of suggestion to stimulate healing, the practitioner helps to bring the patient's self-conscious will into the healing process by instructing them in the techniques that they can use for this purpose. The paternalism that characterizes the practitioner role in most health care systems gives way to a partnership orientation in the holistic health system.[143]

Although the holistic health practitioner primarily acts as a health educator or teacher rather than as a healer, circumstances do sometimes arise in which the practitioner must take an active part in dealing with disfunction. In cases of patient incapacitation, responsibility for treatment shifts from the patient to other individuals—first, to those who may be classified as the patient's significant others (family members, friends, etc.) and then to those classified as practitioners. This way of constructing the chain of responsibility is designed to insure that the control of the patient's body/mind/spirit remains as close to the patient as possible.

Macro Structure: The Structure of Medical Practice

The patient-practitioner Relation of any health care system cannot be understood in isolation from the broader structure of medical practice to which it is related. In any health care system (and *all* social systems, for that matter), the micro and macro dimensions exist in dialectical relation to one another with each dimension defining the other. The precise meaning of this statement will emerge in the course of discussing the relationship between the patient-practitioner Relation and the structure of medical practice in the holistic health system.

In the previous section, we saw that the central feature of the patient-practitioner relationship is the dominant power position of the patient: patients are responsible for making decisions about their health and they exercise control over all health producing actions relating to their own body/mind/spirit. The practitioner, on the other hand, is the subordinate power holder in the relationship: s/he merely provides the knowledge that patients need to reach their health care goals. The contradiction in this relationship involves the practitioner's control over the key resource in the health production process. As the primary source of medical knowledge, the practitioner occupies a potentially powerful position vis-a-vis the patient— individuals seeking to achieve their health care goals can do so only with the cooperation of practitioners. Although the power that derives from controlling medical knowledge is an inherent feature of the practitioner role, the degree of power varies according to how medical practice is structured. In the holistic health system, the occupational organization of medical practice is structured so that the inherent power of the practitioner is minimized.

In order to understand this aspect of the holistic health system, we must consider again the nature of knowledge distribution in this system. A variety of medical perspectives exist within the holistic health framework, and all of these medical perspectives are granted equal legitimacy. Consequently, in the holistic health system, no one medical professional group enjoys a monopoly over the right to practice medicine (a monopoly that is granted by social or legal sanction). All professional groups are granted the legal right to offer their knowledge and technique to those who need these resources to attain their health care goals. Such a structure is believed to afford patients the best opportunity to attain the knowledge that is most appropriate to their own unique health care needs and to provide a truly comprehensive system of knowledge and technique.

Another advantage of this kind of professional structure is that it serves ✓ to reduce the collective power of practitioners. Competition among different professional groups for the opportunity to provide their services to patients, undermines the ability of the practitioner collective to maintain a monolithic, interest-oriented professional structure. The nature of health and illness is such that many therapeutic alternatives exist for effectively dealing with a given health problem. Patients who for any reason are not satisfied with the help and advice they receive from a particular practitioner can always select from among a variety of approaches available within the holistic health system. The fact that patients always have this option forces practitioners to be attentive to their patient's needs.

CONCLUSIONS

In the preceding pages, a medical countersystem has been described that can be used for the analytical and practical/political purposes set forth in the first part of this volume. This system is best understood as a "constructed type" that is based on, but not identical with, pre-existing medical models currently used by practitioners or advocates engaged in actual medical intervention. I have borrowed elements from three distinct models. From the public health perspective, I have adopted the emphasis on the ultimate causal variables involved in human biological function—those aspects of the ecological and social systems that impinge upon the human organism's exchange of the crucial elements it needs for survival. In accordance with the public health approach, the countersystem embraces the proposition that primary emphasis should be placed on these ultimate factors, particularly with respect to practical efforts to improve human health.

From the biopsychosocial medical model, I have borrowed the concept of the multidimensional nature of human health and the concern for exercising rigorous standards of empirical research in our efforts to assess medical theories and practices at all levels and to expand medical knowledge. The countersystem shares the·biopsychosocial model's emphasis on the central importance of the person within the systems hierarchy, the understanding that the person "represents at the same time the highest level of the organismic hierarchy and the lowest level of the social hierarchy" (Engel 1980, 537). Equally important to the countersystem viewpoint is the concern to avoid a reliance on medical dogma, a principle theme in the biopsychosocial model but an unfortunate tendency in the holistic health movement.

The third empirical reference for our countersystem is the perspective of the holistic health movement. The majority of the substantive medical concepts that make up the countersystem come from my content analysis of this perspective. The countersystem incorporates holistic health's broad conceptualization of the various dimensions that make up the human Gestalt and its holistic (or dialectical) epistemological approach. With the merging of these various components of the three existing medical models, we have constructed the medical countersystem/utopia that will guide the remaining analysis and, hopefully, the practical and political efforts of the incipient collective representing the interests of the patient population.

CHAPTER FIVE

The Traditional Medical Model

Having synthesized an alternative medical model to be used as a reference point for analysis, we can now begin the analytical phase of the study. The goal of the next two chapters is to analyze the network of Relations making up the dominant system of medical practice in the United States during most of the twentieth century. These Relations are analyzed through the countersystem method: elements of the utopian, holistic health model are contrasted with traditional medical knowledge and practice, a procedure that helps to identify the core features of the traditional system. The analysis is also concerned with three more substantive goals. First, in the present chapter, which deals with the cognitive elements (presuppositions, concepts, etc.) that make up the medical knowledge system, the logical connections between the elements of the medical scientific paradigm are explored. In chapter 6, various relational (dialectical) identities and contradictions between the different facets of the medical practice system are identified. Finally, I attempt to discover the principle by which the medical system is organized—the principle of organization of the health care system as a whole.

Before beginning this part of the study, however, attention must be directed to an important theoretical problem associated with the analysis of the relationship between the ideal and material domains of the medical practice system. While modern medical practice is tied to the medical scientific system of knowledge, I will avoid treating the relationship between the medical science and actual medical practice as a static Relation. The relationship between a particular system of knowledge and the practice patterns associated with this knowledge is constantly evolving in one direction or another, and our analyses of such relationships should reflect this fact. Therefore, I have found it useful to treat the medical scientific model as an ideal type that diverges from the reality of modern medical practice in some important ways. The actual behavior of patients, physicians, and other health care workers is influenced by a variety of ideational factors even in a system in which one medical paradigm is hegemonic. Medical science has been the principle ideological influence in modern medical practice but not the only one. An attempt to capture the diachronic dimension of the relation between medical science and medical practice—to describe changing character of this relation over time—is of the utmost importance.

The dialectical paradigm supplies concepts that are particularly well-suited for this type of analysis. From a dialectical perspective, the relationship between medical science and modern medical practice is best conceived of in terms of a "developing Relational identity." Although a significant discrepancy existed between the dictates of medical science and the actual system of medical practice in the early decades of this century, the trend over the last eighty years has been for medical practice to become increasingly identical with the medical scientific model. As I will document later, the other ideological influences on the practice of allopathic physicians, although strong in earlier decades, have steadily waned in more recent decades. This transformation of the knowledge/practice Relation has, of course, been shaped by a number of social structural forces. A central concern at this point is to identify these social structural forces and to describe precisely how they have impacted on the Relation between medical knowledge and practice.

We begin with a description of the medical scientific paradigm followed in chapter 6 by a discussion of the structural relations of health production and a specification of the principle of organization of the traditional medical model. The order of presentation in these chapters differs from that of the previous chapter, reflecting the shift to a new stage in the study: in the remaining chapters, we engage in critical analysis rather than synthesis.

THE MEDICAL SCIENTIFIC PARADIGM

The analysis of the knowledge dimension of the traditional medical model focuses on the dominant medical paradigm within this model, the medical scientific perspective. This knowledge system is best understood as an ideal type. Both systems are logical constructs that are analytically distinct from any actual system of medical practice. In the case of medical science, however, the ideal nature of the perspective is less pronounced due its paradigmatic status within the medical practice system that has prevailed in the United States over the last eighty years. Despite this fact, it must be kept in mind that any formal medical model that we may identify must be treated as a caricature of the actual knowledge that is employed in medical practice.

In what follows, I have employed the countersystem method to elucidate the principle elements of medical science. We begin with the most important issue—the problem of defining health.

The Definition of Health.

As noted in the previous chapter, the definition of health is the most fundamental concept of any medical paradigm because it delineates the substantive goals of the health production process within the system in question. The anatomo-clinical definition of health differs from the utopian definition in two fundamental ways. While health is viewed as an ongoing process in the utopian system, it is a state of being in the traditional system. One is either healthy or nor healthy in this system. A healthy state can be achieved by adopting a proper course of health-producing action, and once this state is reached, one need not concern oneself with further health-producing efforts. The utopian and anatomo-clinical definitions of health differ in some additional ways. In the utopian system, health is defined as the process of maintaining and developing human species being and maintaining balance. In the anatomo-clinical system, however, health is defined as merely "the absence of bodily disfunction" (or the absence of disease, with disease being defined strictly in organic terms).[1] In the anatomo-clinical system, health and organic disfunction are two mutually exclusive conditions. If organic disfunction exists, then one is healthy and vice versa. This contrasts sharply with the holistic health approach to this relationship: because health is a process and organic disfunction a state of being, the two are not opposing conditions and, therefore, can exist simultaneously.

There is a second major difference between the utopian and anatomo-clinical definitions of health. Within the utopian system, health production is a multidimensional process involving action that is directed towards many different spheres of human existence. By contrast, health producing action in the anatomo-clinical system is distinguished by its reductionist character: because health is defined as freedom from organic disfunction, all health-producing activity involves the manipulations of various organic systems or processes. Healthy individuals need never concern themselves with any aspect of their existence other than the functioning of their bodies.

In summary, the two medical perspectives incorporate very different definitions of health, and these definitions account for some fundamental differences in the nature of health-producing action in the two systems. In the utopian system, health production action consists of an ongoing process of maintenance and development, a feature that distinguishes this system as a preventative health care approach. In the anatomo-clinical system, health-producing action takes place only in the context of biological/organic crisis. The anatomo-clinical definition of health, therefore, serves as the cognitive foundation for a crisis care medical system.

The Role of Subjective Consciousness in Health Production

Another important element of the anatomo-clinical paradigm is the conceptualization of the relationship between the patient's subjective consciousness and the objective conditions that are the focus of health production action. In the previous chapter, we saw that the holistic health approach to this problem reflects the dialectical conceptualization of the relationship between subject and object. In the same way, the anatomo-clinical approach to this issue also emerges out of a specific epistemological approach to the relationship between subject and object.

The epistemological system that undergirds the anatomo-clinical paradigm is the positivist, objective approach discussed in chapter 1. In contrast to the dialectical conception of subject and object existing in a necessary but opposed relationship, the positivist approach views these two realms in dualistic terms. This latter conceptualization has important implications for any kind of human science. The subjective realm is assumed to have no determinant influence over the objective realm; therefore, all aspects of the human condition are explained in terms of the determinant influence of objective, external forces. Consciousness, meaning, etc., are regarded as epiphenomenal factors in this system. Within the anatomo-clinical paradigm, this notion takes the form of a dualistic view of the relationship between mind and body. Body function is governed and influenced by a whole host of external, objective factors, but the mind has no causal influence whatsoever over the body. Mind and body are two distinct realms and although consciousness allows us to sense and perceive events that occur in the body, mind cannot determine those events.

The implicit assumptions that a medical paradigm makes about the subject/object relationship are intimately related to the essential problem addressed by the system. In the holistic health system, the essential concern is the problem of how to increase the degree of conscious awareness and control that an individual exercises over all aspects of his or her existence (including the body). This concern seems appropriate only if one accepts the dialectical conception of the subject/object relationship. By the same token, the essential concern of the anatomo-clinical paradigm reflects its dualistic assumptions about the nature of the subject/object relationship: medical perception focuses on the problem of discovering the objective conditions that give rise to the subjective sensations that we know as patient complaints (defined as symptoms in this system).[2] In other words, the problem is to objectify the subjective sensations of the patient.

This task is accomplished by translating all illness (i.e., the patient's subjective sense of abnormality) into disease. As we will see in the next section, disease is defined strictly in terms of morbid anatomy: all diseases can (or should) ultimately be associated with specific abnormalities of gross or microscopic anatomical structure.[3] Accordingly, anatomo-clinical diagnosis attempts to establish a link between all of the patient's subjective sensations and a specific anatomical lesion, either directly or indirectly.[4]

Another instance of the objectification of the patient's subjective sensations can be seen in the process of assembling clinical data:

> To decide that a particular symptom or sign exists, the clinician goes through a process of contemplating sensation, adding specification and selecting designation. For a symptom, sensation describes the actual phenomenon perceived by the patient, such as a discomfort in the chest; specification adds such further description as substernal location, provocation by exertion, and prompt relief with rest; designation gives a name to the specified sensation—in this instance, angina pectoris.[5]

As this passage indicates, the principle concern of medical perception in the anatomo-clinical system is to locate all symptoms within some specific part of the body; in fact, the sensation is even designated in terms of a particular anatomical location.

To understand how associating subjective sensations with specific anatomical phenomena serves to objectify them, we must consider again the nature of the human Gestalt. Recall that the human Gestalt is conceptualized as wholes within wholes, with each of the different dimensions of human existence defined as a distinct whole (with all of the characteristics of wholes that we discussed in previous chapters) that subsumes as parts all of the less emergent wholes below it. This means that while the body is a distinct whole in and of itself, it is simultaneously a part of the more emergent whole of the mind; the mind, in turn, is subsumed by the more emergent whole of society. From this perspective, the only whole within the human Gestalt that does not include the subject (consciousness) as one of its parts is the whole of the body. This dimension is the most emergent whole that one can designate and still exclude the subject. In all of the more emergent levels of the Gestalt (mind, society, spirit, etc.), the subject is included as a part and, by virtue of this fact, has causal influence on the nature of these whole. Hence, by locating disease strictly within the whole of the body and by reducing all subjective patient complaints to a disease condition thus located, the anatomo-clinical approach succeeds in objectifying those symptoms.

Associating symptoms with conditions of the mind, society, or the spirit, as the holistic health approach does, makes the subject a causal factor in the emergence of symptoms.

Herein lies the essential difference in how the holistic health and anatomo-clinical systems define the role of the patient's subjective consciousness in the phenomena of health and illness. Holistic health regards the patient's consciousness (the subject) as a crucial causal factor in all facets of health and illness, and it seeks to employ knowledge and technique for the purpose of increasing the individual's conscious control over all of the factors that impinge on physical, emotional, and spiritual well-being. In contrast, the anatomo-clinical approach posits that the patient's consciousness plays an insignificant role in the phenomena of health and illness. Illness is, by definition, the patient's subjective impressions of events that take place exclusively within the realm of the body. Therefore, the patient's consciousness acts as nothing more than a mirror or indicator of the disease process—and a rather distorted indicator at that. Consciousness or subconsciousness cannot be a causal factor in the disease process nor can it play any part in the healing process.

The principle goal of anatomo-clinical medicine, then, is to develop a rational and comprehensive classification system that associates all subjective sensations with specific anatomical locations, which can be joined with more objective indicators (signs) to designate particular varieties of morbid anatomy. Implicit in this approach to illness is the notion that only those who possess a working knowledge of this classification system can exercise any control over the disease process. Therefore, the patient, as a conscious subject, must play a passive role in medical action. As we will see in a later chapter, this concern with objectifying patient complaints has implications not only for the structure of the patient role but also the professional status of medical practitioners.

The Nature of Organic Disfunction.

Recall that within the holistic health system, all of the organic conditions associated with illness (physiological disfunction, tissue lesion, etc.) are merely reflections of a state of metaorganic imbalance. In contrast, the anatomo-clinical system views organic disfunction as unrelated to any condition within the metaorganic realms. In this system, the focus is directed toward the microscopic rather than the macroscopic end of the continuum. Of the many different kinds of conditions that could be associated with illness, the phenomenon of disease is considered to be the most fundamental. Moreover, this latter condition is defined in very strict terms: disease always refers to a particular form of morbid anatomy, a form of tissue lesion. Any condition associated with illness that cannot be defined in terms of gross or micro anatomy and that cannot be further distinguished as abnormal is not a disease.

The histopathological definition of disease allows many of the entities that could possibly be defined as diseases (and in different historical contexts were viewed as diseases, such as fever, cyanosis, consumption, etc.) to be classified, instead, as clinical manifestations.[6] Similarly, when an illness condition consisting of a set of simultaneously occurring clinical manifestations cannot be associated with a specific tissue lesion, the condition is defined as a syndrome rather than a disease. Not surprisingly, a major goal of the anatomo-clinical paradigm is to eventually translate all syndromes into diseases—in other words, to discover the pathological anatomy that gives rise to the particular set of clinical manifestations.[7]

The fact that disease is defined in terms of morbid anatomy creates some special problems for those who endeavor to classify human diseases. Observing the disease process (for purposes of classification, diagnosis, etc.) is particularly problematic because histopathologically defined diseases are always hidden within the body. In addition, the opaque character of the disease makes it impossible to objectively identify its onset—the principle method for detecting the presence of disease is to rely on the patient's subjective sensations of illness (the symptoms that lead patients to believe that they are sick). The difficulties involved in observing morbid anatomy mandate that disease classification must involve additional categories of evidence beyond the identification of tissue lesions.

The kinds of evidence used in the anatomo-clinical classification of disease indicate very clearly the organo-reductionist thrust of this paradigm. In the holistic health system, a broad range of evidence is considered relevant to the observation and classification of illness: organic evidence, subjective sensations (symptoms), the condition of the individual's extended energy field, mental/emotional state, social state, and spiritual state. In the anatomo-clinical system, by contrast, only four categories of evidence can be used to classify disease: (1) clinical; (2) physiological; (3) pathological; and (4) causal information.[8] Let us examine more closely each of these categories of evidence.

Symptoms (defined as "subjective sensation[s] or other observation[s] that a patient reports about his or her body or its products)[9] are necessary criteria of disease classification because the patient's subjective sensation of illness is almost always the first step in the disease detection process. However, symptomatic evidence, although an unavoidable criterion of disease classification, is generally regarded as the least valuable form of evidence. A major concern of the anatomo-clinical approach is to either translate symptoms into signs (defined as "an entity objectively observed by the clinician during physical examination of the patient")[10] or, at least, conjoin symptoms with signs to form a more objective body of clinical evidence.[11]

Implicit in this approach to signs and symptoms is a unique way of distinguishing between these clinical phenomena and the phenomenon of disease, a method that contrasts sharply with the one used to establish this distinction in the holistic health system. In the latter system, tissue lesion, symptoms and signs are all believed to be manifestations or reflections of imbalance in one of the metaorganic realms. Moreover, signs and symptoms can occur either prior to or after the development of tissue damage. In the anatomo-clinical system, disease (tissue lesion) is always prior to signs and symptoms. Treated as "indicators" of a host afflicted with disease[12], these clinical data are used in three different ways in clinical reasoning. In diagnosis, they suggest causative diseases; in prognosis and in general therapeutic strategy, they indicate comparable patients; in subsidiary therapy, they indicate specific targets of treatment.[13] This way of conceptualizing clinical phenomena and disease reflects, once again, the core presupposition of this perspective—the assumption that morbid anatomy is the ultimate cause of all illness phenomena.

The use of physiological evidence as a criterion of disease classification is yet another indication of the importance of anatomical location in the definition of disease. Within the whole of the body, anatomy and physiology refer to the structural and functional aspects of the system, respectively. In the body system, as in every system, structure usually implies function and vice versa so that disease conceived of in terms of anatomical pathology leads inevitably to an interest in observing and measuring physiological disfunction as well. Evidence relating to the adequacy or inadequacy of physiological functioning is, therefore, crucial for the classification of specific diseases, especially considering that it is often much less difficult to measure physiological function than it is to observe the anatomical structures involved in physiology.

The category of evidence receiving the greatest amount of attention in the classification of disease is, of course, pathological evidence. According to the logic of anatomo-clinical reasoning, neither of the preceding categories of evidence possess any value for designating disease unless they can be associated with specific kinds of morbid anatomy. Tissue lesion is the source of all illness phenomena: when body tissues take on abnormal characteristics, organs cannot function properly, the body equilibrium is threatened, homeostatic/defense mechanisms are activated, and the individual experiences the subjective sensations of illness (pain, discomfort, etc.). Within the anatomo-clinical system, physiological disfunction, symptoms, and signs are regarded as mere manifestations of the more essential condition of pathological anatomy.

This way of designating disease makes disease classification a difficult enterprise. The inaccessibility of histopathology to the observing medical eye has prompted the development of a whole host of practices designed to deal with this problem. Chief among these is the post-mortem examination, a practice that historically played a crucial part in disease classification. As Foucault and other medical historians have noted, the practice of opening up human corpses was one of the most important developments in the evolution of the anatomo-clinical system.[14] Only after this practice became routine could disease classifiers correlate their clinical findings with actual observation of the tissues. Once the human tissues came under the scrutiny of a systematically organized medical consciousness, a complex, esoteric vocabulary developed for describing these inner spaces, and the concept of disease became firmly wedded to the human body.

As anatomo-clinical medicine developed, the post-mortem examination was supplemented with additional techniques for observing human tissues. The purpose of most modern diagnostic instrumentation and procedure, such as x-rays, angiograms, catheterizations, etc., is to aid the practitioner in locating tissue abnormalities that will account for specific clusters of symptoms and signs. These techniques are not as useful as the post-mortem examination in providing direct observational information about the tissues, but they have the advantage of allowing the practitioner to observe anatomy in the living as opposed to the nonliving organism. The development of this kind of diagnostic instrumentation and procedure has served to further solidify the belief that morbid anatomy constitutes the core feature of the disease entity.

The last category of evidence used in the classification of disease is causal information. As with the other aspects of the disease concept, the anatomo-clinical approach to locating the causes of morbid anatomy contrasts sharply with the holistic health approach to this problem. In the latter system, tissue lesion (or any other condition of the body, for that matter) is believed to arise from the interaction of a large number of factors that make up the conditions of one's existence. In contrast, the anatomo-clinical system adopts a single cause model in which all forms of tissue lesion are causally linked to a single factor.[15] Moreover, the anatomo-clinical perspective recognizes only two entities as legitimate causal agents: genetic defect and microbiotic attack.[16] None of the metaorganic disfunction-producing factors emphasized by the holistic health system (vital energy, mind, emotions, social factors, etc.) are causally linked to disease in the anatomo-clinical system. This restrictive approach to disease causation allows the anatomo-clinical perspective to establish both "formal and informal models that represent disease as classifications of causes and effects."[17]

In summary, what is most noteworthy about the anatomo-clinical approach to disease classification is not the kind of evidence *included* in the designation of a disease but, rather, that which is *excluded*. Assuming that all aspects of the human Gestalt are relevant to the problems of perceiving organic disfunction, identifying the sources of disfunction, etc., one could ask why the anatomo-clinical perspective adopts this exclusionary approach. To answer this question, we must explore some implications of the differences between the holistic thrust of the utopian perspective and the reductionist thrust of the anatomo-clinical perspective.

Just as the holistic health method of classifying organic disfunction implies a specific approach to controlling disfunction, the anatomo-clinical approach to disease perception and classification is also related to a distinctive method of disease control. Control of organic disfunction that excludes the direct use of subjective factors is not possible within the holistic health system, but it is viewed as the preferred method for dealing with disfunction in the anatomo-clinical system. As with any other naturally occurring phenomenon, disease can be made the subject of rational, systematic inquiry, leading to a system of verifiable knowledge about the disease process. The assumption that all disease-related phenomena can be reduced to an essential micro-level condition makes such knowledge about disease possible. For example, by removing the subject (the psychological/emotional realm) as a causal factor in disease, a major source of "particularism" is dispensed with, and disease can be conceived more as a universal phenomenon (a necessary requirement of universally valid knowledge). By the same token, the reduction of tissue abnormality and abnormal biochemistry to either genetic defect or microbiotic attack allows one to avoid the indeterminacy associated with more emergent phenomena. As Edmund Murphy notes,

> Foreign organisms are the best external, and Mendelian inheritance the best internal, instances of naturally discrete phenomena, the effects of which come to the attention of the clinician. Both microorganisms and genes behave, for the most part, as discrete units.[18]

Again, assuming that the subject of analysis consists of discrete entities serves as an essential prerequisite for the development of a knowledge system made up of discrete categories that are universally applicable to those objective entities.

One distinction embraced by the anatomo-clinical perspective is an especially important presupposition for its claim to the status of universally valid knowledge. Implicit in all of the concepts that refer to the various aspects of disease, i.e., the concepts of illness, physiological disfunction, morbid anatomy, and abnormal biochemistry, is the assumption of a clear-cut distinction between normal and abnormal. In the holistic health system, such a distinction cannot be made: because of the unique character of every individual's Gestalt (including even the biochemical dimension), the distinction between normal and abnormal is always an arbitrary determination. Such an approach to the normal/abnormal distinction clearly does not accord with the anatomo-clinical effort to develop conceptual categories applicable to all diseased individuals in all times and places. If human diseases are to be treated as truly objective phenomena, then it is imperative to employ a rigorous method for distinguishing normal tissues from abnormal tissues.[19] Although this problem has been the subject of much theoretical debate in the medical literature (cf. Murphy 1976, 123–132), anatomo-clinical medicine generally relies on the statistical concept of "the normal range" as the most practical method of establishing this distinction.[20]

We find, then, that these three assumptions—the location of disease within the organic realm exclusively, the reduction of all disease phenomena to the core condition of tissue lesion (conceived as the direct effect of genetic defect or microbiotic attack), and the distinction between normal and abnormal—all lend logical support to the claim that the anatomo-clinical system is a body of universally valid knowledge. As we will see, this claim is a crucial element in the development of a medical profession entrusted with the task of controlling disease. These three assumptions are, however, only a small part of a broader logical structure that functions to give the anatomo-clinical system its universally valid character. This logical structure consists of a set of concepts and assumptions that are not unique to the anatomo-clinical system, per se, but are associated with the broader tradition of positivist science.

Perhaps the biggest change in medicine in the twentieth century was the introduction of biomedical science into medical theory—the shift from "medicine as an art" to "medicine as a science."[21] This topic has been the subject of must discussion in the philosophy of medicine. For present purposes, the most important thing about this shift is the support it has provided for the idea that disease is a process governed by universal laws of nature that can be understood in terms of rational rules of logic.[22] For example, the anatomo-clinical system employs a number of scientific concepts that implicitly deny any indeterminacy in the phenomenon of disease (since indeterminacy makes it impossible to apply rational rules of logic): a medical event is conceptualized as something that "has a certain intrinsic continuity from its beginning to its end. Two events can be recognized only if there is a discontinuity between them."[23] Similarly, in order to avoid the indeterminacy associated with nonlinear, holistic conceptions of causation, morbid events are defined in terms of linear series. This accords with the more general commitment to conceiving all causal relations as unidirectional cause-and-effect relationships.[24] Finally, probability distributions are used to deal with aspects of empirical medical reality that exhibit "irreducible objective indeterminacy," an indeterminacy that defies categorizing efforts.[25]

One aspect of the anatomo-clinical system has been subjected to particularly intense efforts to make it "more scientific"—the area of disease taxonomy. Nowhere has the contradiction between medicine as an art and medicine as a science been more manifest than in this area. Alvan Feinstein acknowledges this contradiction and notes that all clinicians, because they are human observers, are proned

> to vary greatly in the way they perform and interpret their examinations. . . . Problems of the observer variability are neither the eyes nor the ears of the observers. We all see and hear essentially the same things, but each observer uses different ingredients in his criteria for description and interpretation of the observations.[26]

The inherently subjective nature of clinical observation means that clinicians tend to develop their own unique systems of clinical classification, systems that are "nonreproducible or even indescribable."[27] Despite this tendency, contemporary adherents to the anatomo-clinical method generally agree that future development of the perspective will require a reorganization of the disease classification process to accord with basic scientific principles: "To be able to discern natural phenomena with predictable precision is surely one of the hallmarks of science, even though the work is purely clinical."[28]

A variety of measures have been taken to achieve this end, including such things as applying the "principle of exhaustiveness" to the disease sample space: "a classification should be constructed in such a way that every member of the group to whom it applies will fit into one class of the system. The classification is then said to exhaust the sample space."[29] Similarly, disease classifiers have incorporated the "principle of disjointness" into the classification system: "disjointness implies that no particular case should fall into more than one class."[30] In situations in which no standardizing principles can be applied without doing violence to the essential character of the disease, statistical techniques can be used:

> The absence of classification must mean that each member . . . belongs to his own unique class. However, it is still possible to allow an infinite

number of classes, while keeping the whole manageable by constraining in a different way. The existence of continuous distributions and the techniques that may be applied to them, such as regression analysis, solve the problem in many cases.[31]

These are just a few of the many ways of making disease taxonomy more scientific. These measures serve the more important goal of objectifying the disease classification system: categorical distinctions established according to their principles are not simply the arbitrary reference points of a subjective observer; rather, they correspond to real (objective) disease entities whose essential character is determined by universal laws of nature.

As this analysis reveals, incorporating scientific principles into the anatomo-clinical perspective lends legitimacy to the claim that this body of knowledge can provide universally valid explanations of disease. This claim implies further that those who are trained in this system of knowledge can make accurate predictions about the course of the disease process and, therefore, can take the necessary steps to control it.[32] Hence, if the disease process is to be controlled at all, it must be controlled by an individual who has acquired an extensive understanding of this system of universally valid knowledge. Individuals afflicted with disease can turn their fate over to the knowledgeable physician with the confidence that the physician's interventions into their existence will be "functionally specific" or focused only on the treatment of disease. This also suggests that the potential for conflict between the values of the patient and those of the physician is minimal because the process of defining disease is a value-free enterprise.[33]

Before we leave the subject of science in medicine, one more issue requires attention. The incorporation of scientific principles into the anatomo-clinical system gives this perspective a special kind of legitimacy, but an even more direct link exists between anatomo-clinical medicine and the scientific tradition. Medicine, like any other applied science, needs theoretical knowledge; it must rely on some theoretical system in designating its perceptual reference points (All practical endeavors require such a theoretical system even though, in many cases, this system is not explicitly acknowledged.) The interventionist thrust of anatomo-clinical medicine also brings with it a need for the kind of medical instrumentation developed by scientists engaged in specialized biomedical research. The need for both theory and medical instrumentation creates an intimate link between medicine and the basic biological sciences (such disciplines as physiology, genetics, microbiology, biochemistry, etc.). Through the use of theory and technological principles, basic scientists produce medical instrumentation that become incorporated into "the subjective body of the clinician as a new transcendental structure or a new form of tacit 'knowledge' resulting in new powers of observation and direct interpretation."[34] In contrast to what is commonly believed, basic science does not serve an explanatory role for the clinician; rather, it creates the space of possible medical events. As Heelan notes,

> the basic science that makes possible good clinical science is developed not by clinicians . . . but by microbiologists, biochemists, geneticists, physiologists and others working in close association with clinical medicine and its dependent technologies.[35]

From the perspective of holistic health, the most important issue here concerns that fact that only the biomedical sciences serve the function of "creating the space of possible medical events." This contrasts sharply with the belief that the multidimensional nature of disease makes many social and behavioral sciences, and many nonscientific disciplines, relevant to the problem of designating the perceptual space of health and illness.

Diagnosis of Disease.

In the realm of diagnostic methodology, the holistic health and anatomo-clinical systems differ in two fundamental ways. The first difference involves the kind of data used as diagnostic criteria. In both systems, diagnostic criteria are essentially the same as disease classification criteria. For example, the holistic health approach to diagnosis reflects the holistic conceptualization of illness. Consequently, no fact of an individual's existence is considered to be irrelevant to the problem of diagnosing illness (although it is recognized that diagnosis inevitably involves selective attention to some facts over others).

In contrast to this multidimensional approach, the anatomo-clinical approach to diagnosis is distinguished by its reductionist nature. The anatomo-clinical conceptualization of illness as nothing more than the subjective manifestation of histopathology impels the physician to search for the source of a patient's illness in a specific tissue lesion. However, the fact that tissue lesions are hidden in the inner spaces of the body forces the physician to rely on more observable kinds of evidence. Of first importance is evidence concerning the patient's physical condition collected through unaided observation (eyes, ears, touch, etc.)—the signs of the patient's disease (histopathology). Physicians also rely on their patients' own subjective sensations of their diseases, i.e., the symptoms of disease. The general categories of signs and symptoms can be further broken down into the subcategories of (a) "objective symptoms"—entities observed by both the physician and the patient (such as jaundice) and (b) "iatric signs"—entities delineated only through the use of specific clinical techniques of examination (such as retinal exudate, prostatic nodules, cardiac murmurs, etc.). Objective symptoms can be further designated as either "corporeal," located within the patient's body (such as a skin rash, a palpable superficial lump, etc.) or "effluent," consisting of various visible products that emerge from the patient's body (such as a bloody sputum, green vomitus, brown urine, and tarry stools).[36]

All of these categories of evidence share a common feature: each refers, in one way or another, to the patient's organic condition. The anatomo-clinical practitioner elicits diagnostically relevant information from patients by asking questions about their physical state only; information regarding their psychological/emotional state, the nature of their lifestyle, or the quality of their spiritual life cannot be included in a formal diagnosis. Just as disease classification considers only those aspects of the Gestalt defined as direct manifestations of morbid anatomy, diagnostic criteria are also limited to the indicators of the condition of the patient's tissues.

The timing of diagnosis in the anatomo-clinical system also reflects the basic logic of this perspective's approach to disease. In the holistic health system, the diagnostic process is directed toward detecting metaorganic imbalance, and, therefore, almost all diagnostic activity occurs well before the onset of tissue damage. By contrast, virtually all diagnostic activity in the anatomo-clinical system occurs only after the onset of tissue damage. If illness is the manifestation of disease and disease is defined in terms of morbid anatomy, then diagnosing an illness before tissue damage has occurred is logically impossible. The use of signs and symptoms as the principle diagnostic criteria in the anatomo-clinical system also indicates the priority of histopathology in the diagnostic process. In the holistic health system, various access points exist within the whole of the body that can yield information about the dynamic changes taking place before the appearance of tissue lesion. The anatomo-clinical perspective does not accept the legitimacy of such a diagnostic approach and, therefore, lacks any method for anticipating the onset of tissue abnormality. This post-histopathological diagnostic approach partly accounts for the anatomo-clinical system's status as a crisis care system.

Response to Disease

In every medical system, notions about what constitutes a proper response to disease can ultimately be traced back to the specific conceptions of health, disease, and the relationship between the two. One aspect of the anatomo-clinical definition of disease is particularly important for understanding the appropriate response to disease in this system. The significance of the post-mortem examination in the historical emergence of the histopathological definition of disease was described earlier. In addition to producing data relevant to the classification of disease, this practice accounts for one of the fundamental features of the disease concept. As Edmond Murphy points out, the practice of studying the "natural history" of disease by starting with the post-mortem records and working backwards has led inevitably to a negative prognosis for most diseases.[37] By virtue of the central place of the post-mortem exam in the classification process, disease is unavoidably associated with death and has come to be seen as a form of death incorporated into the living organism. While disease can co-exist with life for a time, it has the potential for ultimately overtaking life. The appearance of disease always signals a potential shift from life to death, a shift that every human being must eventually experience.[38]

Just as the holistic health and anatomo-clinical systems differ in the way that disease is conceptualized, so do they differ in designating the necessary response to disease. In the former system, disease is inherent in nature: it reveals the existence of an imbalance that has not been properly resolved. Consonant with this notion, one appropriately responds to disease by treating it as a feedback message, which indicates the direction in which one should modify ongoing balancing activities. Organic disfunction is rarely dealt with directly; health-related endeavors most often focus on the three health-producing activities of maintenance, growth and development, and balance.

In the anatomo-clinical system, however, disease is viewed as the antithesis of nature. Although this view reflects indirectly the tendency in Western culture to view life and death in terms of the nature/anti-nature dichotomy, it relates more specifically to the link established by the anatomo-clinical perspective between death and disease. Disease is death incorporated into the living organism, and, therefore, one responds to disease by dealing with it directly; one intervenes to eliminate histopathology and return the organism to its natural, living state.

What we find in this analysis, then, is a direct logical connection between the anatomo-clinical conception of disease as anti-nature and the interventionist trust of this approach. Other aspects of the anatomo-clinical definition of disease also influence the nature of medical intervention. In particular, the assumption that the disease process is an objective phenomenon governed by universal laws of nature ultimately frees the individual afflicted with disease of any direct responsibility for either the onset of disease or its elimination. If intervention to eliminate disease takes place, it cannot be initiated by afflicted individuals themselves (as it is in the holistic health system); rather, it must be initiated by one who possesses knowledge of the natural history of disease and the consequences of medical intervention on disease. The anatomo-clinical conceptualization of disease, therefore, provides the logical justification for the belief that disease is "the proper object of external and impersonal medication" which, in turn, empowers medicine to intervene and sever the alliance between personal responsibility and health.[39]

Treatment of Disease

The last aspect of the anatomo-clinical conceptual system we will consider involves ideas relating to the treatment of disease. I have chosen to discuss this topic last because the approach to disease treatment in the anatomo-clinical system (as in all medical systems) relies on all of the concepts and assumptions discussed up to this point.

When the appropriate circumstances exist for the initiation of disease treatment in the holistic health system, the approach adopted can best be described as the "natural/noninvasive" method. The defining feature of this method of treatment is its emphasis on modalities that work to enhance the various self-healing mechanisms of the human Gestalt. In contrast, the anatomo-clinical approach reveals an almost total disregard for the self-healing process. This system adopts a more direct approach by calling for action to deal with the "essential feature" of the disease process—the tissue lesion. This emphasis on the external manipulation of the tissue lesion results in anatomo-clinical treatment techniques that are often radically invasive. In order to "get at" the specific tissues that constitute the site of disease, it is often necessary to violate the physical integrity of the body. Two general techniques are used for this purpose. In surgical manipulation, the most obviously radical of the two techniques, the body is opened and the lesion exposed to the knowing eye of the physician. Advocates of surgical intervention believe that diseased tissue associated with specific physiological disfunction should be removed and, if necessary, replaced by either artificial or natural tissue. Justification for such an approach is provided by the "machine" metaphor for the body—the notion that the body is essentially a machine consisting of individual parts, which may be defective or may occasionally "wear out." What is somewhat ironic about this is that the effectiveness of surgical intervention depends on a specific self-healing process: surgery is a viable technique only because the body has the capacity to recover from the surgical assault.

The second general technique for treating disease in the anatomo-clinical system is biochemical manipulation. Although this technique would appear, at first glance, to be a natural alternative to surgical manipulation, drug use in the anatomo-clinical system generally assumes an invasive character. Drugs are used for two major purposes in this system: first, to treat a specific pathological condition (tissue lesion) and, second, to treat the clinical manifestations of the pathological condition (symptoms).[40] In contrast to the holistic health (or, more specifically, homeopathic) method of prescribing drugs for the whole body, the anatomo-clinical method uses drugs to treat a particular pathologic condition. One consequence of such drug use is that almost all drug treatment involves "side effects": although a drug may have the desired effect on the lesion for which it is prescribed, it can also have a negative effect on other parts of the body. This disregard for the systemic effects of lesion-specific drugs accounts for this technique being labeled as unnatural and invasive. In the same way that the integrity of the body is violated by the knife in surgical manipulation, it is violated by the toxic effect of drugs in biochemical manipulation.

A second form of drug use within the anatomo-clinical system can also be designated as unnatural in character. Recall that in the holistic health system, symptoms are manifestations of the body's self-healing mechanism attempting to deal with organic disfunction. In this system, drugs are prescribed not for the symptoms but rather to aid the body's self-healing efforts. In contrast, a significant proportion of the drugs used in the anatomo-clinical system are designed to suppress symptoms. Drug treatment in this system generally works in opposition to the body's self-healing mechanisms: a patient with fever is given drugs to reduce the fever; if the patient has vomiting and diarrhea, then drugs are given to suppress these symptoms.

We find, then, that the common feature of therapeutic techniques in anatomo-clinical medicine is their unnatural and invasive character. Although the self-healing potential is recognized as an inherent feature of the human system, the anatomo-clinical therapeutic approach does not focus on self-healing processes, and, in some instances, therapy even works to undermine these processes. The logical/conceptual justification for this approach is the notion that the essential aspect of disease—the tissue lesion—can be dealt with through direct intervention (either biochemically or surgically), an approach that is viewed as much more efficient and effective than any of the self-healing processes. As we will see later, this approach to therapy has important implications for the issue of who controls the disease treatment process.

In addition to the differences between holistic health and anatomo-clinical systems relating to the kinds of therapeutic techniques used, these two approaches also differ with respect to where treatment is focused. The latter difference, like many discussed thus far, reflects different epistemological principles upon which each system is based: the holism of the holistic health approach vs. the reductionism of the anatomo-clinical approach. When treatment is initiated in the holistic health system, it focuses on the whole of the body or on a more emergent level of the human Gestalt—never on a more reduced aspect of the body. In contrast, treatment in the anatomo-clinical system focuses on the most reduced aspect of illness—the tissue lesion. The anatomo-clinical conceptualization of disease as an objective phenomenon and the related notion that all diseases can be grouped into standard categories leads to an emphasis on the treatment of disease cases rather than patients. As one medical scientist notes, a central element of therapeutic reasoning is the idea that the patient is a case—"a representative instance of disease and illness."[41] In rejecting the idea of standard diseases, the holistic health approach defines the reduction of the patient to a disease case as illegitimate. In this system, every disease condition is the manifestation of the interaction between the individual and some environmental factor. Because every individual is unique, every disease condition is also unique, which means that treatment must always focus on unique patients. Consequently, the holistic health approach always takes into account the problem of the differential susceptibility of different patients while the anatomo-clinical approach generally disregards this problem.[42]

CHAPTER SIX

The Structural Relations of Health Production

Having described the ideal typical system of medical knowledge that serves as the dominant paradigm for modern medical practice, I now direct attention to the social structure of contemporary medical practice in the United States. As in the previous section, the medical countersystem will serve as the reference point for the analysis of this dimension of the system. The principle concern at this juncture is to describe the character of health production in the traditional medical model and the relational structure that makes up the broader system of health care within which medicine is practiced. A key Relation in this system is the relationship between the medical knowledge perspective just described and the social structure of medical practice. Although historically discrepant, these two dimensions have become increasingly identical in recent decades, a fact that has had important consequences for other aspects of the health care system.

The first step in the analysis of the traditional medical model is to examine the distribution of medical knowledge in this system. After a brief discussion of this feature, I then describe the nature of the health production process, highlighting those social structural aspects of the traditional medical model that interpenetrate (that are dialectically identical with) the cognitive elements described above. These social relations together with their cognitive expressions, reflect most clearly the principle of organization of this system.

THE DISTRIBUTION OF MEDICAL KNOWLEDGE

I begin by making explicit, once again, my reference point for analyzing knowledge distribution within the traditional medical model. Knowledge is distributed in the holistic health system in a way that accords with key elements of the holistic health conceptual system. Health and illness are multi-dimensional phenomena; therefore, it stands to reason that no one medical perspective can adequately account for all aspects of this reality. The

119

eclectic approach to organizing the medical knowledge base of the holistic health model reflects this way of thinking about health and illness: a variety of different modalities and perspectives can be used in this system, and all of these different perspectives are sanctioned, both legally and socially, as potentially legitimate. Although these perspectives have some core presuppositions in common (which accounts for their inclusion in the holistic health metaframework), the different empirical foci and different conceptual make-up of the various perspectives provide a knowledge reservoir from which concepts can be selected that best apply to one's own unique health requirements.

In contrast to the pluralistic nature of knowledge distribution in this system, the traditional medical model is characterized by perspectival hegemony. This difference can partly attributed to anatomo-clinical assumptions about the possibility of a single, comprehensive, and universally valid system of medical theory. The conceptualization of disease as an objective phenomenon governed by universal laws of nature, means that conceptual categories can be generated that exactly correspond to the elements of this objective reality; therefore, a body of universally valid knowledge concerning the "natural history of disease and the effect of medical intervention" emerges as a realistic possibility. We have seen that all of those factors that threaten the objective status of the disease concept have been excluded from the anatomo-clinical definition of disease. The essential aspect of disease is morbid anatomy—clearly an objective condition; all other factors related to this condition are merely its manifestations.

Claims about the universal validity and comprehensiveness of anatomo-clinical medicine have helped to maintain this system's hegemony over all other medical perspectives that have emerged in modern American society. However, these claims are not sufficient alone to guarantee the maintenance of this hegemony. The hegemony has been so enduring because such claims have been backed up by legal sanction (medical licensing laws) and by a systematic effort on the part of the medical profession to designate most competing perspectives and practices as "quackery." These issues will be addressed in more detail in a subsequent section.

THE HEALTH PRODUCTION PROCESS

The analysis of the contemporary system of health production starts with the countersystem presupposition that health is a process, not a state of being. In accordance with this presupposition, the analysis will focus on the health production process, which will be described both in general terms and in the context of the traditional model. In theoretical terms, the health production process involves two essential inputs: medical knowledge and action. Health is produced through the ongoing actions of individuals responding to some health-producing agenda which, in turn, reflects a particular system of medical beliefs that specifies the precise goals and methods of health production. As compared to the process of industrial production, health production can be distinguished as a labor intensive process: health production does not require raw materials, as demanded by industrial production, but it does require the action of some one who possesses skill and knowledge.

In order to identify the various parties that supply the required inputs in health production, we must move beyond this abstract level to the level of a concrete medical practice system. Within the countersystem, we have seen that knowledge and action are ideally supplied by individuals who endeavor to produce their own health. Following the dictates of the holistic health perspective, people undertake a program of health production by maintaining existing capabilities, seeking to develop new capabilities, and maintaining balance. To the extent that medical practitioners or other health care workers contribute to this process, they serve in the capacity of facilitators by helping or instructing individuals in their health-producing efforts. Within the countersystem, then, both inputs in health production are supplied by the same party—the individual who desires health.

In contrast, the traditional model is organized around two distinct social roles—practitioner and patient—with the former supplying medical knowledge and undertaking the most significant action required for health production. In this system, health-producing action on the part of the patient is limited in scope. As Talcott Parsons (1964) has pointed out, the behavior of sick people is structured by a normative environment that defines illness as a form of deviance and requires that the infirmed individual seek the help of a competent practitioner. Sick people are generally expected to try to "get well" and follow the doctor's directions for accomplishing this end. Beyond this limited set of actions, patient behavior does not directly contribute to health-production.

Correlated with the passive role of the patient is the activist role of the practitioner. The practitioner applies his or her skills in a direct course of interventionist action to produce health. These actions, which take the form of either physical, surgical, or biochemical manipulation of the patient's body, accord with the practitioner's knowledge of the disease process and other factors that s/he believes relate to health. Medical professionals are the sole possessors of the knowledge required to diagnose and treat patients' health problems by virtue of their membership in a collective that has maintained strict control over the development and transmission of this knowledge. In short, both inputs required for health production are supplied by the practitioner with limited contributions being made by patients and, in some cases, by ancillary health care workers (who also act in accordance with doctors' orders).

The unique character of the medical scientific approach requires an additional input for health production. This input, which is not a universal requirement of health production but derives from this particular system of medical practice, directly reflects the biologically reductionist nature of medical science. The reduction of illness to a condition of the body tissues (disease) creates a logical justification for the use of various medical technologies in health production, basically technologies that allow the physician examine the hidden spaces of the body. Although these technologies were rather simple and inexpensive in the earlier decades of this century, they have become increasingly complicated and costly in recent decades. Thus, health production typically involves not only medical knowledge and action (the two components of medical labor) but medical equipment as well. This trend has brought the process of health production closer to the dominant model of production in the industrial sector: with the increasing reliance on medical equipment in the health production process, industrial and health production are presently distinguished only by the former's requirement for raw materials.

The growth of complex technological resources in health production constitutes an important historical development because it has given rise to a central contradiction within the health care system. In earlier times when a physician could carry all of the tools needed for medical practice in the doctor's bag, the suppliers of medical labor (physicians) exercised complete control over the equipment required for health production. As the equipment used in diagnosis and treatment has become more complicated and costly, however, it has increasingly come under the control of the "capital intensive medical sector"—that portion of the health care system made up of "bureaucratic organizations that assemble large amounts of capital and hire labor and strive to accumulate surplus" (Brown 1979, 212). Most of these organizations were publicly financed in past decades, but recent changes indicate greater control over this sector by private interests, a trend that some describe as the "corporate incursion" into the health care industry (Starr 1982). As we will see later, elements of the capital intensive medical sector have become extremely influential in determining the direction of change in the health care system, ultimately challenging the traditional authority of the medical profession in these matters.

This analysis of the traditional model from the countersystem perspective points to an important but largely ignored feature of the health production process within traditional medicine. Insofar as laypersons do not possess medical knowledge and skill and cannot gain access to or use the technology required for medical diagnosis and treatment, they are *separated* from the means of health production. The inputs required for health production are controlled by parties other than the individuals who seek to produce their own health. Medical knowledge and skill belongs to the medical profession, and medical equipment falls under the control of public and private bureaucratic organizations. The health of the lay public, therefore, depends on the contribution of these outside parties and organizations.

To understand that laypersons are separated from the means of health production is an important first step in the critical analysis of the traditional model. More important, and more difficult, however, is explaining how this situation was created and how it is maintained. Among the various factors that contribute to this state of affairs, the most important are key elements of dominant the medical knowledge system within the traditional model. As noted in the previous chapter, the anatomo-clinical perspective relies on two central propositions: the notion that health is the absence of disease and the related idea that disease can ultimately be traced to morbid anatomy. To the extent that these medical beliefs prevail within the general population, they have several important consequences for the health-producing behavior of laypersons. People who believe they are healthy if free from disease lack any incentive to engage in active campaign of health production as called for by the countersystem perspective. The experience of disease-produced illness is rather episodic for most people (except for those at the lowest levels of the economic scale), and medical labor is employed only on an irregular basis as well. Consequently, this medical belief system offers little justification for the lay person to acquire medical knowledge and skill.

The general pattern of separation from the means of health production incorporates a more specific contradiction emerging within the traditional model—the lay public's separation from the means of illness treatment. This contradiction derives, in part, from the idea that all illness can be traced to a condition of the tissues (disease). As a histopathological condition, disease is typically hidden from the observing eye of the infirmed individual. The individual may be aware of disease symptoms, but the tissue abnormalities that cause these symptoms typically reside in the deep recesses of the body. Illness can be treated only after the causally prior disease condition has been identified (diagnosed) by someone who possesses the complex knowledge and equipment required to "see" into the opaque domain of the human body.

The complex and esoteric nature of anatomo-clinical medical knowledge means that all but the most basic medical principles are beyond the grasp of the average lay person. Consequently, most people must rely on medical professionals specially trained in the nature of morbid anatomy to diagnose and treat their illnesses. Few human experiences hold the same potential for anxiety as that of confronting the gulf between one's own ignorance and the physician's brilliance in this sense. In the usual medical encounter, patients who possess a fundamental fear of a potentially dire medical prognosis often listen to physicians discussing their fate in what amounts to a foreign language. The impenetrable nature of medical terminology and theory to the lay person makes it impossible to include medical science in the stock of knowledge internalized during normal socialization.

Another dimension of the separation from the means of illness treatment involves the equipment that is required for anatomo-clinical therapy. The reductionist focus of the medical scientific paradigm creates a need for various technologies for examining body tissue, technologies so elaborate and costly that they have come under the control of organizations with large amounts of capital at their command. Physicians are granted access to these technologies through a number of formal arrangements between themselves and organizational authorities, relationships that range from consulting agreements to employee/employer arrangements. However, no formal arrangements exist for making medical technology accessible to members of the lay public who wish to engage in self-treatment. The lay person's general ignorance of medical knowledge also renders this technology of no particular use to patients because most of the equipment can be effectively employed only by individuals who possess an understanding of medical science. Even patients who *do* possess adequate knowledge to make use of medical equipment or the information produced by such equipment are typically denied access to it. A case in point is the controversy over patient access to information in medical records. The results of lab work and other diagnostic tests can often be easily interpreted by lay people, but patients cannot usually obtain the results of these tests without first consulting with their physicians. In the traditional model, patients act as passive consumers of health care. Separated from medical knowledge and the capital-intensive technology required for medical diagnosis, they lack the resources to treat their own illnesses.

The growing complexity and expense of medical equipment relates to another separation that has become an important feature of the contemporary health care system, a feature that I alluded to earlier as a central contradiction within the system. With the steady increase in the amount of capital required to assemble complex medical technology, medical equipment has gradually come under the direct control of those who can supply these large amounts of capital. In earlier times physicians themselves or groups of physicians could provide the financial resources for medical equipment, but the rising cost of such equipment and the division of labor it creates, has placed it beyond the economic grasp of many physicians. At the present historical juncture, members of the corporate class and organizations with control over public finances function as the chief suppliers of capital for medical equipment which has greatly expanded their control over medical facilities. Consequently, physicians and patients are beginning to find themselves in a similar position vis-à-vis the suppliers of capital-intensive medical technology. Increasingly separated from the equipment input in the health production process, physicians as well as patients have become more and more distanced from the means of disease diagnosis.

Among the various ideational factors that function to separate people from the available means of illness treatment, one has been especially obscure to analysts who have examined the traditional medical model without the aid of the holistic health countersystem. I am speaking of the medical scientific paradigm's reliance on the dualistic presuppositions of positivist science. As noted previously, the holistic health perspective rejects dualism in favor of a dialectical conception of the relationship between subject and object: it sees mind and body as a dialectical unity, as two opposing moments of the same Relation. This conceptualization underlies several other important holistic health ideas, including the notion that people possess a variety of mental capacities for exercising control over bodily processes (which is the foundation of such modalities as biofeedback, autogenic training, etc.) and the idea of personal responsibility for health (see chap. 4). From the countersystem perspective, one of the most important resources available for dealing with illness is the capacity that all people possess for mental control over bodily function. The existence of this capacity helps to establish the ideal of self-care as a reasonable possibility.

In contrast to this dialectical conception of the mind/body relationship, the medical scientific paradigm defines the relationship in dualistic terms and, therefore, eliminates any possibility of subjective determination in the disease process. Disease possesses an objective character because the actions or thinking of the subject play no part in its emergence (apart from actions that put people in contact with disease agents). Disease arises from the attack of microbial agents or the toxic effects of genetic abnormality, substance intake, etc. As we saw in chapter 5, this way of conceiving of disease relates to other elements of the traditional model—the belief that effective disease diagnosis must focus as much as possible on objective signs rather than subjective symptoms, the notion that people are not personally responsible for their illnesses (and the related elements of Parsons's sick role), and the nonactivist character of the patient role.

Most important, however, are the implications of this objective definition of disease for people's access to the means of illness diagnosis and treatment. Potential patients who have internalized the medical scientific definition of disease possess no incentive to explore and develop their potential capacities for the mental control of bodily processes. Consequently, they are separated from these important resources for the treatment of illness. To posit that people experience this form of separation is not to suggest, however, that mental factors play an insignificant role in the experience of illness or healing within the traditional model. Phenomena such as the "placebo effect," psychosomatic illness, and the therapeutic benefits of the practitioner's authoritative demeanor can be regarded as evidence of mental determination in illness and healing within the traditional model. Unfortunately, the way in which mental capacities for healing are marshalled in traditional medical practice serves to deny patients control over this process. Control is usurped by practitioners who either consciously or unconsciously manipulate the patient's belief system to bring about the desired biological outcome. W. I. Thomas's famous dictum appropriately describes the dynamic operating here: "What men believe is real, is real in its consequences." When people come to *believe* that they are being helped by a sugar pill or their physician's healing ministrations, they may set in motion the psychic processes that actually bring about healing.

We see once more that the separation of the means of illness treatment from the subjects of treatment, which here takes the form of the separation between mind and body, creates new opportunities for practitioners to extend their control over the health production process. If members of the lay population generally reject the notion that mental states are causally associated with disease conditions and, as a consequence, never develop these capacities, then their dependency on those who possess expert knowledge of the disease process increases. However, the medical scientific definition of disease as an objective phenomenon serves additional functions that go far beyond the medical profession's desire to control the health production process. The removal of the subjective dimension of disease (i.e., the "objectification of disease") not only frees individual patients from bearing any responsibility for their condition but also frees any other subjects from responsibility for illness.

At issue here is the role of medical theory in helping to establish blame for the existence of illness. From the perspective of the countersystem, the blame for illness lies with people, either as individuals or as collectivities. The person who bears the most immediate responsibility for illness is the person experiencing the illness, but to assign responsibility in this way is not to adopt a "blaming the victim" approach as claimed by some critics of the holistic health movement (Brown 1979, 236). This criticism applies only to the "nonsociological" conceptualization of personal responsibility for health, which assumes that individuals are autonomous entities without social connections and social histories. The countersystem approach, in contrast, emphasizes personal responsibility within a social context: individuals have immediate or proximate responsibility for their illnesses because they choose, perhaps, to conform to a socially defined lifestyle that involves significant risks to health or because they fail to engage in collective political action against other collectivities whose actions threaten the health of the population (through the marketing of dangerous products, degradation of the environment, etc.). In short, this perspective sees subjects other than the victims of illness themselves as being ultimately (as opposed to proximately) responsible for illness.

The medical scientific approach to illness, in contrast, eliminates any subjects, acting either as individuals or as collectivities, from the range of factors that can be blamed for the existence of illness. Illness is the subjective experience of disease, and disease involves the breakdown of normal bodily function due to tissue defect or destruction. If a pattern of illness develops within the population, such as coronary artery disease or a new type of cancer, then medical science looks for the "culprit" within the microbiological domain rather than the social/ecological domain. This way of assigning blame for illness serves to absolve any human individual or group from responsibility for the existence of medical infirmity. By removing the subjective dimension entirely and thus objectifying disease, medical science serves to insulate from blame not only those human actors who bear proximate responsibility for illness (sick people themselves) but also those who are ultimately responsible—powerful actors and interest groups that shape the predominant lifestyle patterns of a society and determine the quality of nutrition, the ecological environment, and so on.

These considerations direct attention to the role of medical theory and medical practitioners in the construction of meaningful experiences among people who share a society and culture. As Paul Starr (1982, 4) notes, "(Physicians) serve as intermediaries between science and private experience, interpreting personal troubles in the abstract language of scientific knowledge." Although the process of interpreting personal troubles involves many different concerns, one of the most important is assigning responsibility and blame for the individual's troubles. In this regard, the medical scientific perspective succeeds as a "blame the germ or the victim's genes" approach. By assigning blame in this fashion, medical science serves the ideological function of protecting certain human actors from culpability for disease and ultimately supporting existing socio-economic arrangements.

Finally, one last factor contributes to the lay public's separation from the means of health production. This source of separation resides outside of the system of medical practice, and involves the elements of modern industrial society that impede people's ability to pursue the health production agenda defined by the countersystem approach. Scattered references to this division found throughout the previous discussion reflect the fact that each form of separation discussed in this analysis is relationally identical with every other form. This last type of division is unique in that it is tied to a structure of interest group relationships more complex than any discussed thus far.

In dealing with this set of structural factors, we begin charting conceptual territory that is the chief domain of classical Marxian theory. As revealed in his theory of alienation, one of Marx's primary critical concerns is to demonstrate that the productive process under capitalism serves to thwart the development of species being, i.e., those elements of human nature that remain dormant within the individual unless externalized and developed through labor. Viewed from the countersystem perspective, the human potentials that constitute species being involve the very same capacities that one should endeavor to develop in the health production process. The process of maintaining existing capabilities and developing new ones (two of the three processes involved in health production within the countersystem model) serve to externalize human species being in the true Marxian sense. Thus, structural features of the capitalist mode of production that impede the growth of human potential are the very same factors that limit people's ability to pursue the countersystem health production agenda.

As neo-Marxists have often noted (see especially Braverman 1974; Ollman 1971), the long-term trend in the development of the capitalist productive process has been an increasing rationalization of the work process for the purpose of maintaining or increasing profit. This has involved a general movement away from the "craft" model of production in which work assumes a more holistic form to the industrial mode, which differentiates and automates the labor process and reduces work to simple, repetitive tasks. In Braverman's brilliant analysis of labor under capitalism, this historical transformation in the character of work is described in terms of a number of more specific trends, including the growth of the "detail division of labor," the increasing separation between "conception and execution," the "deskilling" of work and, most importantly, a shift away from worker control over the conditions of work toward capitalist control of the work process. As a consequence of these changes, work ceases to be a means by which human capacities and skills are developed and instead becomes a stultifying and dehumanizing experience that people engage in only to insure physical survival and/or a high level of consumptive power. In short, the capitalist productive process minimizes the possibilities for human growth within the realm of work, at the same time that it enhances the possibilities for accumulating profit (surplus value).

The analysis can be extended even further by considering other lifestyle factors that impact on people's ability to pursue a health production agenda within capitalist society. As many workers will readily testify, a fundamental impediment to their ability to develop whatever interests (capacities) they may have is the shortage of time away from work. In an economic system (capitalist or otherwise) that is geared to maximize the productivity of workers, time not working or not specifically preparing for work constitutes "unused economic capacity." While a number of structures have evolved within the capitalist system to take up this slack in productive capacity, perhaps the most important is the prevailing structure of consumption. Insofar as workers are alienated from their labor, work possesses none of the intrinsic satisfactions that would motivate people to work any more than they have to. What *does* motivate people to devote significant time and effort to work is the understanding that the more they work and the higher they climb on the career ladder, the greater their potential for consumption. Moreover, this commitment to high consumption is maintained by other structures within the system, which range from socialization encouraging people to believe that their purchasing ability determines their personal worth, to the barrage of commodity advertising that circumscribes every facet of people's existence. These structures help support a commitment to focus one's time and effort around the labor process and to minimize the time devoted to pursuits that don't increase one's consumption capabilities. As many careerists will readily testify, work is so all-encompassing that little time exists for any pursuits outside of work, whether it be for the development of new skills and capabilities (in the process of health production) or even for the enjoyment of the consumer items they work so hard to acquire. Thus, the structure of consumption may rationalize the worker's lifestyle to a greater degree than any of the economic structures explicitly designed for that purpose.

The rationalization and intensification of work has further implications for people's ability to engage in health production. In addition to diminishing the possibilities for maintaining and developing human capabilities, the emphasis on increased worker productivity also impacts on efforts to maintain balance within the human Gestalt (the third process involved in health production). As we have seen, most discussions of balance within the countersystem paradigm focus on the problem of "stress." Psychological stress, it is posited, is a causal force in biological functioning, and optimum function requires neither too little nor too much stress.

In a comparative perspective, modern capitalist society is properly located at the "high stress" end of the continuum. The logic of capitalist production and consumption dictates that expectations for individual productivity be open-ended, that individual production goals be ever-expanding. In other words, the more an individual worker can produce, the better (assuming that a market exists for the goods being produced). In earlier stages of capitalism, greater worker control over the conditions of labor (through the worker's control over craft knowledge and skill) served to limit the demands that employers could make on their employees. With the further development of capitalism, however, these sorts of limits were steadily eroded through various rationalizing mechanisms used by employers to gain control of the work process. Technological mechanisms for governing the pace of work (for example, the assembly line), bureaucratic structures that divide workers and increase competition for advancement, the promotion of careerism among workers, and other devices for increasing the productivity of workers (cf. Edwards 1979) have all contributed to especially high levels of stress within the work place. These features, along with the structures within the broader socio-cultural system that legitimize a high stress social environment, work in opposition to forces that contribute to the maintenance of balance within the human Gestalt.

A critical analysis of modern capitalism thus reveals a structural logic within this system that promotes people's separation from the means of producing their own health. The structure of production and consumption and the various social relations that support this structure diminish people's opportunities for developing and maintaining any of those human potentials not directly related to labor productivity. At the same time, these structures increase the degree of social psychological imbalance that people experience in their daily existence. Although the factors just discussed belong to the category of general social system elements, they are directly tied to elements of the health care system that also separate people from the means of health production. In order to fully understand the nature of these ties we must next turn our attention to the system of interest group relations within modern American society.

INTEREST GROUP STRUCTURE AND THE TRADITIONAL MEDICAL MODEL

A central premise of the present study is the idea that all knowledge systems reflect the social structural environment in which they emerge. They reflect, more specifically, the character of interest group relations by providing ideological support for some interests and undermining other interests. In accordance with this premise, the ideological implications of medical scientific knowledge, which is part of a more general interest in the political economic dimension of the traditional medical model, must be discussed. This section explores how the structure of the traditional model as a whole relates to the existing system of privilege in American society.

Medical Practitioners

The obvious place to begin is with the interest group most directly tied to the existing system of medical thinking and practice—the practitioner group. As noted previously, the reductionist thrust of the medical scientific paradigm has one clear-cut ideological consequence. Insofar as illness is reduced to the level of tissue abnormality and thus relegated to the hidden interior spaces of the body, people experiencing illness must rely on the services of those who possess knowledge of the internal workings of the body and who have access to the technology for peering into those hidden spaces. One important function of medical scientific assumptions, then, is to legitimate the practitioner's control over medical diagnosis and treatment. Moreover, because health is defined in this system as the absence of disease, control over medical diagnosis and treatment translates into control over the health production process.

Medical scientific assumptions serve the more specific purpose of justifying intervention by the practitioner into the patient Gestalt. The medical scientific paradigm posits that illness arises from tissue pathology, which, in turn, produces a breakdown in body function. The mechanistic thrust of this approach leads to an additional assumption that body function can be restored only by "repairing the damage" or "fixing the machine." The most appropriate response to an illness episode, then, is intervention by one who possesses an intimate knowledge of the workings of the machine. Such intervention typically involves the use of either biochemical or surgical therapies for manipulating body tissues.

The practitioner's interventionist goals and control over the health production process, combined with the passivity of the patient role, form the social basis of the practitioner's professional status. The logic of the traditional model dictates that patients will be highly vulnerable in their dealings with practitioners. As individuals who suffer from ailments that only physicians fully understand, patients must be assured that the physician's interventionist efforts will be undertaken in the patient's best interests. Patients do not possess the knowledge required for an accurate assessment of their physician's good intentions in individual patient/practitioner encounters;

therefore, a formal structure has arisen to assure that the patient's vulnerability will not be abused. This structure involves the various professional features of the practitioner role.

Much has been written on the professional structure of the medical practitioner group, including a significant amount of recent research focusing on the ideological dimension of medical professionalism. Perhaps the most influential of these latter analyses is Eliot Freidson's (1970) classic study of the profession of medicine. Freidson was the first scholar to go beyond the morphological study of medical professionalism to explore the structure of medical practice in more critical terms. By adopting a critical orientation towards the medical profession's position within the division of labor (i.e., its. autonomous status), he was able to pose a question not previously asked—how is the medical profession's control over the conditions of its own work created and maintained? In answering this question, Freidson points to the ideological function of professionalism within the practitioner group:

> A profession's position in society does not necessarily (though it may) reflect a distinctively and especially superior skill, theoretical learning, or ethical behavior on the part of all or most members of the occupation. . . . What the status reflects is society's *belief* that the occupation has such attributes and society's belief in the dignity and importance of its work (Freidson 1970, 42).

While laudable as a first effort to critically analyze medical practice, Freidson's study does not fully describe the social functions of medical professionalism. The principle shortcoming of the analysis is Freidson's failure to extend his critical orientation beyond the issue of autonomy to issues related to the character of medical treatment itself. He challenges the common-sense belief that professional autonomy derives from the very character of medical work but the assumed necessity of medical intervention by practitioners and their control over the health production process is not questioned. Consequently, Freidson fails to appreciate that practitioner intervention and control must be legitimized just as autonomy is.

In offering this criticism, I do not wish to minimize the importance of professionalism as a mechanism for legitimizing the autonomy that doctors have traditionally enjoyed. Professionalism may serve several ideological functions, some of which are more important than others. The most fundamental problem faced by both patients and practitioners, a problem that arises anew in every encounter between patient and practitioner, is the question of whether the doctor's intervention will ultimately benefit or harm the patient. Both parties have a profound interest in this problem: patients want to be reassured that the pain or discomfort (physical or psychological) associated with medical intervention will be justified by an improvement in their condition while physicians want their patients to be likewise reassured in order to maintain a thriving practice. Only after this problem has been potentially resolved do physicians have the luxury to concern themselves with their position within the division of labor.

This analysis points to the critical importance of the relationship between the medical scientific paradigm and the professional dimension of medical practice. Professional characteristics are made necessary by the interventionist nature of modern medical treatment and this intervention is legitimated by the medical scientific perspective. The interests of the practitioner group are, therefore, most fundamentally tied to the latter perspective—without the ideological support of medical science, the practitioner's control over the health production process would be more tenuous.

We can extend this perspective further by also focusing on the collective organization of the practitioner group, in particular, the interest group actions of organized medicine. As past studies have suggested, the actions of physicians as an organized collective have been a crucial force in the development and maintenance of their professional status. State and local medical societies and the highly visible American Medical Association (AMA) serve the formal function of creating and maintaining professional standards. However, the critical perspectives of Freidson and others (Berlant 1975) have called attention to an important discrepancy between the formal function of these practitioner groups and their actual activities, suggesting once again that the real function of practitioner organizations is to advance the interests of the profession.

The present analysis differs from the existing critical literature only in terms of how the particular interests of organized medicine are defined. Freidson sees the issue of practitioner autonomy as the principle concern of physicians' organizations. While these organizations assign a great deal of importance to this issue, the problem of maintaining control over the health production process is of even greater concern. Practitioners have controlled this process for most of the twentieth century because they supply one of the crucial inputs in health production—the knowledge/skill component. Maintaining a firm grasp on this resource has been, therefore, critically important to the continued viability of medicine as a consulting profession. Consequently, the AMA and state professional organizations must place the highest priority on practical problems related to the development and transmission of medical knowledge and skill.

The organized profession, then, represents another example of a structure that serves multiple functions, although some functions take priority over others. Moreover, a closer examination of the set of functions fulfilled by the dominant practitioner organizations points to a fundamental irony, which has become an important feature of the contemporary medical practice system. While economic issues may be secondary to the issue of controlling the process of health production, the medical profession, nevertheless, experienced a significant improvement in its economic position during the middle decades of this century. The efforts of organized medicine to increase demand for physicians' services, to restrict the supply of doctors, and to advance legislation favorable to the profession's economic interests have allowed the medical profession to attain a highly privileged position in the occupational structure. Paradoxically, the profession's success in economic matters has contributed to an emerging threat to its primary interest—its concern for maintaining control over the health production process. As the costs of physicians services rise along with the steady increase in the average physician's salary, and as patients have become increasingly inconvenienced in their dealings with physicians (i.e., long waiting times, inflexible scheduling, etc.), ever larger numbers of people have started to question the authenticity of the profession's claim to public service and medical competence. As physicians have become more autonomous and more highly rewarded in their work, the ideological value of professionalism has diminished.

In this emerging climate of doubt about the real motives and capabilities of the medical profession, other groups are making inroads into the profession's monopoly control over the health production process: alternative medical practitioners and perspectives are becoming more popular with the lay population, a form of self-care has emerged as a component of the "new health consciousness," and patients have become less passive in their dealings with physicians. These changes correlate with a general loosening of ties between patients and their practitioners, a relationship that has been the foundation of the dominant practice system in American medicine during most of this century. Consequently, the private practice system is currently giving away to other forms of health care delivery, consisting primarily of organizational alternatives that were tried in earlier historical periods but which failed to attract patients away from private practitioners until very recently (cf. Starr 1982). In another ironic development, as these new health care delivery organizations have gained a greater share of the market for medical services, they are also becoming increasingly attractive working environments for physicians. Many doctors who wish to avoid the difficulties of establishing and maintaining a private practice are now choosing the wage earner alternative, a trend that may signal a decrease in the autonomy of physicians. The very *success* of past efforts to achieve autonomy, then, has contributed indirectly to the potential for a significant loss of autonomy among medical practitioners in the future. The relationship between physician control over health production and professional autonomy, and the many other structural factors that impact on this relationship will be discussed in more detail in a later chapter.

The Owners of the Industrial Means of Production

The next step in the examination of the various social groups whose interests are tied to the medical scientific paradigm brings us to another body of literature that deals with the health care system from a critical perspective. In several studies undertaken by Marxist scholars (cf. Navarro 1977; Brown 1979), attention has been directed to the relationship between the structure of the traditional medical model and the interests of the capitalist class. These scholars propose that the traditional model persists over time because its structure supports the interests of the ruling economic class. Although this proposition contains a kernel of truth, traditional Marxist analysis of the corporate interests involved in the existing medical model tends to gloss over the complexity of the problem. The complex of interrelations between elements of the health care system and the larger social system in which it is located cannot be understood in such simple terms. An adequate account would require identification of the numerous relational identities and contradictions involved in the relationship between the traditional medical model and interests of the capitalist class, as well as an explanation of their development in terms that avoid the "conspiratorial" thrust of some Marxist analyses.

Valuable insights can be extracted from the Marxist literature if we remain cognizant of the distinction between the knowledge system embraced by medical practitioners and the social structure of the medical profession itself. It must be stressed that the medical scientific paradigm is of much greater value to corporate interest than is the medical profession's control over the health production process. As a guild-like labor organization, the medical profession has developed interests that are generally opposed to the interests of the corporate class. At the same time, however, the knowledge system that undergirds medical professional practice is an important capitalist resource. Medical science serves as a powerful supporting ideology for capitalist interests in the struggle for control over economic and political institutions.

The ideological content of medical science is best understood by relying, once again, on the countersystem method. By using the countersystem perspective as a reference point for identifying the various dimensions of health and illness emphasized by the medical scientific model, as well as those it ignores, the political implications of this particular way of designating the essential parameters of health and illness can be considered. The countersystem places primary emphasis on the role of ecological and social environmental factors in biological function, arguing that optimum function is achieved when the elements of the environmental system exist in a state of balance (e.g., balance defined in terms of the quality of nutrition, air, water, and the character of social and psychological experiences). The medical scientific model, in contrast, effectively excludes these factors from the realm of medical discourse and, in doing so, makes an important contribution to the maintenance of the existing system of socio-economic relations.

By reducing disease to morbid anatomy, the medical scientific perspective achieves several specific ideological ends. First, it directs attention away from the factors that the countersystem defines as the most important determinants of health—imbalances in nutrition, elements of the ecological environment and the social psychological realm—as well as the sources of these imbalances. The latter include a social stratification system in which a significant proportion of the population is denied the economic resources needed for adequate nutrition and shelter, specific industries that generate environmental toxins or market food products and drugs that have a negative impact on health, and social groups and organizations that foster a high stress social environment in order to maximize the productivity of workers. Thus, the medical scientific paradigm rests upon a set of assumptions that ultimately support the interests of the corporate class. Insofar as members of capitalist society embrace the medical scientific definition of health and illness, they will be must more inclined to accept the threats to health posed by imbalance in the ecological environment and to conform to the structure of inequality and work/leisure that prevails under capitalist economic relations.

One important dimension of this phenomenon, discussed earlier in this chapter, involves the process of assigning blame for illness. The medical scientific model objectifies the blame for illness by attributing illness to the existence of disease and by defining the causal determinants of disease in terms of microbes and defective genes. Under the domination of medical scientific ideology, the sick are inclined to blame their condition on a germ or virus rather than blame corporate or political leaders whose actions contribute to the emergence or maintenance of a social/ecological environment that increases people's susceptibility to disease. Consequently, threats to public health do not serve as rallying points for political or social movement activity to bring about fundamental social change.

The phenomenon of objectifying the blame for illness is related to another concern of medical sociologists in recent decades—the trend towards an increasing "medicalization" of social problems. To account for the growing tendency to define and treat as forms of disease, problems that were regarded in earlier times as social or moral issues, analysts of American medicine have emphasized the desire of the medical profession to extend the range of its expertise and service. While few can doubt that the professional agenda has contributed to the trend towards the medicalization of social problems, this analysis of the "interest" dimension is too narrow. The ideological value of this trend to members of the corporate class must also be taken into account. To define people's problems in medical scientific terms is to adopt a very specific approach to assigning blame for the problem. Problems that in earlier times could be defined as "someone's fault" (either the fault of the individual suffering from the problem or some other individual or group) can now be blamed on nonsubjective entities like biochemical agents or genetic factors. The assigning of blame to these objective factors thus serves to remove the problem from the realm of moral or political discourse.

To illustrate this point, we could consider the history of alcohol abuse as a social problem. In the earlier decades of this century and before, the abuse of alcohol was regarded as a moral issue best dealt with as a private matter. People who abused alcohol were viewed as spiritual failures who lacked the moral fiber to resist the temptations of the bottle. In the ideology of the period, the blame for an individual's problems with alcohol rested squarely with the individual himself. The blame was attributed to a subject—the subject who was also the victim.

In the latter half of the twentieth century, alcohol abuse began to lose its moral connotations and become a problem best explained by medical science. The medical scientific perspective provides a more "progressive and informed" understanding of alcoholism as a disease rather than a form of moral failure. The most important social consequence of this medicalization of the problem is that the causes of alcohol abuse shifts from the subjective to the objective realm. In the current orthodoxy, the blame for alcoholism rests *not* with the victim's soul but rather with the victim's genetic constitution: it is nobody's fault that people succumb to alcoholism—some people's genetic makeup dictates that if they drink at all they will become alcoholics. This objectification of the blame for alcoholism accomplishes two important social/political ends: first, it frees people who suffer from problems with alcohol from the tyranny of the earlier religious/moral perspective which would seek to sanction them for their transgression; and secondly, it absolves any *other* subject (or group of subjects) from blame for the existence of alcohol abuse. Subjects who would be held accountable for the existence of alcohol abuse under the countersystem perspective, i.e., corporations that mount aggressive advertising campaigns to increase the level of alcohol consumption, or employers and managers who create high stress work environments in order to maximize worker productivity, are freed from any responsibility for the problem. By objectifying the blame for this and other "medicalized" social problems, the medical scientific paradigm helps to dissipate political energy that might be used to challenge existing economic arrangements and the corporate interests that benefit from these arrangements.

One could, perhaps, conclude from this argument that corporate actors have engaged in an organized conspiracy to obscure reality for the purpose of advancing their interests. Indeed, the tendency of past studies within the neo-Marxian tradition has been to implicitly support just such a conspiratorial viewpoint. This is reflected, for instance, in E. Richard Brown's (1979, 119) analysis of the ideological implications of medical science, in which he posits that "the medical profession . . . accepted the capitalist definition of health as the capacity to work." As Paul Starr (1982, 227–28) has noted, "one must . . . have a deep appreciation of the fragility of capitalism" to imagine that its maintenance requires the legitimating function of medical science. Starr's criticism of the Marxist interpretation is well taken, but he is incorrect in suggesting that there is *no* causal connection between corporate class interests and the medical scientific paradigm. While the medical profession has never accepted the capitalist definition of health—after all, there is a clear distinction between this latter definition and the medical scientific approach (in which health is defined as the absence of disease)—this does *not* mean that the two definitions of health are causally unrelated. Within the broader framework of the dialectical paradigm, the relationship between these two definitions, as well as the more general link between medical science and corporate ideology as a whole, can be conceptualized in a way that accurately captures the causal connections involved.

In introducing the dialectical paradigm, I discussed two conceptualizations that allow us to deal with causality or determination within the social realm—the concepts of relational identities and relational contradictions between different facets of the social whole. The former concept is especially relevant to the present problem. By describing the corporate and medical scientific definitions of health as relationally identical, we emphasis the mutually supportive nature of the relationship between them. To borrow a term from Max Weber, one could say that an "elective affinity" exists between the two definitions (Weber 1965, 284): the two definitions can coexist in a stable relationship because there is no tension between them, tension of the sort found within relational contradictions. A central axiom of the dialectical perspective holds that tensions between facets of the social whole are the wellsprings of social change while identities (and lack of tension) between those facets give rise to social stability.

In adopting this approach to causality, we must avoid reifying social system elements, especially those of a cognitive nature like the definitions of health under discussion here. Nothing about these definitions intrinsically makes them either identical or contradictory. What gives a relationship between cognitive elements either one or the other of these qualities is the character of the behavioral and interest structures to which they are tied.

For example, Robert Crawford (1984) documents the coexistence of several definitions of health in contemporary American society and explains their persistence by pointing to the relationship between these definitions and the broader cultural and economic structures of capitalist society. The two conceptualizations of health he discusses, health defined as self-control and release, capture the personal views of health embraced by two segments of the American population. Crawford persuasively argues that these opposing views of health reflect the more fundamental contradiction between requirements of production and consumption under capitalism. Both definitions persist because they are consistent with the structural demands of the broader political economic system.

Crawford's analysis applies equally well to the medical scientific definition of health. This definition may be just one of several currently embraced by members of American society (as Crawford suggests), but it is unquestionably one of the more influential forces shaping most people's thinking about health. If the medical scientific definition leads workers who adopt it to engage in action that undermines the interests of their employers, then the relationship between this definition and corporate view of health can be appropriately described as contradictory. In contrast, if the medical scientific definition leads workers to act in ways that do *not* undermine and, perhaps, even enhance the interests of their employers, then the two definitions are relationally identical. The latter statement best describes the actual relationship between the two views of health.

This conceptualization of the causal relationship between the medical scientific and corporate definitions of health can be extended to the link between medical science and corporate ideology in general. To posit that corporate elites have engaged in efforts explicitly designed to coopt medical science for ideological purposes is to ignore the true complexity of capital's relationship to medical science. Corporate elites have provided crucial support for the medical scientific paradigm (as documented by Brown 1979), and medical science serves an important ideological function in the maintenance of capitalism. However, this is a product of the elective affinity between medical science and the interests of the corporate class rather than the result of a conspiratorial effort by corporate leaders and medical scientists.

The Bureaucratic Imperative

Classical Marxian theory holds that capitalist society is arranged according to a single "principle of organization"—the structural relationship between the capitalist and worker in the productive process. This Relation is regarded as the most fundamental feature of the social system because it pervades (or is reflected in) every facet of the social whole. Marx's own exploration of this idea yielded a general perspective that has had a substantial impact on the world of ideas as well as the world of people. However, as influential as Marxian theory has been in the history of ideas, this perspective cannot fully account for the character of contemporary postindustrial societies. The present analysis, therefore, must employ a modified framework.

The chief limitation of the classical perspective is its assumption that capitalist society possesses a single principle of organization. While Marx's own analysis emphasizes the capitalist productive principle, analysts of modern society have increasingly recognized the importance of another social principle—the principle of bureaucratic organization. No less pervasive in modern American society than the productive relations of capital, the bureaucratic model is an organizing principle for virtually every sector of the system. The medical sector shares this characteristic with the other major institutional domains; therefore, our analysis must examine the relationship between medical science and bureaucratic structure.

Although much discussion within sociology has focused on the importance of the bureaucratic model in modern society, the characteristics of social organizations classified as bureaucracies are now widely understood to vary significantly from one domain to another. Indeed, some have suggested that organizational structure may even vary from one part of a bureaucracy to another, especially within medical bureaucracies such as hospitals (Twaddle and Hessler 1987, 298). Despite this variation, certain general features of the bureaucratic model can be identified. In the modern adaptations of the classical Weberian framework (cf. Pfeffer 1981) bureaucracies are defined in terms of the following characteristics: a hierarchical system of offices in which power and control is centralized and specified by formal rules; organizational goals that are reasonably consistent across different groups of actors; routinized and codified job specifications; a decision-making process organized according to standard operating procedures; and people that are assessed (either personnel or clients) according to the norm of universalism (i.e., hiring based on formal qualifications and clients treated according to need rather than social characteristics).

A pattern of relational identity between the medical scientific paradigm and these organizational characteristics can be observed along several different dimensions. First, the ordering of the illness experience in terms of the reductionist concepts of medical science makes the treatment of illness within a bureaucratic context much more manageable. This point can be more fully appreciated by returning to the contrast between the countersystem and medical scientific models. Within the countersystem model, practitioners deal with patients as entities with a unique biological constitution and unique location within a larger socio-ecological whole. Patients conceived in this way would constitute a problem for provider organizations that place a premium on well-defined goals, standard operating procedures, routinized, and codified job assignments. The attention to the complexity and uniqueness of each patient would frustrate efforts to deal with them through such standardized, efficient means.

In contrast, the medical scientific conceptualization of the patient is well-suited to the bureaucratic requirement for specification and standardization. Because the patient is defined within the traditional model as a typical instance of a typical disease, one can justifiably separate the patient from his or her social/ecological Gestalt and make the problem more bureaucratically manageable. By largely ignoring the social and psychological dimensions, complexity is greatly reduced, patients can be relegated to standard disease categories, and treated in routine ways. For medical organizations that possess the bureaucratic features identified above, processing standard diseases is much easier than processing people.

Another important facet of this relationship involves a theme that has been much discussed in the literature dealing with the socialization and practice of physicians—the "uncertainty" theme. One of the most difficult problems that physicians face in their daily practices is the inherent uncertainty of medical diagnosis and treatment. As Rennee Fox (1957) notes, this uncertainty derives from two distinct sources: the physician's inability to completely master all available medical knowledge and the limitations of current medical knowledge. Implicit in much of the past research on this topic is the notion that medical uncertainty arises as a problem for physicians only because they naturally abhor the experience of uncertainty in their work. While there may be some validity to this assumption, the issue is more complex than this. Insufficient attention has been given to the influence of the organizational context on the uncertainty problem. Most current medical practice occurs within a bureaucratic environment, and this structure defines to a considerable extent the conditions of work and role expectations of health providers. Perhaps nothing is more of an anathema to the bureaucratic model than the phenomenon of uncertainty. The greater the uncertainty in the problems addressed by the organization, the more difficult it is to maintain the rational and consistent standards that are so central to the bureaucratic approach. If physicians and other providers seek to limit uncertainty in their work, it is due, in part, to the influence of a bureaucratically structured work environment that forces them to adopt this approach.

In considering the problem of how uncertainty is managed, some researchers have presented findings that bear on the present concern with the role of medical knowledge in the health care system. Donald Light (1979), for example, suggests that physicians often seek to escape from uncertainty by adopting the somewhat circumscribed approach to medical diagnosis and treatment dictated by a "specialist" perspective. Indeed, even within medical specialities, physicians often gravitate to a particular school of thought, which then minimizes the number of competing treatment alternatives from which they must choose. By adopting the broader perspective of the countersystem approach, we can see that this function is served not only by specialization and subspecialization but by the medical scientific paradigm in general. Excluding from the realm of medical discourse such dimensions of the human Gestalt as the social and ecological environment, mind, and energy, allows medical scientists to restrict the range of variables that have to be considered in diagnosis and treatment. Within this delimited field, competing alternatives are reduced and uncertainty can be more easily controlled.

The fundamental affinity between medical science and the bureaucratic model in relation to the uncertainty issue involves a mutually supportive link between knowledge and organizational structure. The medical scientific paradigm serves to effectively reduce uncertainty; therefore, its use within medical organizations helps to address a critical bureaucratic problem. The identity between the bureaucratic and medical scientific models along this dimensions, in turn, results in a high degree of stability in the relationship between these two dimensions, which contributes to the persistence of both models.

An identity between these two models exists on another level as well. The bureaucratic emphasis on the norm of "universalism" requires the use of a diagnostic and treatment perspective in medical organizations that excludes particularistic elements from the realm of discourse. Analysts have recognized the importance of such professional norms as universalism and "functional specificity" (Parsons 1951), but the interconnections between these norms and the knowledge and organizational dimensions of medical practice have not been made explicit. In order to practice universalism in their dealing with patients, physicians must adopt a "universalistic" conception of illness; that is, they must possess a perspective on illness that discounts social psychological variables as causal factors in illness and objectifies the blame for medical infirmity. By reducing illness to morbid anatomy and defining disease causation in terms of genetic defect or microbial attack, medical science provides the belief structure required for the norm of universalism. In the course of diagnosing and treating patient problems, physicians need not attend to such particularistic concerns as the patient's race, class, or outlook on life. From the medical scientific perspective, these factors are causally irrelevant to the condition of the patient's tissues. In short, physicians seek to be universalistic in their dealings with patients not only because they believe it is "a good idea" (normatively speaking) but, more importantly, because "good medical practice" dictates that they do so.

In making this connection between medical science and the normative dimension of medical practice, I am not suggesting that universalism is simply a manifestation of the medical scientific conception of health and illness. The commitment to this norm cannot be explained solely in terms of either the professional orientation of autonomous medical practitioners (as past researchers have implied) or in terms of the determinant influence of the medical knowledge system embraced by physicians. Universalism in medical practice results most proximately from the interpenetration of both the knowledge system and an organizational structure that defines the basic agenda followed by members of the organization. In the case of modern professional medicine, the norm of universalism represents a point of convergence (identity) between the medical scientific and bureaucratic models. The use of nonparticularistic criteria in dealing with personnel or clients is a feature of bureaucratic organization that accords with the overall rationalistic character of the model. In the same way that the phenomenon of uncertainty is an anathema to both the medical scientific and bureaucratic models, particularism is excluded as an element of either model as well.

In summary, we have considered a number of distinct ways in which medical science relates to the bureaucratic principle of organization. The notion of relational identity best describes the nature of the relationship between the medical scientific paradigm and bureaucratic organization, but it also makes sense to describe medical science as a supporting ideology for bureaucratic interests. To fully understand this point, one could rely on a modified version of E. Richard Brown's perspective on medical science as capitalist ideology. Beyond its support of the more specific capitalist interests discussed above, Brown sees medical science serving the ideological function of helping to "unify and integrate industrial society with technical values and culture" (1979, 122). Had he adopted the present view of bureaucracy as a principle of organization no less pervasive than the principle of capitalist productive relations, he may have preferred to substitute the term bureaucratic society for industrial society in his statement. The analysis in this section demonstrates how medical science helps to unify and integrate bureaucratic society both cognitively and normatively. Insofar as both providers and patients view health and illness in medical scientific terms, they are naturally inclined to organize their actions in accordance with the logic of bureaucratic organization.

In addition to analyzing the relationship between medical science and bureaucracy at this abstract level, I wish to focus more concretely on the role of medical science in specific medical bureaucracies. Space limitations make it impossible to consider all types of medical bureaucracies, but one type is so common within the health care system that it cannot be ignored. I refer, of course, to hospital bureaucracies. The previous discussion provides the foundation for a new perspective on the role of hospitals in the health care system.

The various facets of the relational identity between the medical scientific and bureaucratic models are all tied to a common concern: they are all related to a general effort to reduce health and illness to a more microscopic level (in contrast to the macroscopic thrust of the countersystem model). As hospitals have evolved over time into bureaucratically organized "institutions of medical science" (Starr 1982, 147), the reductionism principle has emerged as a dominant feature of the hospital model. As the preceding discussion suggests, hospitals function as medical organizations whose chief goal is the management of diseases (as opposed to the management of people). Moreover, the bureaucratic approach to achieving this goal involves efforts to reduce the complexity of illness, to minimize medical uncertainty, and to remove particularistic elements from medical diagnosis and treatment. These efforts, in turn, allow for a clear definition of the more specific organizational goals (i.e., managing specific diseases grouped into standardized categories) and for the pursuit of these goals by organizational actors fulfilling routinized occupational roles and following standardized procedures and norms (in particular, the norm of universalism).

An examination of the functioning of hospitals reveals a formal (if not an actual) commitment to these methods of operation. A closer examination, however, reveals another dimension of organizational function that accords with the general reductionist thrust of bureaucracy/medical science Relation but is virtually unique to the hospital model itself. In addition to functioning as a central location for medical technology and the medical personnel that uses the technology, hospitals are preferred environments for the application of medical science to client problems because of one crucial fact—health providers can control the environment of hospitalized patients, but they have virtually no control over the environment of patients not hospitalized.

In the hospital, the patient's social, psychological, and nutritional exchanges can be regulated as the doctor wishes. What doctors desire most, of course, is to create an environment for patients that maximizes the chances that their healing efforts will be effective. Consequently, the perspective embraced by the physician comes to dictate the agenda for controlling the patient's environment. The reductionist medical scientific approach employed by physicians can be applied most effectively in an environment in which patients are isolated, as much as possible, from those social, psychological, and ecological factors that are causally related to their illnesses—factors excluded from the purview of the medical scientific paradigm. Hospitals have relied on such institutionalized practices as "visiting hours" to restrict patients' social contacts. Particularistic factors associated with the patient's social identity are controlled by requiring patients to exchange their own clothing for standard hospital gowns and by restricting the use of personal items, the wearing of jewelry, etc. Within the psychological domain, control is often exercised through the biochemical means: patients experiencing either physical or psychological distress (the boundary line between these two realms is never clear-cut) are given mood altering drugs to meliorate the distress. Most important, perhaps, is the regulation of the patient's behavior: the normal social routines that define the patient's unique lifestyle are replaced by a highly regimented schedule of eating, sleeping, and associating with others. Even the patients' nutritional intake is controlled; they eat only what the doctor wants them to eat (a significant source of irritation for many patients).

This analysis suggests that the hospital, as a unique type of bureaucratic organization within which medical care is rendered, provides something akin to a "controlled experimental situation" for the use of medical scientific techniques. Just as potentially valid scientific hypotheses are unlikely to be confirmed by experimental data if "extraneous variables" are not controlled, medical scientific treatments of some illnesses are unlikely to achieve any positive practical effects if extraneous medical variables (social, psychological, and ecological factors related to the illness) are not controlled. Although some medical scientific therapies have positive effects on certain illnesses even in the absence of such environmental controls, other therapies are effective only if the social, psychological, or ecological correlates of the patient's medical problems are bureaucratically managed. For some medical problems, the overwhelmingly negative impact of metaorganic factors on the patient's health is not meliorated by biomedical manipulation alone.

To view the hospital's therapeutic function in these terms serves to clearly illustrate the dialectical or mutually determinant character of the relationship between the medical scientific and bureaucratic models. We have seen how medical science lends ideological support to the bureaucratic form of organization, but we also find that hospital bureaucracies provide organizational support for medical science. The legitimacy of medical science as an applied medical perspective cannot be maintained solely by the political maneuvering of the practitioner group that uses it. For some members of the lay public, professionally influenced impressions of the value of medical science will always be tempered by data from their own personal experience of the efficacy of this approach. Consequently, advocates of the perspective make an effort to create a structural context for its application that will maximize the possibilities for positive results. For practitioners of medical science, the creation of an environment that insulates patients from the influence of extra-biological factors has resulted in a degree of efficacy that could not be attained otherwise. Thus, the hospital has played an important role in helping to maintain the legitimacy of medical science.

INTERRELATIONS BETWEEN INTERESTS GROUPS

Although the present study focuses on the medical knowledge dimension as an analytical facet through which the traditional medical model can be examined, the general perspective developed here has implications for a number of other problems that have concerned analysts of American medicine. One of the more widely discussed of these problems involves the structure of interest group relations within the medical sector. I have examined the various relational identities that exist between the medical scientific perspective and each of the most powerful interest groups in the health care system, but I have touched only briefly on the issue of how these groups relate to one another. A more systematic examination of this latter problem is now in order.

We can start by looking, in general terms, at the relationship between interest groups that are tied to the two major structural principles of organization in American society—the capitalist mode of production and the bureaucratic model. The relationship between these two dimensions is a complex one that is not well-understood by contemporary social scientists. Consequently, the present effort to examine this relationship must be limited in scope. I will attempt to highlight only those features of the relationship that bear directly on the interest group structure of the medical sector.

As with most Relations that sociologists study, the relationship between bureaucracy and capital can be analyzed from several different perspectives.

Two separate approaches to this problem can be distinguished, both of which ultimately derive from classical theoretical traditions within sociology. The two approaches, the Marxian and Weberian perspectives, differ most fundamentally over the issue of which principle of organization is structurally dominant. Within the Marxian framework, the mode of production is regarded as the dominant principle in a socio-economic system. This is *not* to suggest that it determines the character of all other aspects of the system (as proposed by the "vulgar" Marxist viewpoint) but to posit that all aspects of the system are organized around the basic logic of the mode of production. Conversely, the Weberian perspective gives priority to the organizing principle of bureaucracy or, more precisely, proposes that the bureaucratic form of organization and the capitalist mode of production are both manifestations of the more general historical trend toward the increasing rationalization of social life. In short, two different models of the relationship between capital and bureaucracy can be described, depending on whether one sees the "means of production" or the "means of administration" as the most fundamental principle of organization in modern society.

One of the most well-crafted applications of the Marxist perspective to the bureaucracy/capital Relation is Richard Edwards's (1979) study of workplace organization. Through a careful analysis of data from labor history studies, Edwards describes the historical transformation of the workplace in terms of the various mechanisms of control used by capitalists to defuse worker discontent and increase productivity. Although each control mechanism functioned effectively for a time, we have witnessed a steady progression of new control strategies in the twentieth century. This evolutionary process has been driven by two basic factors: the responses of workers to resist their employers' control efforts and structural changes within work organizations that undermine an existing control strategy. Edwards acknowledges the true complexity of the control issue by noting that control mechanisms are specific to particular economic sectors and types of work organizations. Some of the mechanisms that evolved in earlier era continue to be employed in some sectors but not others. Edwards constructs a typology that specifies these control strategies and the sectors in which they dominate.

Within this framework, the bureaucratic model is designated as the structure employed most recently by owners to control workers within the advanced "primary" sector of the labor force. With its emphasis on formal rules and operating standards, the bureaucratic model allows for a degree of control in large, multisegmented work organizations that could not be achieved by the face-to-face supervisor/employee control strategies charac-teristic of small work organizations. In addition, the hierarchical authority structure of bureaucratic organizations serves to undermine any potential for the development of "class consciousness." By establishing a complex hierarchy of job categories distinguished in terms of incremental differences in status and income, owners encourage "level consciousness" rather than class consciousness among workers. Insofar as workers regard the minor status and income differences between themselves and those directly above and below them as important, they are not likely to recognize their common interests in opposing capitalist exploitation. Bureaucratically created divisions within the working class, therefore, serve the purpose of removing potential resistance to capitalist domination.

In opposition to this view of the bureaucratic model as simply an organizational tool used by capitalists to dominate the working class, the classical Weberian perspective treats the bureaucratic form of organization as the central imperative of modern society. In Weber's view, capitalists do not stand above the social system and select either one or another set of structural arrangements for organizing the productive process. Rather, the capitalist system itself has emerged as the very embodiment of the rationality principle. This principle has been fully realized within the political sphere with the evolution of the modern bureaucratic state and has now started to completely dominate the economic realm as well: "As a type of bureaucracy, the large corporation is rivaled only by the state bureaucracy in promoting rational efficiency, continuity of operation, speed, precision, and calculation of result" (Gerth and Mills 1965, 49). Moreover, in contrast to the Marxian view of socialism, Weber posited that the public expropriation of the means of production would simple extend the rationalizing trend within the economic realm: in a socialist system, the economic sector becomes bureaucratized to the same degree as the political sector within the modern state.

While it is beyond the scope of the present study to determine which of these two perspectives offers the more valid explanation of the bureaucracy/ capital Relation, a few observations about these opposing viewpoints relate specifically to the concerns of this volume. First, if we look beyond the differences between these two perspectives to identify lines of convergence, we find one obvious point of agreement: Both perspectives emphasize a trend toward the coalescence of the bureaucratic and capitalist models. Whether it is because capitalists have used the bureaucratic model as an organizational tool to advance their interests or because of the inexorable movement of bureaucratic rationality throughout all domains of social life, the fact remains that bureaucratic and corporate interests and ideology have become increasingly identical. This is reflected in the language of capitalist ideology, which is more and more the language bureaucratic administration: owners speak of the need to rationalize their productive operations, to promote standard operating procedures, formal task assignment, rational calculation, speed, and efficiency. This ideology promotes an explicit goal of organizing productive operations in a way that maximizes profit or the implicit goal of increasing the owner's ability to exploit the productive power of workers.

Secondly, the issue of determining which principle of organization has causal priority in modern society may be resolved by considering the possibility of sector-by-sector variation in how capitalist and bureaucratic relations evolve and become intertwined. In some sectors, the market domination of more archaic forms of production may occur long before significant bureaucratization of the sector takes place. In such cases, corporate owners probably make explicit decisions to employ rationalizing strategies for increasing the profitability of their operations when they deem it necessary to do so. In other sectors, however, the encroachment of the bureaucratic model into the sector may occur well before capitalist enterprises seek to establish market power in that area. In this case, existing bureaucratic organizations may establish an ideological and institutional structure that increases the ease with which corporate groups can move into the sector.

These considerations suggest several avenues for exploring the relationship between the various interests groups that have some stake in the United States health care system. The latter version of how capital and bureaucracy are related best captures the situation in the medical sector: the evidence would suggest that the bureaucratic model emerged as the dominant challenging principle within the medical sector long before any significant corporate incursion into this sector. Robert Alford has assembled data from several decades before 1970 indicating that the chief structural interest challenging the dominance of the "professional monopolists" in the United States health care system were the "bureaucratic reformers." The groups tied to this latter structural interest—including medical schools, public health agencies, insurance companies, hospitals, and health planning agencies —promote an ideology that stresses "a rational, efficient, cost-conscious, coordinated health care delivery system" (1985, 204). The general concern of all who adopt this ideological position is to promote the further bureaucratization of the system. This ideology also advances the individual interests of the top administrators in such bureaucracies who wish to extend the range of their power and control over the system.

Alford's study captures an important phase of a long-term process of bureaucratic encroachment into the health care system. In the medical sector, then, the Weberian perspective seems to best explain the structural changes that have occurred in recent decades. As one of the few remaining economic sectors in the twentieth century where market power and authority was still organized according to the guild model, the system was destined be transformed by modernizing forces. The principle thrust of this modernization process has been the steady growth of bureaucratic organizations and persistent calls for a rationalization of the entire system, a transformation that would remove power and control from the medical profession and place it in the hands of administrators. Until the last decade, most of the medical profession's attention and resources have been dedicated to dealing with the threat posed by bureaucratic rationalizers, who have variously emerged as advocates of such programs as socialized medicine, national health insurance, Medicare/Medicaid, and the like. As a consequence of this preoccupation with bureaucratic rationalizers, the medical profession has been largely blind to the threat posed by another major challenging group—advocates of the corporate model.

Alford's study also lends support to the earlier suggestion that structural change in modern American society involves a coalescence of the bureaucratic and capitalist models. At the time of Alford's study, the portion of the health care system under direct corporate control was only a vestige of what it is today. Yet Alford was able to accurately decipher "the writing on the wall" to describe the coming transformation of the system. In his words, this change involves,

> a move toward transforming the present professional monopoly into a corporate monopoly, with new health corporations taking various forms and seeking to turn individual entrepreneurs (the doctors) into employees. The slogan of "social responsibility" may be used to justify taking away some of the powers of the private physician to charge what the market will bear and to transfer these powers to the hospital, the insurance companies, or the medical corporation (1975, 217).

At the heart of this most recent trend is a convergence between corporate and bureaucratic forces around the same structural interest—the desire for greater cost-benefit efficiency in the delivery of health care. In order to fully understand this transformation, however, a number of related issues must be considered, including the identification of the precise ways in which the two models converge, the sources of tension between them, and, most importantly, the specification of forces that have led corporate organizations to make renewed attempts to gain control of the medical market even though such efforts have largely failed in the past. To address these problems, we must carefully examine the relationship between the corporate order and the medical profession.

The medical profession's relationship to corporate interests has been a major focus of concern in medical sociology for the last two decades. Freidson's (1970) classic study of the medical profession, although not directly concerned with the relationship, helped to draw attention to the problem by focusing on the medical profession's place within the division of labor, i.e., the medical professional's control over the conditions of their own labor. Later writers have adopted Freidson's general political economic approach, but they question his assumption that professional groups acquire privileges by simply convincing the lay public of the intrinsic worth of the services they provide. For instance, Marxist analysts (cf. Navarro 1984) dismiss the idea that consumers of health care have the power to dictate the structure of the health care system and focus instead on the real source of power in capitalist society—the corporate elite. In this view, practitioner autonomy must be understood as a privilege bestowed on the medical profession by those corporate figures who wield both economic and political power within capitalist society, a privilege they grant because it serves their interests to do so. In accordance with this view, Brown (1979, 4) describes the historical transformation of the medical profession as a case in which the interests of practitioners and the corporate class "developed independently, coalesced, and then clashed."

Midway between Freidson and the Marxists is a third perspective articulated by Paul Starr (1982). Starr directs attention to the role of the corporate order in the development of the medical profession, but he rejects the idea that there has been a coalescence of interests between these two groups. In his view, professional autonomy is a consequence of the medical profession maintaining the upper hand, until recently, in an ongoing battle with corporate groups seeking to gain control of the market for medical services. The source of the medical profession's power in this struggle has been its strong ties to the patient population.

While fundamental disagreements can be found in the literature on this subject, one thing is clear: the relationship between corporate forces and the medical profession is currently undergoing a fundamental transformation. In the span of little more than a decade, analysts have gone from describing the practitioner group as the archetype of an autonomous profession to heralding a "corporate takeover" of medicine in which physicians are increasingly being turned into wage earners. Whether or not wage-earner status will greatly reduce physician autonomy is presently unclear because these changes are so recent. One finds complete consensus, however, about the monumental significance of the changing relationship between capital and the medical profession.

In structural terms, the current relationship between the corporate order and the medical profession is best understood as an antagonistic one in which corporate interests are presently ascendant, although antagonism has not always characterized the relations between these two groups (as we will see in the next chapter). This latest development derives from a number of structural changes that have served to polarize the interests of these two groups. One source of conflict has been the perception by corporate groups that the medical profession has played an important role in diminishing corporate profits. The practice of providing a portion of worker compensation in the form of health care benefits—which serves corporate interests by keeping the work force healthy and therefore more productive— means that a large percentage of the money funneled into the health care system comes directly from employers. This strategy has resulted in significant increases in labor costs over the last two decades as the price of health care has steadily increased. With inflation running higher in the medical sector than the economy as a whole and ever greater percentages of the Gross National Product going to health care services, many corporate elites have concluded that the traditional structure of the health care system is seriously flawed. The feature of the traditional system receiving most of the attention, of course, is the dominance and control of the medical profession (Starr 1982).

Although physicians' incomes have increased with the overall increase in health care costs, corporate leaders have generally accepted the profession's claim that physician compensation represents only a small proportion of the overall increase in costs. What is of greater concern to employers, however, is the medical profession's dominance within the health care system—their monopoly control over the health production process and their influence in matters relating to the structure of the system. Employers see the guild-like character of the profession impeding any effort to rationalize the system (as dictated by the capitalist model) in order to make it more cost-efficient. From the corporate perspective, the high cost of health care is a testament to the inherent inefficiency of noncorporate forms of economic organization. What corporate leaders regard as the solution to these problems is, of course, a dismantling of the structures that maintain professional dominance and a rationalization of the system through the promotion of market forces.

If the structural factors that have produced the "cost crisis" in health care explain, in part, the renewed efforts by corporate organizations to enter the health services market, other structural factors account for the unprecedented success of these recent efforts. One such factor involves the previously noted relationship between the bureaucratic and corporate interests within the medical sector. Structural change in the medical sector has involved a steady growth in bureaucratic organizations and an increasing tension between these organizations and the medical profession. While the medical profession was particularly successful in earlier decades of this century at keeping corporate organizations out of the health care business, it has been unable, and largely unwilling, more recently to mount efforts to stem the growth of such bureaucratic entities as public health organizations, hospitals, and medical school complexes. One important consequence of this increasing bureaucratization of the system has been the steady accumulation of organizational and ideological resources that could be exploited by corporate entities seeking to enter the medical market. Capitalist groups calling for greater corporate involvement in health care delivery or seeking to justify their own incursions into this domain employ essentially the same ideology that has been promoted by bureaucratic rationalizers for many decades. Both groups speak of the need to coordinate the system, to do away with redundancy in manpower and technology, and to provide services in a more cost-effective manner. At the same time, preexisting bureaucratic organizations such as nonprofit hospitals, nursing homes, and clinics have often been targeted by corporate groups that either contract to manage them or take them under direct corporate ownership. Such organizations provide a means of entry into the health care system for corporations wishing to market health care services.

One can conclude from these considerations that the bureaucratization of the medical sector has made the system ripe for an incursion by corporate organizations. Certainly in the ideological domain, a coalescence of interests between the bureaucratic and corporate realms has occurred, a coalescence that justifies Alford's use of the term *corporate rationalization* to describe the common ideological perspective embraced by these two groups. As Brown notes (1979, 204–206), three distinct groups promote this ideological perspective—one interest group made up of the "functionaries of bureaucratically organized medical care" (academic physicians and public health officialdom, advisers, planners, and consultants); another interest group consisting of "industries with a direct economic stake in the medical market" (hospitals and health insurance carriers); and the "corporate class," which includes "those who own or manage the nation's corporate wealth and foundation trustees and officers who supervise the expenditure of that portion of the wealth that is devoted to managing social institutions." With all three of these groups providing material resources to help spread the rationalization ideology, the corporate agenda has won many converts within the legislative and lay public domains. Consequently, in the battle of ideologies between the professional monopolists and the corporate rationalizers, the tide has started to turn in favor of the latter group.

The conflict between groups promoting different health policy perspectives has been emphasized by several analysts of the medical sector, but the struggle for control of this sector obviously involves much more than just a battle of perspectives. Which policy perspective gains the greatest number of converts is much less important than the actual help-seeking behavior of members of the lay public. Undoubtedly, the hegemony of either one or the other policy viewpoint influences patterns of help-seeking behavior within the population: insofar as potential patients internalize the ideology of corporate rationalization, they may be more inclined to rely on corporate health care organizations rather than private practitioners. However, many other factors also shape help-seeking behavior patterns, which means that one's choice of a health care provider may be inconsistent with one's beliefs about the appropriate political economic arrangements in the health care system. Some scholars emphasize other dimensions of help-seeking behavior that relate to interest group relations within the medical sector, but they fail to appreciate the importance of another ideological factor that impinges on such behavior. I refer to the ideological system that has been the chief concern of this volume—the medical scientific knowledge system.

Paul Starr typifies those scholars whose analyses of interest group conflict within the medical sector emphasize the market consequences of individual patient decisions about medical services. Although his impressive study examines this issue in a broad historical perspective (covering several centuries), his analysis of the most recent transformation involving the decline of professional dominance and the rise of corporate dominance is most salient to the present discussion. Starr argues that the moderate success of more recent attempts by corporate organizations to establish a foothold in the medical market is best explained in terms of the changing character of the patient-practitioner relationship. In the earlier decades of this century, an era in which the ties between patients and their practitioners were very strong, corporate health care organizations failed because they could not attract patients away from their private physicians. Even though corporate groups could provide services at a cost savings to prospective patients, most patients preferred to pay more for what they regarded as higher quality medical care rendered by private practitioners. In contrast, the general weakening of ties between patients and private practitioners in recent decades has provided a new opportunity for corporate groups to market health care services. In the new climate of rising health care costs and weak attachments between patients and practitioners, the cost savings offered by for-profit health maintenance organizations and other corporate alternatives have become attractive to potential patients: more and more people now believe that the extra expense of a private practitioner does not necessarily carry the dividend of better care.

Starr identifies a number of structural factors that have stimulated these changes in the patient-practitioner relationship, chief among them being the decline in the "cultural authority" or physicians. One crucial factor in the transformation, however, has been ignored by Starr and other analysts of this relationship—the role of the medical scientific paradigm in structuring the interactions of patients and practitioners. As we have seen, the physician's control over the health production process depends upon two basic factors: (1) the physician's possession of a culturally legitimate body of applied medical knowledge that supports the physician's role as healer and (2) a social structural arrangement that allows practitioners to apply this knowledge to particular human problems. The latter involves, more specifically, a patient-practitioner relationship in which practitioners can personally mediate between the medical knowledge system and the people who bring their problems to them. While there has been a growing recognition of the steady disintegration of the personalized nature of the patient-practitioner relationship (cf. Alford 1975, 193), the important connection between this change and the hegemony of the medical scientific definition of health and illness is little understood.

As I will describe in the next chapter, one dimension of the historical evolution of the medical practice system involves an increasing identity between the dominant medical knowledge system (the medical scientific paradigm) and actual medical practice. Accordingly, it is appropriate to describe medical science as currently hegemonic within modern medical practice: the scope of the paradigm has been broadened to include more and more domains of human existence, the system has been steadily refined and elaborated, and the training of physicians—their induction into the work of medical science—has become increasingly sophisticated. At no time in history have individual physicians been more predisposed to a medical scientific view of patient problems than they are now. My content analysis of medical science makes it possible to specify the precise consequences of this view of human problems for the interaction of practitioners and patients. Consonant with the reductionist emphasis of the medical scientific perspective, the practitioner directs the diagnostic eye toward the hidden spaces of the body. The practitioner's task is to establish a conceptual link between patients' subjective experience of their problems (symptoms), the practitioner's own clinical observations of patients (signs), and possible histopathological conditions that could cause such an array of symptoms and signs. Consequently, patients are not perceived by practitioners as individual human beings with human problems but as "representative instances of typical diseases." This way of perceiving the patient has undermined the strong ties between patients and their private practitioners more than any other single factor. To underscore this last point, I will rely once again on the logic of countersystem analysis. Within the countersystem model, the interaction between patients and practitioners is directly shaped by the practitioner's perception of patients as multidimensional entities who experience problems that reflect their interconnections to broader metaorganic wholes (society, culture, economy, ecology, etc.) as well as the organic dimension of their bodies. Thus, the practitioner's understanding of the patient as a person, that is, as a unique sociobiological entity with a complex social, psychological, and biological history, is critical for the resolution of the patient's problem. In this system, the relationship between patient and practitioner *must* be personalized if an effective course of therapy is to be identified.

There is little question that some version of this latter form of patient-practitioner relationship is what many contemporary Americans want and what some allopathic physicians actually provide. On the practitioner's side, however, the personalized approach to patients and their problems directly contradicts the "ideal-typical" model of knowledge and practice, which has been the focus of their training and serves as the principle reference for defining competent medical practice. While patients who bring their problems to physicians may wish to describe themselves and their difficulties in spiritual, social, or social-psychological terms, the model that guides medical perception designates information about these domains as irrelevant to the proper diagnosis of the problem. This is not to deny that some individual physicians, as a personal matter, might regard the conditions of their patients' social or spiritual existence as important elements in the etiology of medical problems. In their formal role as practitioners of medical science, though, physicians must discourage any discussion of these aspects of the patient's existence, for it can only interfere with their ability to perceive the possible histopathological source of the patient's problem. From the patient's perspective, the practitioner exists as an anonymous and dispassionate observer of a hidden and mysterious domain of the patient's existence. The patient has no personal connection to the practitioner because of the latter's ignorance of, and lack of interest in, any of the personal knowledge that forms the basis of primary relations in modern society. Consequently, in the same way that services such as having one's hair cut or one's shoes fitted can be provided by competent strangers, patients increasingly feel that their bodies can also be serviced by anonymous individuals who need only to provide formal documentation of their competence (i.e., a medical degree).

With the growing identity between the medical scientific model of medical practice and the actual clinical behavior of medical practitioners, the social structural basis of the physician's control over the health production process has steadily eroded. The personalized relationship between practitioners and patients necessary for maintaining strong ties between these two groups is undermined by the model of diagnosis and treatment dictated by the medical scientific perspective. Patients feel little attachment to their private practitioners, who deal with them not as people with a distinctive social, psychological, and biological histories but as universalistic disease categories.

At the same time that the medical scientific perspective conflicts with the personalized patient-practitioner relationship emphasized by the ideology of the professional monopolists, it is perfectly consistent with the logic of the corporate-bureaucratic model of health care delivery. By reducing human problems with a complex, metaorganic etiology to the level of discrete disease conditions, medical science makes it possible to organize a delivery system in a rational, efficient, and mass-oriented fashion. The choices that patients now face in their efforts to secure medical services are clear-cut. They increasingly perceive very little difference in the type of care they are likely to receive from either private practitioners or staff physicians in a corporate organization. They *do* see a significant difference, however, in how much they will pay for these services. As health care consumers, patients are increasingly attracted to corporate providers who can organize services more efficiently and therefore offer them at a lower price.

In summary, the current state of affairs in American health care involves an interest group structure in which the principle line of tension exists between the medical profession and those groups organized around a common interest in corporate rationalization. The development of corporate rationalization as the chief antagonist to the interest of the medical profession is of fairly recent origin. As we will see in the next chapter, interest group relations have been constantly shifting in the medical sector with the interests of some groups converging at one point in time but diverging at other times. While in an earlier era, the interests of the medical profession and the corporate class were mutually supportive and both groups were generally aligned against bureaucratic interests, a gradual shift in the interest network has led to greater tension between the medical profession and the corporate class and greater identity between the latter and medicine's old enemy, the bureaucratic rationalizers.

The recent convergence in bureaucratic and corporate interests has not eliminated the incipient differences between these two groups, however. Bureaucratic groups established a foothold within the medical sector long before corporate groups did, which allowed bureaucratic functionaries to largely dictate the parameters of the policy alternatives. Whereas corporate groups have used bureaucratic ideology and organizational structures as a springboard for gaining access to the health care system, they have also increasingly redefined the parameters of the rational model of health care delivery. In the present relationship between these two groups, corporate interests are apparently calling the tune to which bureaucratic rationalizers dance. Starr, for example, describes a tendency for nonprofit hospitals and other delivery organizations to model the behavior of the corporate health maintenance organizations (HMOs) and hospital chains because failing to adhere to the corporate definition of rationalization often results in the inability of noncorporate organizations to compete and survive. The question that remains is, How long can the present identity between bureaucratic and corporate interests be expected to remain stable. At what point will the bureaucratic rationalizers based in medical schools, public health agencies, and health planning agencies begin to focus on the irrationalities of the corporate model of health care? Although it is difficult to know precisely when a divergence between these two groups will take place, it will very likely occur at some point in the future.

THE PRINCIPLE OF ORGANIZATION

The last issue to be addressed in this chapter is the problem of specifying the principle by which the traditional medical model is organized. In accordance with a basic presupposition of dialectical theory, this principle is to be found in the relationship between the consumers and providers of health. Recent change in the structure of health provision helps to reveal in stark form the true nature of the organizing logic of the traditional model. When the provision of health was the exclusive domain of private practitioners, who may have served as proxies for other powerful groups in society but who took on the appearance of autonomous professionals, discerning the essential character of the medical model's principle of organization was more difficult. Now that medical practitioners have increasingly come under the direct control of corporate-bureaucratic forces, which have also gained almost exclusive control over capital-intensive health care resources, it is much easier to penetrate the hazy character of the relationship between health consumers and providers. The essence of this relationship is the fundamental opposition of interests between health consumers (patients) and health providers, an opposition that is defined in terms of the conflict between patients' interest in holistic health production and providers' interest in reductionist health production.

As demonstrated in the preceding chapters, the concept of health can be defined in many different ways, and every definition of health supports a particular interest structure. From the perspective of patients, health is a conceptual reservoir for all that people value in opportunities for personal fulfillment and growth. Illness, by contrast, is a category that refers to personal troubles, which, by their very nature, derive from many difference sources—biological, psychological, social, and spiritual. While Americans today may possess only a vague awareness of their interest in defining health and illness in these terms, such a conceptualization nevertheless constitutes a powerful ideology that supports the structurally defined interests of patients.

In contrast, the interests of health providers dictate that health and illness be defined in strictly reductionist terms. The rendering of health care by a provider group requires that health and illness be reduced to the level at which standardized knowledge and technique can be applied to the task of manipulating discrete units. In addition, this process must be carried on in fashion that does not threaten the existing structure of privilege. Conversely, providers cannot serve patients' structurally defined interests without undermining their own claims to exclusive control over medical knowledge and technique and placing themselves at odds with powerful interests the larger social system. While individual practitioners at various times *do* adopt elements of the holistic approach in an effort to serve their patient's best interests, such acts lead to conflict between these practitioners and their professional organizations as well as sanction by corporate interests who may be threatened by them. This conflict is almost always resolved in a way that serves to maintain existing patterns of medical practice and social arrangements.

The structural opposition of patient and provider interests is a dynamic revealed in every facet of the traditional medical model, from micro- to macro-structural levels. The struggle between these opposing interests is often difficult to recognize in some domains but is always there in at least incipient form. Consider, for example, the typical encounter between patients and their doctors. Patients efforts to explain their problems to physicians are often explicit statements of personal troubles in terms of social, psychological, and spiritual parameters. Moreover, many patients are amenable to approaches for dealing with their problems that would focus on these dimensions. The practitioner's primary professional commitment, however, is to translate patients' troubles into the language of medical science and, in doing so, reduce social, psychological, or spiritually based problems to the level of body chemistry and tissues. While there is little surface evidence of struggle between opposing interest in such an encounter, a closer examination reveals a fundamental conflict between the two parties, one involving the central concern of many people who seek the help of professional consultants—to find relief from the emotional and physical pain of social living and to achieve a sense of balance and purpose in their lives.

In defining this opposition of interests between patients and providers as the organizing principle of the traditional model, several additional issues emerge. As I have demonstrated, the resources that can be used in the struggle between patients and providers are not equally distributed between the parties involved. On the provider side, practitioners and the managers of health care organizations (both corporate and noncorporate) possess power based on collective organization. Such organizationally based power is virtually nonexistent within the patient population. Provider resources also include the practitioner's control over medical knowledge and administrator's control over medical technology and the medical division of labor. Once again, no comparable resources are found on the patient side. The absence of a medical ideology favoring patient interests to counter the ideology of medical science is particularly problematic because such a system would allow patients to articulate in more explicit terms ideas and feelings about their problems that already exist in incipient form. As a practical matter, the holistic health countersystem is designed to fulfill precisely this function.

The unequal distribution of resources between patients and providers accounts for the dominance of the latter group in the health production system. Providers have used their dominant position to direct patient energies away from the production of well-being and towards a production agenda that best serves the interests of the most privileged groups in American society. Patients under the control of providers do not invest energy in maintaining and developing existing capabilities and establishing balance (in accordance with the countersystem definition of health); rather, they invest their energy in the production and consumption of goods and services in a fashion dictated by those who control the means of production and distribution and who benefit most from this system. If energy is invested in the production of health within this system, it typically takes the form of the patient's consultation with a physician to establish a therapeutic course of action. This approach is unique insofar as it is minimally disruptive to the patient's socially defined tasks, the most crucial of which are the patient's production and consumption functions. This system of health care thus creates the possibility for an expropriation of human energy for the purpose of protecting and enhancing existing political-economic structures. The system allows for a rationalization of social life that serves to free up a maximum amount of human energy for the production of surplus wealth.

In positing that the opposition between patient and provider interests is the organizing principle of the traditional model, I do not wish to downplay the importance of other conflicts within the health care system. I have dedicated significant attention in this chapter to the lines of tension that exist within the provider group—the conflict between practitioners, administrators and corporate owners. However, while the struggle between these groups plays a role in shaping many of the most fundamental characteristics of the health care system, the changes that arise from this struggle do not alter the basic principle by which the system is organized. Regardless of whether practitioners exercise monopoly control over the provision of care or they are under the direct control of corporate or noncorporate administrators, opposition between the interests of patients and providers (providers broadly defined) is still the most salient feature of the relationship. Despite the differences that exist between them, providers have a common interest in imposing reductionist definitions of health and illness and related therapeutic procedures on patients. The outcome of current battle for control over health care provision makes little difference to patient interests. As long as practitioners remain committed to medical scientific ideology, patients will continue to be exploited by a system that expropriates their energies for the pursuit of goals that are inconsistent with their own basic interests. The health care system functions as one more institution within modern capitalist society that reduces people to a narrow and constrained existence, sacrificing the opportunity for a full development and exploration of human species potential for the purpose of helping to produce ever greater amounts of capital.

CHAPTER SEVEN

Diachronic Analysis of Medical Practice

In the previous chapter, I described the United States health care system in terms of the various "synchronic Relations" that make up the traditional medical model. This type of analysis requires that time be held constant in order to identify the interrelated set of structures that constitute the whole of the medical model. While this procedure is a necessary part of the methodology I have employed, it obviously violates a central premise of the dialectical paradigm—the notion that change is ubiquitous within the social domain. To insure a comprehensive dialectical analysis of the medical practice system, an examination of the "diachronic Relations" of the traditional medical model is now necessary. In the present chapter, I undertake this form of analysis by describing the historical development of the biomedical model.

One of my central concerns at this point is to explore the consequences of the evolving relationship between medical science and medical practice for the social structure of the health care system. By once again using the countersystem as an analytical reference point, we will come to see this changing relationship in terms of a movement away from contradiction and toward identity. The countersystem method will also allow us to view other aspects of the history of medicine in a new light. With the insights of the previous chapter forming the basis of a new perspective, historical data on a variety of topics relating to health and medicine can be reinterpreted. My goal is not to provide a detailed analysis of any particular aspect of the history of medicine but rather to show how the general perspective developed in previous chapters can be applied to various kinds of historical data.

The relationship of the present to the past is, of course, just one type of diachronic Relation of interest in this study. Attention must also be directed to the relationship between the present and the future by examining the emerging trends within the medical sector in relation to the pragmatic possibilities for creating the ideal health care system articulated in this

163

volume. The combined analysis of the past and future of the traditional medical model makes it possible to transcend a static view of the system to a conception of it as a dynamic entity in a state of "becoming." After examining the historical Relations of the medical scientific model in the present chapter, I direct attention to future Relations in chapter eight.

THE EVOLUTION OF HEALTH STATUS

Among the variety of issues addressed by medical historians, perhaps none has had greater ideological significance than the phenomenon of the "demographic transition"—the dramatic improvement in health status and life expectancy in Western societies during the last three centuries. Moreover, this topic has come under renewed scrutiny recently with the emergence a new body of research that challenges the conventional wisdom about the historical change in health status. The traditional view of this historical pattern among historians of medicine is consistent with the common-sense orientation of most members of Western societies, an orientation that reflects the influence of medical professional ideology on this subject. This view attributes the vast improvement in health in the nineteenth and twentieth centuries to scientific, technological medicine, with the decrease in disability and early death due to disease directly correlating with the advancement of medical scientific knowledge and technology (cf. Schwartz 1972; 1975). Unfortunately, the progenitors of this perspective have offered little empirical support for their central premise. When empirical evidence *has* been systematically examined, a very different picture has emerged.

The effort to empirically assess the traditional viewpoint has been undertaken by several scholars more recently (Eyer 1984; McKeown 1979; McKinlay and McKinlay 1977; Powles 1973). McKeown, for example, adopts a simple and direct method for determining if there is a causal connection between the development of clinical techniques and the improvement in health by looking at the exact timing of the changes in both domains. When evidence relating to the decline in mortality from specific diseases is compared to the historical record on the introduction of specific clinical procedures for dealing with these diseases, a consistent pattern emerges: For almost all of the diseases that McKeown examines, mortality rates started to decline well in advance of the development and use of the clinical techniques for treating those diseases.

More generally, McKeown's data points to several important conclusions. First, the evidence indicates that the overall decline in mortality and the increase in life expectancy during the eighteenth, nineteenth and early twentieth centuries was primarily due to the decline in epidemic diseases. This decline, in turn, had little to do with the development of medical science and medical cures but was chiefly due to three significant changes: the improvement in food supplies and thus the quality of nutrition in the eighteenth century, the institutionalization of sanitation measures by the later nineteenth century, and the development of birth control techniques, which made it possible keep population growth from negating the effects of the improvement in the standard of living. Clinical techniques introduced in the twentieth century did help to accelerate the improvement in health status caused by these other factors, but this latter component was the least important of the four causal factors.

As this and other similar studies clearly demonstrate, little empirical support exists for the traditional view of the relationship between clinical medicine and the improvement in health. The data suggest the need for an alternative, socio-economic model of the historical change in health status. Reductions in mortality and morbidity rates can be viewed as direct manifestations of social and economic changes during the last three centuries, changes that were associated with a dramatic improvement in the standard of living. This socio-economic model and its supporting evidence is particularly relevant to the concerns of the present volume. Just as the traditional view of the historical change in health status is directly tied to the medical scientific model, the alternative, socio-economic viewpoint is directly tied to the countersystem medical model and the broader framework from which the latter is derived, the Marxian perspective. Although the connections between these conceptual models have not been explicitly established in the past, I will show that they can be integrated with one another to form a broader perspective that is clearly supported by the data.

The most important link between the socio-economic explanation of increasing life expectancy and the countersystem medical model is each perspective's emphasis on the influence of metaorganic factors in the organic functioning of the body. Social and economic structural arrangements that impact on the quality of nutrition, the quality of air, soil, and water and the relationship between population size and available resources are defined by both models as the ultimate determinants of biological functioning. Consequently, the historical evidence supporting the socio-economic view of change in health status can also be taken as empirical validation of the countersystem perspective. As the holistic health perspective hypothesizes, the most important determinants of health status are those characteristics of the more emergent wholes to which human beings belong, factors that influence the body's self-healing capacities. In contrast, the invasive techniques of healers would be expected to have very little effect on the health of the population because these techniques rarely enhance the self-healing propensities of human organism.

The analysis can be taken a step further by considering the implications of this historical data for a more general model of historical change. A socio-economic analysis would attribute the improvement in the population's health over the last three centuries to the ongoing realization of a dynamic potential within industrial society—the potential for a rational and efficient exploitation of nature leading to an accumulated material surplus of unprecedented size in human history. With the steady development of the productive potential of capitalism, a long-term increase in the standard of living of most members of capitalist society has occurred, a change consisting of improvements in food supplies and nutrition, in the quality of shelter and clothing, and in the distribution of work and leisure time. The health status of the population within Western society may therefore be used as a parameter of long-term social change. By doing so, we establish a reference point for critically assessing the general tendencies of socio-economic change, specifying both the destructive trends as well as the progressive potential that exists within the evolving socio-economic order. This type of assessment is, of course, crucial for the advancement of the praxis approach to social change, an approach that emphasizes conscious human authorship as a key element of social/historical change.

Examined in terms of variables that relate directly to organic functioning (i.e., mortality rates, morbidity rates, life expectancy, etc.), the development of capitalist productive relations has involved several positive and negative trends. The positive tendencies in the evolution of capital have been noted—the decreases in mortality and morbidity rates associated with the growth in material resources such as food, shelter, and clothing. This pattern of improving organic function has not followed a smooth linear curve; periods of widespread death and disease in the last three centuries can be indirectly tied to the evolution of the mode of production (i.e., the epidemic diseases that spread through Europe as the population became more urbanized and experienced greater exposure to urban filth). The overall trend, however, has involved a general improvement in organic functioning for most members of capitalist society as revealed by the dramatic increase in the life expectancy rate from 1900 to the present (from 48 years to approximately 75 years). This trend constitutes one dimension of a more general development emphasized by classical Marxian theory—the movement within the capitalist system towards a state of "superabundance."

Embedded in this pattern of improving health, however, are several negative trends. In addition to the tendency of capitalist economies to create ever-increasing amounts of surplus wealth, a related tendency had produced a radical maldistribution of that surplus. The basic logic of the capitalist production process requires that significant amounts of the value that workers create be placed in the hands of those who own the means of production, the corporate elite who constitute only a small part of the population. Equally necessary to capitalism is the existence of a sizable population of unemployed or underemployed workers ("surplus labor"). What this means for the economic status of members of capitalist society is significance variation in the standard of living between different segments of the population. In addition to radical lifestyle differences between members of the capitalist class and those individuals belonging to the surplus labor pool, recent research has identified a structurally induced disparity in the standard of living of the professional/managerial classes (the "primary sector" of the labor force) vs. those poorly paid members of the "secondary sector" (Montagna 1977). These differences in economic status make it impossible to speak of a "general" standard of living within capitalist society.

The structural logic of the capitalist productive process produces mortality and morbidity patterns that roughly correlate with the distribution of wealth in this type of society. Epidemiological studies focusing on variations in death and disease rates across different social groups have found dramatically higher incidences of illness and premature death among those groups at the lower end of the economic scale. Members of the black population in the United States, who are disproportionately represented among the poorer classes, experience greater disease and disability than whites and have a lower life expectancy for both males and females. Moreover, the infant mortality rate for blacks is two and one-half times greater than the rate for whites. In fact, the mortality rate for blacks is higher than it is for whites for both sexes in all age categories. Within the white population, we also find variations across class categories: in general, the lower one's economic status, the more likely one is to experience disease and early death. The disparity in health between the lowest and highest economic groups among whites approaches the disparity that exists between whites and blacks in general. The overall pattern revealed in the epidemiological data is clear-cut: the higher one's economic standing, the less likely one is to experience disease and disability and the longer one can expect to live (National Center for Health Statistics 1980; Antonovsky 1972).

As Marxist scholars point out, the vast accumulation of wealth that becomes concentrated in the hands of the capitalist class is only possible because certain segments of the working class experience significant material deprivation. This insight can be easily extended to other disparities related to the differential distribution of wealth, including the health-related phenomena presently under discussion. One could posit that the low rates of death and disease among some social groups within capitalist society have been achieved at the expense of other social groups: good health among members of the higher social classes goes hand in hand with poor health among members of the lower social classes. Stated more dramatically, the relatively low rates of mortality found among white infants are possible only because large numbers of black infants die from the various social and biological consequences of poverty. This may seem outrageous from a common-sense viewpoint, but this insight is rooted in an understanding of the structural imperative of capitalism, a logic that allows for the development of vast personal fortunes for the owners of the means of production and a high standard of living for the agents of corporate owners (the managerial and professional groups) through the direct exploitation and impoverishment of those who produce wealth in society.

The uneven distribution of disease and disability across race and class groups is the most obvious negative health trend in capitalist society but not the only one. Additional data from social epidemiological studies reveal patterns of mortality and morbidity that point to other health-threatening features of modern society. One such pattern involves the rise and decline of various types of diseases across the last several centuries. Perhaps the most important occurrence in the history of human diseases was the dramatic rise and eventual decline of the epidemic diseases of the seventeenth, eighteenth, and nineteenth centuries. As noted above, the emergence of these diseases was directly tied to the movement of human populations from rural areas to the growing cities of the European continent. This population shift was, in turn, related to structural changes in economic conditions involving the growth of mercantilism and industrialism, which created for the first time in human history a broad-based demand for contract or wage labor. As more and more people crowded into European cities looking for work, the ecological and population conditions required for the rapid spread of contagious diseases were created. The rise of epidemic diseases was, therefore, a socially and historically determined phenomenon. In the same way that certain social and political developments were made possible by the ongoing evolution of the forces of production, the major plagues and epidemics of the seventeenth and eighteenth centuries were directly tied to the demographic and ecological changes wrought by the development of these same forces.

The decline of the epidemic diseases can also be explained in terms of the social/historical dynamic just described. I have already noted how the improving standard of living that accompanied the development of industrialism throughout the nineteenth and twentieth centuries has contributed to a general enhancement of people's inherent disease fighting capabilities. Another important factor in the decline of epidemic diseases involved activism on the part urban authorities—the enactment of public health measures to improve the quality of water and air in the growing cities. These efforts were also directly related to the developing economic base of the cities in which public health efforts were undertaken.

The decline of epidemic diseases correlates with another broader historical change in mortality and morbidity patterns, one that is especially important for understanding the nature of illness in the twentieth century. This transformation involves a change in the incidence of acute vs. chronic illness. While the social and economic factors just discussed contributed to a significant reduction in the amount of death and disability due to acute illness, an equally dramatic increase in the rates of chronic illness has occurred for reasons not now fully understood. On the one hand, the rise in chronic illness could be a direct artifact of the decline in acute illness: the lower incidence of acute illness has meant that more people are living long enough to begin experiencing disability associated with various forms of organic deterioration. On the other hand, the rise of chronic diseases may also represent the same type of social/historical phenomenon as the rise of epidemic diseases several centuries ago: it may be a direct consequence of new environmental conditions created by the developing forces of production. This latter proposition, which reflects the countersystem viewpoint, deserves further attention.

To describe the various environmental changes that have accompanied the development of the industrial forces of production in the twentieth century, it would help to first distinguish between the ecological and the social psychological dimensions of the environment. Within the former domain, alterations associated with the growth of industrialism have been a subject of much scientific and public concern and, therefore, are well-documented (although not well understood). Among the many effects of industrialism on world ecology, the one that seems to have had the greatest direct impact on the population's health is the rise of environmental pollutants in the air, water, and soil. The increases in environmental pollutants have been particularly dramatic in the last century as the expansion of the world population has created a market potential for consumer goods leading to exponential growth in industrial production. Accompanying this latter development have been the equally dramatic increases in the burning of fossil fuels, which produces numerous health-threatening byproducts (e.g., acid rain, and excessive amounts of carbon dioxide), a rapid accumulation of toxic substances within the air, soil, and water (lead, mercury, kepone, etc.), an increase in atmospheric radiation levels due to the spread of radiation-producing technologies, and many more specific chemical changes in the environment with consequences that we are just now beginning to understand (e.g., the effect of chlorofluorocarbons on the earth's ozone layer). Although many of these ecological changes could have long-term consequences for the ability of the planet to support life, we confront more immediate problems associated with the effect of specific pollutants on the organic functioning of current members of the world population.

Another type of ecological change that may have direct consequences for human health is the increased reliance on synthetic chemicals in the agricultural sector. The introduction of chemical agriculture and food processing since World War II has not only revolutionized the food industry but has also fundamentally altered the nutritional spectrum for most people in industrial societies. The greater reliance on nitrogen, phosphorus, and potassium fertilizers in the postwar period resulted in substantially higher crop yields while, at the same time, making plants more susceptible to assault by insects, fungi, and weeds. This, in turn, has necessitated the use of powerful insecticides, fungicides, and herbicides. The effect of these changes in agricultural practice has been to create a system in which most of the food available to the public is now grown in soil that has had very little organic matter recycled into it during the last forty years. With the evolution of modern agribusiness, profits for companies marketing foodstuffs have steadily increased while, at the same time, unprecedented levels of synthetic chemicals have been introduced into the foods consumed by the public.

Unfortunately, little research has been done on the consequences for human health of the population's increased exposure to environmental pollutants and agricultural chemicals. While we know little about the causal mechanisms that may give rise to environmentally produced disease, the available evidence does reveal some highly correlated historical trends. For instance, as the amounts and range of pollutants and agricultural chemicals have steadily increased in the environment, there has also been a rather dramatic increase in the incidence of various types of cancer. Cancer is now the leading cause of death in children under fifteen while two generations ago childhood cancer was virtually nonexistent. Likewise, a number of chronic degenerative diseases have followed a growth curve similar to that of cancer, including such diseases as hypertension, diabetes, kidney disorders, and heart disease. Again, the most disturbing pattern is the growth of these diseases among young adults and children. As one researcher has pointed out, it appears that "the diseases that use to be the diseases of old people are becoming the diseases of children" (McKee 1987).

The growth in chronic diseases during the twentieth century not only correlates with changes in the ecological environment, the trend is also associated with equally dramatic changes in the social psychological environment. As noted in an earlier chapter, the character of productive and consumptive relations in modern postindustrial societies means that large segments of the population typically live under conditions belonging to the high stress end of the continuum. The economic structures that presently serve to maximize the productivity of workers, involving such things as ideological manipulation (through the media, schools, and other socializing agencies) that emphasizes commitment to increasing one's consumptive power (earning capacity), and the focus on career advancement as the primary measure of self-worth, encourage lifestyle patterns in which high levels of stress become a central feature of daily existence. The scientific community presently knows very little about the precise mechanisms that may be involved in stress-related disease, which accounts for the difficulties we confront in trying to establish a clear-cut causal relationship between stress and specific disorders. However, there *is* a growing consensus that high stress conditions produce deleterious effects on organic functioning and may be directly related to such disorders as cancer and heart disease (cf. Siegrist 1984; Jenkins 1983).

In addition to stress and other psychological phenomena associated with life in modern postindustrial society, numerous lifestyle practices dictated by the structure of modern society appear to be causally related to prevalent forms of disease. Growing evidence suggests that the typical diet of Americans may be associated with specific organic disorders. The heavy reliance on processed sugar, fatty meats, high levels of sodium, and other foodstuffs virtually unique to modern society, may significantly stress critical organs and tissues in the body and is increasingly cited as a possible source of degenerative disease. The notion of "social determination" is important for understanding this pattern. The diet of a typical American may reflect individual food preferences, but it is height of sociological naiveté to assume that individuals form their food preferences in isolation from socio-economic factors. The growing prevalence of some foods in the American diet must be related to the efforts of specific food industries to market their products, creating and/or increasing demand for their products where there was little or no demand before. If we take into account the entire causal sequence between ultimate socio-economic factors and more proximate dietary factors associated with specific disorders, these disorders are properly characterized as endemic features of the existing socio-economic order.

The same can be said for diseases associated with various forms of substance use and abuse. Disorders arising from the use of tobacco and alcohol, i.e., lung cancer, heart disease, hypertension, kidney, and liver diseases, have become increasingly prevalent causes of disability and death in the twentieth century. Like the dietary patterns of the modern era, the growth in the consumption of alcohol and tobacco has been shaped by well-funded marketing efforts to increase demand for these products. One could also argue that the high rates of drug abuse are, to some degree, associated with those elements of modern society that encourage individuals to seek drug-induced stimulation or escape. The image of the factory worker who responds to a work life filled with mindless, stultifying ("alienated") labor by consuming drugs that stimulate the senses or the corporate executive who escapes the stress of a highly competitive work environment through substance abuse are increasingly common pictures of contemporary American life. The growing recognition of the health-threatening conse- quences of widespread drug abuse has led to many well-publicized efforts by public agencies and officials to deal with the problem through regulatory means—by restricting the availability of drugs and by undertaking media campaigns to encourage individual decisions not to use drugs (i.e., the "just say no" campaign). While these measures may lead to some reductions in substance abuse, they are unlikely to contribute to any lasting changes in drug use patterns. Without dealing with the socio-economic factors that lead people to seek stimulation or escape through the use of psychoactive chemicals, the problem is not likely to soon disappear.

In summary, this evidence supports the view that long-term changes in mortality and morbidity patterns are a direct consequence of the socio-economically produced alterations in both the ecological environment and the psychological experience of societal members. The data supporting this view (including much more data than can be reviewed here) also provide an empirical foundation for a diachronic model of changing health status. The data reveal a historical pattern of both positive and negative changes in the health status of members of Western societies. People in these societies are living longer and are enjoying freedom from many of the diseases that have long plagued humankind, but, at the same time, they confront health problems of a type and a degree never before seen in human history. This pattern lends support to a "historical materialist" model of changing health status.

At the center of the historical materialist model of social change is a distinctive emphasis on the dialectical character of evolving human and social potential. As a particular mode of production develops, an inherent potential for progressive social change is realized. However, existing political and legal structures (the relations of production) define who will directly benefit from this new found potential and who, in turn, will have to bear the costs of newly created privilege. In all modes of production, privilege is maintained at the expense of some groups within society and some dimensions of the collective good; positive developments occur hand in hand with negative developments. The tensions (contradictions) that develop between those who benefit from the existing relations of production and those who suffer under these relations is the motor for further progressive change. However, only after the existing political and legal structures are reorganized through political action by oppressed groups in society can the pent-up potential for further human and social advancement be realized.

The historical data on disease patterns taken as a parameter of social change helps to define a central contradiction that has emerged with the evolution of capitalism. With the ongoing development of the capitalist forces of production, the structural capacity for generating material abundance has reached an unprecedented level. The age of superabundance has indeed arrived in most modern capitalist societies. Although most of the surplus wealth produced by this system resides in the hands of the capitalist class, sufficient amounts have "trickled down" to certain segments of the working class to significantly raise their standard of living. This improvement in the standard of living, in turn, may account for a major part of the overall decline in acute illness and early death. However, at the same time that the economic potential for superabundance has been realized under capitalism, the health of some groups has been seriously compromised and the integrity of many organic and metaorganic systems crucial to the maintenance of the health of the whole population has been threatened. The potential exists within the present structure of productive forces to effectively deal with health problems endemic to the current socio-economic system, but this potential can be realized only through the destruction of the existing relations of production and the creation of a new set of social and political arrangements organized to resolve the contradictions of capital. The nature of the potential for further progressive change in the health status of the population and the type of social/political structure needed for realizing this potential will be discussed in some detail in the concluding chapter of this volume, when we "return to the future."

THE EVOLUTION OF MEDICAL KNOWLEDGE

Another topic that has received significant attention from students of medical history is the historical transformation of medical thinking. So much has been written in this area (cf. King 1958; Rothstein 1972; Kett 1968; Coulter 1977) that a comprehensive review of the available literature on this subject cannot possibly be provided here. Nor is it desirable to offer such a review because my main purpose is to demonstrate how the perspective developed in the previous chapter can serve as a general framework for interpreting data relating to a number of topics in the history of medicine. Consequently, I have been selective in assembling the evidence for the present section, focusing on the general characteristics of American medical thought as it has evolved in the last several centuries. What is presently missing in the wealth of research dealing with the history of medical knowledge is a sociology of knowledge model that can explain, in a theoretically informed way, the relationship between one historically specific system of medical knowledge and another. The perspective of the present study can be employed to resolve this problem.

When we examine the entire universe of distinct medical knowledge systems that developed in North America during the last three centuries, we confront a diverse and complex array of medical paradigms. Numerous medical knowledge systems have come and gone over the course of the last two to three hundred years, with each system variously gaining converts among both practitioners and laypersons and losing them to the competing systems that inevitably arise as time passes. Although history presents us with a hodgepodge of different ways of thinking about health and illness, some patterns are discernible in the apparent chaos. A close examination of these patterns reveals a recurring dynamic, which can be understood in terms of the general dialectical model of change employed in other parts of this study.

The argument I wish to make can be summarized as follows: the countersystem perspective helps us to see how medical knowledge has evolved through a dialectical process in which each institutionalized medical paradigm seems to generate the seeds of its own destruction. The use of an applied medical perspective inevitably calls attention to the fundamental principles of medical thinking and treatment that are *missing* in the system, which, in turn, underscores the value of an approach based on the opposing principles. Consequently, the evolution of medical knowledge has followed a pattern of development that accords with a thesis/antithesis dynamic.

Domestic Medicine

In the American experience, one find the dialectical opposition between holism and reductionism emerging as the principle dynamic in the history of medical thinking. The earliest manifestation of the holism/reductionism dialectic was the opposition between domestic medicine and professional medicine during the eighteenth century. The predominant theory of medical practice in this period was the domestic system, an approach that can be properly classified as a holistic orientation because it incorporated some key elements of the countersystem model. The domestic system was based on a naturalistic conception of health and illness, which places emphasis on the natural healing propensities of the body. Accordingly, all treatment within this system was designed to aid the natural healing process. For example, the most widely read domestic medical manual of the late eighteenth century, William Buchan's *Domestic Medicine,* provides an explicit expression of the naturalistic medical philosophy. Buchan states that the role of medicine is to "gradually assist nature in removing the cause of the disease" (Buchan 1771; quoted in Blake 1977, 12).

This system also incorporated a self-care component consisting of a normative commitment to employ family and community members as the chief providers of health care. This latter element of the domestic system might easily be viewed as simply an artifact of the social conditions that prevailed in the period—because of the inaccessibility of professional providers, people were forced to rely on family and community members for health care. In actuality, this is only a small part of the story. As Starr (1982) and others (Blake 1977; Cassedy 1977) point out, the low demand for professional services in the eighteenth century reflected a deep-seated distrust of physicians within the American public. People generally believed that physicians were not likely to help them and could, in fact, do them harm. They were also suspicious of the claim by physicians that medicine was a mysterious art from, and they believed that medical self-sufficiency was politically and morally preferable to medical dependency (Cassedy 1977, 47; Shyrock 1960, 6). The prevalence and intensity of these beliefs was reflected in the thriving market that developed around the commitment to medical self-sufficiency: medical manuals for lay persons, written primarily by physicians who made a point to avoid the use of Latin and medical jargon, were readily available in this period (Shyrock 1960, 5).

In addition to its self-care and naturalistic emphasis, the domestic medical system incorporated many of the other defining elements of the countersystem model. Looking again at Buchan's influential domestic manual, we find an overriding preoccupation with how to encourage a personal preventative approach to health maintenance: the principle topics are the role of diet, cleanliness, and exercise in good health; the influence of psychological factors (the "passions") on the cause and cure of diseases; and the role of collective action in raising the quality of public health (Blake 1977, 12).

The Transition to Heroic Medicine

While the domestic system remained dominant in America throughout the eighteenth and early nineteenth centuries, it was gradually superseded by a system of professional medical practice based on more reductionist principles. In contrast to the natural healing emphasis of the domestic system, the professional system rested on the assumption that healing cannot take place without direct intervention on the part of one who understands the internal machinery of the human body. Accordingly, the best therapy was believed to be that which produces rapid and observable symptomatic changes in the patient. Rothstein (1972, 41–42) notes that the professional system incorporated two basic principles: first, the idea that the symptoms constitute the disease or, at least, strongly indicate the pathological state of the organism; and second, the notion that therapy "produc(ing) desired changes in the gross pathological symptoms of the patient . . . act(s) on the disease" (1972, 43).

In the professional system, intervention into the body to eradicate the source of illness typically involved "heroic" efforts. Practices such as "bleeding," "blistering" and excessive purges exemplify the types of heroic intervention frequently employed by professional practitioners. The use of invasive modalities also directly relates to the professional emphasis on practitioner control over diagnosis and treatment. If healing must involve the use of heroic and, therefore, potentially dangerous interventions into the body, then the self-care approach advocated by the domestic system is simply out of the question. Lay persons lack the knowledge and training to use such invasive procedures safely; they are safe and effective only in the hands of "qualified" individuals.

In addition to the emphasis on heroic intervention, the professional system of the early to mid-nineteenth century incorporated several principles that would later come to be identified with "allopathic" medicine. One such principle involved an approach to the symptoms of disease directly opposed to domestic medicine's stress on the "wisdom of the body" and the self-healing capacity of the human organism. Within the professional system, symptoms were not regarded as part of the body's effort to fight the disease but rather as organic responses that could further complicate the patient's condition and thus do harm. The appropriate therapeutic response to symptoms was to undertake action or use drugs that oppose or suppress the symptoms: for instance, fever can be dangerous to that patient so fever should be suppressed (Coulter 1977, 365). If drugs are to be employed in therapy, they should be used in the aggressive manner dictated by heroic medicine—that is, they must be given in large dosages and be powerful enough to have an impact over the range of idiosyncratic forms in which a particular disease is manifested (Coulter 1977, 701). Once again, the point is not to use drugs to enhance the body's response to disease; rather, it is to employ powerful agents to simply eradicate the disease.

The historical evidence presented here indicates that the decline of domestic medicine and the rise of the professional system involved movement along a continuum of opposing extremes, from a system incorporating holistic principles to one that embraced reductionist principles. Although the transition from domestic to professional medicine has been well-documented by historians of medical thought, little attention has been focused on the dialectical nature of this developmental pattern or the role of the "principle of contradiction" in the transition. The growth of professional medicine was stimulated by a number of important social structural changes in the nineteenth century, including changes that reduced the indirect costs of professional services (i.e., concentration of the population due to urbanization, improvement in transportation and communication technology, etc.), and the growing rationalization of social life, which removed family members from the household where they could care for the infirmed and into industrial organizations where they worked as wage earners (cf. Starr 1982). One causal factor in this transition, however, has been ignored—the fact that professional providers could offer the lay public an approach to medical treatment that was not only radically different from the prevailing system, but one that reflected the defining characteristics of the emerging social order as well.

I have discussed at length evidence that would support the professed efficacy of holistic, natural healing approaches. On the basis of this evidence, there is every reason to believe that domestic medical practice was effective in dealing with certain kinds of illness. However, the paradigmatic principles of domestic medicine blinded lay practitioners to the effectiveness of reductionist, invasive techniques for dealing with other types of health problems. Consequently, lay practitioners were generally helpless in the face of acute illnesses that required quick, heroic efforts to meet the threat. In the context of domestic medicine's hegemonic status, it seems quite natural that professional providers would seek to articulate a medical philosophy and a set of therapeutic practices explicitly antithetical to the domestic system. In doing so, professional practitioners could offer healing services that could not be provided by lay practitioners. Most of the reductionist, invasive practices were clearly ineffective and, in some cases, actually dangerous to the patient (i.e., the practice of bleeding); but some others represented breakthroughs in therapeutic procedure (minor surgical procedures, for example). The use of these new procedures by professional practitioners gave them healing power not possessed by lay practitioners, a feature that made physicians attractive to people who had previously avoided them.

Of course, the opposite was also true—lay practitioners possessed healing power not offered by professional practitioners because it involved the use of procedures considered illegitimate within the new medical paradigm. This fact became increasingly obscured, however, within the newly emerging social and cultural environment of the early nineteenth century. The professional emphasis on aggressive intervention to eradicate the sources of illness was much more in line with the organizing principle of the emerging social order than was the naturalistic emphasis of domestic medicine. As the pace of scientific and technological advancement quickened and new innovations were increasingly incorporated into the industrial production process, an important transformation began to take place in American culture. This transformation consisted of a shift away from an agrarian world-view based on the principle of human beings "living with nature" and toward the new industrial world-view emphasizing the rational control and domination of nature by human beings. The driving force behind the development of this new world-view could be found in the material conditions of people's existence. Everywhere one looked in this period of great industrial expansion one could find evidence of the effectiveness of production strategies based on the rational domination of nature. The growing sense within American culture was that the possibilities for expanding the rational, industrial principle were unlimited—there was no domain in which this principle could not be put to good use.

When physicians began offering an approach to healing that involved aggressive intervention into the human body and produced evidence of the effectiveness of this approach (as limited as this evidence was), they placed themselves on the "cutting edge" of the cultural transformation, which was gathering steam at this point in time. In contrast, domestic medicine was clearly out of step with the emerging social and cultural order, and, as a result, even those lay practices with proven effectiveness began to lose legitimacy. For a period of time, many of the concepts and practices that made up domestic medicine were relegated to the realm of old-fashioned and backward thinking about health and illness.

What we find in the historical transition from domestic medicine to professional medicine, then, is a dialectical developmental sequence shaped by external socio-economic forces. Domestic medicine can be viewed as the direct precursor of professional medicine—the two systems are best understood as contiguous stages of an ongoing developmental process, even though, or rather *because,* they are polar opposites of one another (along the holism/reductionism continuum). Professional medicine took the form it did because its advocates endeavored to define the professional alternative in opposition to the domestic system. The professional system would not have constituted any alternative at all if physicians simply offered the same general approach that lay practitioners had effectively employed for many decades. Physicians had to explore concepts and principles of medical practice not found within the domestic system and develop those modalities that seemed to offer some degree of effectiveness. The fact that they seized on reductionist, invasive modalities is no surprise—this was, after all, the missing dimension of the domestic system.

With the emergence of this fully developed polar opposition between domestic and professional medicine, the socio-economic context began to function as a selective force that determined how the contradiction would be resolved. The domestic system began to lose legitimacy to professional medicine because the latter approach shared an identity with the organizing logic of the newly emerging socio-economic order. This rise of professional medicine was, by no means, inevitable however. While dialectical developmental sequences, like the one just described, are persistent patterns in the course of ongoing social-cultural evolution, the most recently evolved system may or may not supersede the opposing system from which it emerged. The contradiction is resolved in favor of the new system *only* if it accords with the prevailing structure of dominant socio-economic forces. In the opposition between domestic and professional medicine, the new system superseded the old because the former was consistent with the organizing principles of the emerging socio-economic order. As we will see next, the dialectical sequence that followed the domestic/professional shift represents a case of a contradiction being resolved in favor of the old system rather than its opposing alternatives. In this instance, the new alternatives could not attain hegemonic status because they were inconsistent with the prevailing social structural principles.

With professional medicine becoming firmly entrenched by the end of the eighteenth century, the self-care orientation and related holistic elements of the domestic system began to recede from the public mind. Increasingly, Americans would take as self-evident the provision of health care as the work of individuals who have been formally trained for this function rather than a task that lay persons can competently undertake. While professional providers superseded lay practitioners as the principle providers of health care, new schisms developed within the practitioner population, which involved differences of medical theory and philosophy (along with related therapeutic practices). Once again, the new alternatives arose as negations of the prevailing system, as more holistically oriented models that opposed the reductionist emphasis of "regular" medicine.

The Revival of Domestic Principles: Thomsonian Medicine

The new round of dialectical change involved the opposition between regular professional medicine (the system that had emerged in opposition to domestic medicine) and the various forms of sectarian medicine that appeared throughout the nineteenth century. The first significant challenge to growing dominance of the system of heroic therapy practiced by the regulars was the botanic medical system developed by a New Hampshire farmer named Samuel Thomson. Although Thomsonian medicine never claimed more adherents than regular medicine, it had a large enough following within some regions of the United States (primarily the South and Midwest) to significantly threaten the practices of many regular physicians working in those regions (Rothstein 1972, 141). Reaching its zenith before the Civil War, the Thomsonian movement stimulated efforts by the regular profession to restrict its growth through the enactment of medical licensing laws in the early decades of the nineteenth century. However, by 1840, almost all of the licensing laws that had been passed by state legislatures in earlier decades had been repealed and the campaign by the regular profession to delegitimize Thomsonianism had ended in failure (Kett 1968, 31).

For the present analysis, the Thomsonian movement is significant because it developed as a direct response to the growing dominance of regular professional medicine. Rothstein (1972, 127) notes that as the number of medical school graduates increased in the early nineteenth century and regular medicine became more prevalent, public hostility towards the heroic therapeutic practices of the regulars also began to increase. By the 1830s, opposition to heroic techniques reached crises levels, and the public became increasingly interested in medical therapies that eschewed the highly invasive approach of regular practice. Consequently, many nostrum venders and botanical practitioners advertised themselves using slogans that criticized heroic therapeutics (Rothstein 1972, 128). Within this context, the holistic approach of the Thomsonian practitioners was especially attractive as an alternative to the therapy offered by regular physicians.

Thomsonian medicine had much in common with the early domestic medical system that had been supplanted by professional medicine. Although a part of Samuel Thomson's ideas about health and illness reflected his intrinsic interest in the medicinal use of herbs, he was also concerned about the movement away from the naturalist foundations of domestic medicine under the growing dominance of professional practice (Kett 1968, 130–131). In his major treatise on medical therapeutics, he dedicated significant space to an explicit criticism of such heroic practices as bleeding, blistering, and the use of powerful drugs (like opium and calomel). He was generally critical of the professional disregard for the healing power of nature: "invigorate all the faculties of the body and mind, to exert the most laborious efforts that nature is called upon to perform, instead of stupefying, and substituting art for nature" (Thomson 1832, 131; quoted in Rothstein 1972, 134).

In staking out a position on medical therapeutics that opposed regular practice, Thomson did not simply call for a return to the domestic medical system. He embraced many of the basic principles of domestic practice but elaborated these principles in directions that brought his system closer to the countersystem ideal than perhaps any other sectarian approach of the nineteenth century. In addition to emphasizing the importance of the emergent dimensions of the human Gestalt in the phenomenon of illness (i.e., mind, society, spirit) and advocating natural healing, Thomsonian medicine adopted a decidedly radical position on the issue of professional versus lay practice. As we have seen, the prevalence of self-care within the domestic medical system was more a reflection of normative commitments than the unavailability of professional practitioners, but for Thomson and his followers, promoting self-care was the central goal of the movement.

Embracing the commitment "To make every man his own physician," Thomsonians argued that the family, not the infirmary, should be the principle locus of medical treatment. In addition, Thomsonians championed the development of "useful knowledge," which in the medical domain involved the elaboration of practical botanic precepts for self-medication (Kett 1968, 107,110). Such information was spread to the lay population through Thomson's own domestic medical manual entitled the *New Guide to Health* as well as numerous medical pamphlets and bulletins. Medical knowledge for self-care and a stock of basic herbal medicines were marketed to the public, along with automatic membership in mutual aid societies that were organized for the exchange of information and skills in the treatment of illness (Rothstein 1972, 140). With the development of these knowledge and organizational resources, the Thomsonian movement became an effective force for the promotion of self-care practices.

Closely tied to the self-care orientation was another element of Thomsonianism that represented a more fully developed version of an incipient feature within the earlier domestic medical system. As suggested earlier in this study, *all* systems of medical knowledge function as ideological systems. Every medical perspective offers a general explanation of illness and a system of medical therapeutics that either directly or indirectly supports the interests of one or another political-economic group. Within the Thomsonian system, the link between medical theory and the political struggle was explicitly acknowledge. In addition to encouraging medical self-reliance, the Thomsonians embraced a number of political causes organized around a common agenda, that of freeing the working masses from either corporate, professional, or political domination.

One such cause was the emerging feminist movement of the early nineteenth century. Thomsonian journals during this period were filled with articles calling for the expansion of roles for women in American society, echoing the views of increasing numbers of women who were becoming active in women's rights societies. This concern was a natural outgrowth of

Samuel Thomson's early interest in promoting the use of trained female midwives over male members of the regular profession as the chief providers of obstetrical care. Thomson and his followers persistently criticized professional obstetrical care for the inexperience of male physicians in delivering babies, their use of invasive technologies (forceps, etc.), and the high fees they charged. In addition to advocating a return of obstetrics to female control, they argued that women should play a more active part in the provision of all forms of medical care. The proper locus for medical care was the family; therefore, the special role of women within the family made them uniquely qualified to render medical care to family members.

The explicit linking of Thomsonian medical theory and practice to radical politics involved other issues beyond the feminist agenda. Riding the wave of democratic populism associated with Andrew Jackson's rise to power, Thomsonians extolled the virtues of the common man and criticized of all forms of privilege or monopolistic control over resources. While manual labor, useful knowledge, native ability, simplicity, and independence were glorified, Thomsonians had nothing but scorn for "fictitious" wealth (accumulated by nonproducers), abstract theory, artifice, ostentation, and servility (Kett 1968, 109–111). Of special concern to Thomsonians, of course, was the ongoing efforts of elitist groups to secure special privilege and control over the common people through licensed monopoly. While they had a direct stake in opposing the enactment of restrictive medical licensing laws, they were no less concerned with class politics and the promotion of true democracy in all domains of social life.

To summarize, the Thomsonian movement emerged as a system of medical theory and therapeutics that directly opposed the reductionist precepts and techniques advocated by the regular profession. Where regular medicine defined the space of medical events in restrictive terms, focusing attention on the internal contours of the body, Thomsonian medicine revived the notion that the metaorganic dimensions of mind, society, and spirit are important causal forces in health and illness. The regulars embraced a therapeutic approach based on heroic intervention while Thomsonian therapeutics were rooted in a naturalistic philosophy that emphasized the inherent healing capacities of the human system. In regular medicine, reductionist concepts and therapeutics were tied to a political stance that not only promoted professional monopoly but was closely aligned with the other forms of established privilege, even as the advocates of this system claimed that medicine had nothing to do with politics. In contrast, the holism of Thomsonian medicine led its advocates to make explicit the political and ideological dimensions of medical theory and practice and to place themselves in opposition to all antidemocratic, elitist forces within American society. Thus, the opposition between regular medicine and the Thomsonian system in the early nineteenth century represents a clear instance of the thesis/antithesis dynamic, a polarity that can be classified in terms of reductionism versus holism.

The success of Thomsonian medicine for a period of time, even as it was being attacked by the regular profession, was a consequence of several factors. First, the very fact that the regular profession *did* attack the Thomsonians worked to the advantage of the medical sect. As the public became increasingly disenchanted with the heroic practices of regular physicians, the latter's efforts to brand Thomsonianism as quackery only served to call the public's attention to the noninvasive techniques offered by the Thomsonians. Moreover, Thomsonians were able to actually meet the public's expectations for an effective alternative because their techniques often produced positive therapeutic results. In short, the campaign against Thomsonian medicine highlighted its potential as an alternative healing approach based on efficacious principles that had been left out of the system of regular medical practice.

The negative campaign by the regulars may not have been sufficient alone to make Thomsonian medicine a viable competitor to regular practice if the former movement had not also been able to take advantage of important resources emerging from the broader socio-cultural environment. The success of the Thomsonian movement depended in part on its connection to the broader social and political transformations that took place during the Jacksonian era. As several medical historians have noted (Starr 1982; Kett 1968), a profound consistency between medical/political agenda of the Thomsonians and the widespread populist sentiment existed during this period. "The success of the Thomsonians was due to their near monopoly among medical practitioners of popular rhetoric, and to their generally sincere identification with radical causes" (Kett 1968, 116). While the ideological resources emerging from the American political system worked to the advantage of professional medicine over the long-term, for a short period antiprofessional forces were buoyed by the populist ideology associated with Andrew Jackson's political ascendancy.

In the same way that these various forces help explain the success of Thomsonian medicine, they also allow us to understand the decline of the movement. With the widespread repeal of medical licensing laws in the 1830s and 1840s and the failure of the regular profession to restrict sectarian medicine by any other means, the regulars gradually began to abandon their campaign of open warfare with the Thomsonians. As a consequence, movement resources arising from the process of "conflict with the enemy" (cf. Lyng and Kurtz 1985) were no longer available to the Thomsonians—the approach became less identifiable as a unique system of medical practice, and Thompsonians lost public sympathy as the perception of "unjust criticizism" by the regulars vanished. The movement also began to lose the ideological resources emerging from the broader political-cultural environment of Jacksonian America when the populism of this period began to wane. The era of the common man, self-sufficiency and popular democracy gradually came to an end, which sent into decline many of the popular movements that had celebrated these concepts.

Hence, the death knell was sounded for Thomsonian medicine when its resource base started to collapse and the long-term historical forces that were transforming nineteenth century America began to undermine the movement. Although the holistic medical principles of an earlier age blossomed in Thomsonianism and, expressed in this new form, were promoted through an affinity with Jacksonian populism, these principles were clearly antithetical to he new logic of the emerging bureaucratic industrial order. Whereas "knowledge for the common people" and the commitment to self-sufficiency was perfectly suited to the prevailing conditions of the eighteenth and early nineteenth century, specialization, formal education, and credentials were becoming increasingly important within the newly emerging society. Indeed, the tension between the old and the new order became apparent inside the Thomsonian movement itself with the development of a split between those movement members who advocated a more professional approach and those who opposed professionalism in medical practice.

While Samuel Thomson was adamantly opposed to formal medical schools and licensing, a group of neo-Thomsonians under the leadership of Alva Curtis began to charter medical colleges and set up licensing boards in some states in the late 1830s. The new faction not only promoted formal education but also advocated a medical curriculum that included the reductionist disciplines of anatomy and physiology. With these developments, the movement began to decline, ultimately leading to its complete disintegration by 1850 (Kett 1968, 129–130). As we will see, this would be the first of several instances in which a sectarian medical movement would be destroyed by dissension within its own ranks with the emergence of a splinter group advocating the adoption of professionalism and reductionist principles of medical practice.

Also contributing to the demise of the Thomsonian movement were developments taking place in the system of regular practice. Just as Thomsonian medicine was beginning to incorporate principles from the competing system of regular practice, the latter system started to move more in the direction of Thomsonian medicine. The following that Thomsonian practitioners enjoyed within the lay public demonstrated to the regulars the real depth of the public's opposition to the heroic therapeutics of regular practice. Consequently, the regulars began to gradually dispense with such heroic practices as bloodletting, blistering, and drug-induced purges during the second half of the nineteenth century (Rothstein 1972, 181). As regular practitioners began to abandon heroic therapies while, at the same time, Thomsonian medicine increasingly took on the characteristics of regular practice, public support started to swing in the direction of the regular profession. At this historical juncture, the polar opposition between Thomsonian and regular medicine was being resolved through a movement toward synthesis, a resolution that worked to the advantage of the regulars rather than the Thomsonians.

Although the use of heroic therapies in regular practice did decline in the second half of the nineteenth century, regular medicine did not abandon its reductionist principles. After a short period of internal debate and disagreement among the regulars, a consensus was achieved about the need to maintain a commitment to invasive therapy—to offer therapeutics that "make an impression on the patient." Rothstein (1972, 196) describes the system that evolved out of this new found consensus as the "New Vigorous Therapy." This new approach relied on radical intervention, but it employed techniques that were not as dangerous to the patient as the earlier heroic procedures. The regulars made increasing use of such things as antipyretics, analgesics (especially opium) and tonics in place of the bleeding and blistering techniques of their predecessors (Rothstein 1972, 187–197).

The reductionist medical paradigm thus became ascendant once again as the Thomsonian movement collapsed, although it was a somewhat different form of reductionist medicine than the previous professional system. The hegemony of the New Vigorous Therapy would be short-lived, however, as a new and more significant sectarian challenge arose in the latter half of the nineteenth century. Even more threatening than the challenge posed by Thomsonian medicine was the competition offered by another alternative system rooted in holistic principles—the homeopathic approach.

The Challenge of Homeopathic Medicine

Although the life spans of the homeopathic and Thomsonian movements overlapped by a decade or so in the mid-nineteenth century, homeopathic medicine reached its zenith about fifty years after Thomsonian medicine was at the height of its popularity. The founder of the homeopathic system, the German physician Samuel Hahnemann, was inspired to define new principles of medical practice by the same set of concerns that motivated Samuel Thomson to develop his system. Both men felt there was a need for some alternative to the invasive and often dangerous therapeutics of regular medical practice. Hahnemann was especially critical of the tendency of regular physicians to base their therapies on an "imaginary and supposed *material* cause of disease" (Rothstein 1972, 152, emphasis added). In developing his new system, Hahnemann embraced several concepts that were also prominent elements of domestic medicine and the Thomsonian system.

Foremost among these ideas was the notion that the body possesses a reservoir of inherent healing capacities from which all healing derives. This idea was the core element of the homeopathic model, and most of the other concepts and practices of this system could ultimately be traced to it. For instance, the nature of therapeutic action was structured by the natural healing orientation: it was believed that practitioners should prescribe drugs and engage in actions that enhance the natural healing processes of the body. The heroic, invasive procedures practices by regular physicians had no place in the homeopathic system.

The notion of natural healing had a somewhat different meaning within the homeopathic system than it did in any of the other sectarian systems. Rejecting the regular profession's belief that diseases were caused *only* by material forces, homeopathy relied on a vitalist explanation of disease causation. Homeopaths conceived of the vitalist principle as equivalent to nature, which should always be defined in holistic terms:

> Nature could be spiritual or material; it could refer to the physiological processes or to a nonmaterial force that imbued the body . . . or to a force altogether outside of the body which beneficently restored health (Kett 1968, 134).

In accordance with the naturalistic emphasis, the homeopathic model also adopted a unique approach to symptom evaluation and the use of drugs. Homeopaths believed that the patient's reporting of their symptoms was crucial to a correct diagnosis because these were the direct manifestations of the body's effort to fight the disease. Indeed, the homeopath's sympathetic attention to patient reports was one of the factors that accounted for their popularity with the lay public (Starr 1982). The homeopathic response to patient symptoms also contrasted with the regular approach in another way. The regulars tended to prescribe medicines or engage in action that worked in the opposite direction from the symptoms—an approach that Hahnemann labeled as "allopathic" therapy (Rothstein 1972, 157). Homeopaths, in contrast, followed the principle of *similia similibus curantur* or the "law of similars": medicine or therapeutic action should work in the *same* direction as the symptoms because the symptomatic response represents the body's effort to deal with the disease. Similarly, drug use within the homeopathic system was not focused on the direct biochemical elimination of disease, as in allopathic medicine, but involved an effort to aid the symptomatic response. Homeopaths used drugs in small doses and prescribed them for the body as a whole, which was the antithesis of the disease-specific and large dosage approach of allopathic medicine.

In general, the homeopathic system can be characterized as a holistic, noninvasive medical perspective that stood in direct contradiction to the reductionist, invasive techniques employed by followers of the new Vigorous Therapy. The homeopathic model receives this holistic designation not only because it emphasized self-healing capacities but also because of its diagnostic and therapeutic orientation to the whole of the body as well as the metaorganic dimensions of the human Gestalt (mind, spirit, etc.). In fact, this holistic emphasis led some homeopaths to develop an interest in such mind-oriented cults as mesmerism, which reflected their "desire for a more profound approach to the mind-body problem" than regular medicine could offer (Kett 1968, 142). The holistic underpinnings of the paradigm were also manifested in explicit linking of medical practice to events taking place within the political domain. Like the Thomsonian system before it, advocates of homeopathic medicine were consistently allied with radical political movements (Kett 1968, 155). In this respect, homeopathic medicine embraced a central principle of the countersystem model—the notion that social activism is required for any effort to improve health because there is a political dimension to most medical problems.

One of the great ironies of the homeopathic movement is the fact that its most effective therapeutic practice—the noninterventionist, natural healing or "therapeutic nihilist" approach—was chiefly the result of homeopaths' commitment to a set of goals having very little to do with therapeutic nihilism. The centerpiece of Samuel Hahnemann's system was his regimen for establishing the dosage levels for various drugs. Hahnemann's experimentation with drugs led him to conclude that the large doses administered by regular physicians increased the severity of existing symptoms and hid the true symptoms of a disease by producing additional drug related symptoms. The solution to this problem was to rely on very low doses of drugs and to avoid combining different drugs in a single administration. As Hahnemann continued to experiment with drug therapy, his recommended doses became smaller and smaller, to the point that a patient receiving the typical "homeopathic dose" experienced virtually no actual exposure to drugs. The unintended consequence of this practice was the development of a therapeutic approach that could take advantage of the recuperative powers of nature:

In his eccentric fashion, Hahnemann made one of the great discoveries of his time: he established that, given the existing state of medical knowledge, the absence of therapy was vastly superior to heroic therapy. The fundamental soundness of his perception is clearly manifested in the positive and negative hygienic and therapeutic measures that he advocated: he accepted the medically valid therapies of his time, and he recommended the use of fresh air, bed rest, proper diet, sunshine, public hygiene, and numerous other beneficial measures at a time when many other physicians considered them of no value. He opposed bloodletting, blisters, large doses of drugs, and the whole host of heroic therapy. Unfortunately, Hahnemann misinterpreted his great discovery and attributed his success not to drugless therapy, but rather to his homeopathic doses (Rothstein 1972, 157–158).

Despite the paradoxical fashion by which some efficacious homeopathic practices were established, the rise of this medical sect in the latter half of the nineteenth century represented a continuation of the trend that had started with the Thomsonian movement in the first half of the century. The homeopathic movement was initially stimulated by many of the same resources that helped spur the development of Thomsonian medicine. Both movements initially took form as negations of the prevailing system of heroic practice: the progenitors of both medical paradigms sought to organize their systems around a set of medical truths ignored by regular practice, and the patrons of these sectarian systems viewed them as representing clear alternatives to heroic medicine. While the Thomsonian movement followed a course of development characterized by rapid growth and equally rapid decline, homeopathy's development was slower and took place over a much longer period of time. At a point when the Thomsonian movement started to wane, homeopathy was steadily gaining in strength, reaching its zenith a good thirty years after the collapse of Thomsonianism.

To account for the homeopathic movement's different pattern of growth, we can look again to the dialectical model of social movement development. As noted above, a central force in the production of movement resources for Thomsonianism was the intense conflict between movement partisans and members of the regular profession in the early decades of the nineteenth century. By the same token, the decline of the movement can be largely attributed to the abatement of this conflict as the regular profession gradually ceased to regard Thomsonian medicine as much of a threat. While homeopathy was initially perceived by the regular profession as less of a threat than Thomsonianism, it eventually came to represent a much greater challenged to the legitimacy of regular medicine. Consequently, the regulars were not inclined to adopt a more accommodative stance towards homeopathy until the latter decades of the century—and, as an ironic consequence, the continuing conflict only served to strengthen the homeopathic movement.

Homeopathy emerged as a more significant challenge to regular medicine than Thomsonianism for several reasons. First, many of the principle advocates of homeopathic medicine were former members of the regular profession itself, which meant that their criticisms of regular practice carried much more weight than the criticisms offered by the lay advocates of Thomsonianism. Secondly, the social characteristics of the client populations of each medical sect were very different: while Thomsonianism appealed mostly to rural and lower class segments of the population, homeopathy was popular among members of the urban middle and upper classes. "The wealth and influence of homeopathy's clientele assured it a degree of success and longevity unattainable by the other social movements, and made it a far greater threat to the regular profession" (Rothstein 1972, 165).

These resources allowed homeopathy to claim a degree of legitimacy unmatched by any other sectarian perspective and forced the regular profession to regard the sect as a real threat. However, the more that the regulars tried to sanction and control homeopathy, the stronger the movement became. For instance, a principle impetus for the development of homeopathic medical organizations was the decision by the regular profession to expel homeopaths from their own organizations (Rothstein 1972, 172). The campaign by the regular profession to undermine the homeopathic movement generated other resources as well. As was the case with the Thomsonian movement, the effort by the regular profession to brand homeopathy as quackery helped to create sympathy among the lay population for homeopaths and stimulated further interest in what they had to offer. Moreover, homeopathy's affiliation with the educated and well-to-do segments of the population helped to create the impression that it was a progressive challenge to medical orthodoxy, that perhaps regular physicians felt threatened by it only because of their own backward thinking about medical matters. In paradoxical fashion, then, the hostility that the regulars directed towards homeopathy contributed significantly to its popularity in the late nineteenth century.

Homeopathy was not to make the transition from a social movement to an institutionalized system however. The same broad socio-cultural forces and internal dialectical processes that undermined Thomsonian medicine eventually sent the homeopathic movement into decline as well. In fact, the similarity of circumstances under which the two sectarian movements declined is quite striking. Following the same course that the Thomsonian movement had charted half a century before, the homeopathic movement eventually split into two separate factions: the "high dilutionists" versus the "low dilutionists." Although the conflict between these two factions appeared, on the surface, to involve a disagreement about the degree of dilution required for the most effective drug dose, this issue belied the true character of the controversy. The real conflict centered on opposing views of the future of the homeopathic movement—the question of whether homeopathy was going to maintain its distinctiveness as a naturalist, holistic system or be remade in the image of the reductionist model of regular medicine.

The initial distinction between the high and low dilution factions developed as a result of experimental work that Samuel Hahnemann conducted in the later years of his life. As he continued to experiment with different drugs and dosage levels, Hahnemann eventually came to believe that increasing the dilution factor of certain drugs actually made them more potent. One group of practicing homeopaths, the high dilutionists, embraced this principle and began to employ dilution levels of a thirtieth, a thousandth and even a millionth in their drug therapy (Rothstein 1972, 239). The opposing faction of low dilutionists not only rejected this part of Hahnemann's teachings but also moved steadily away from the traditional principles of homeopathic practice. The low dilutionists were not simply defenders of the status quo in homeopathic practice—guarding against the unreflective application of the most extreme teachings of the master; rather, they represented a new wave of change in the movement as they gradually abandoned the established principles of homeopathic practice.

The changes brought about by the low dilutionists led to both new therapeutic approaches as well as new professional organizational arrangements. The primary therapeutic change involved an increasing willingness to substitute palliative medications (preferred by allopaths) for the homeopathic drugs. As more and more homeopaths began to employ drugs traditionally associated with regular practice, the size of the dose ceased to be the primary issue. By the end of nineteenth century, a distinctive *materia medica* for homeopathic practice no longer existed as most homeopaths were prescribing palliative drugs as often as homeopathic drugs (Rothstein 1972, 245).

The low dilutionists also raised the ire of their opponents by proposing some sweeping changes in the structure of homeopathic training. The new faction wanted to see more of the basic medical sciences incorporated into medical school curriculum. Accompanying this change would be a greater emphasis on such allopathic techniques as aggressive surgery and the use of sedatives and antipyretics. The conflict over this issue became so intense, in fact, that separate high and low dilutionist medical schools were established in some regions (Rothstein 1972, 242). Closely related to the battle over medical education was an equally intense struggle over the organizational structure of the profession. Consonant with the integration of basic medical science into homeopathic training and the subsequent move towards a more reductionist model of medical practice, the low dilutionists favored a reorganization of the profession into a system of interrelated medical specialties. This interest in encouraging more medical specialization stood in direct contrast to the traditional commitment (maintained by the high dilutionists) to a profession made up almost entirely of general or family practitioners.

The split between the high and low dilutionists was a critical event in the history of the movement for two reasons. First, at this point the movement lost its most important resource in the battle with the regular profession: the loss of solidarity and cohesiveness within the collegium was a blow that would critically injure the movement. Second, this split also reflected the influence of powerful forces within the broader socio-cultural environment on the movement's development. Despite the popularity of homeopathic practitioners, their holistically oriented medical approaches were inconsistent with the dominant social and cultural principles of the time. While sectarian perspectives such as Thomsonianism and homeopathy (as well as naturopathy and eclecticism) were emphasizing medical concepts and techniques rooted in the naturalistic philosophy of the preindustrial era, American culture and society in the late nineteenth century increasingly reflected the influence of the emerging industrial order.

Industrial social life and culture, with its emphasis on dominating nature, controlling the course of events, and aggressive intervention to achieve specific goals, penetrated the homeopathic movement through the agenda proposed by the low dilutionists for upgrading the profession. Thus, the broader socio-cultural environment of late nineteenth century America worked against homeopathy in two ways: it was more supportive of the competing allopathic medical perspective and it contributed to dissension within homeopathic ranks. Regular medicine may have produced its own antithesis in the form of the homeopathic sect, but the original homeopathic system had moved away from the dominant social/cultural principles of organization rather than toward these principles. This contradiction was ultimately resolved through the transformation of the movement itself, which, in turn, served to hasten its ultimate demise.

The similarity in the pattern of decline within the Thomsonian and homeopathic movements extends beyond the development of opposing factions within both movements. Another element that contributed to the disintegration of both movements was the adoption of an accommodative strategy by the regular profession. Toward the end of the nineteenth century, some members of the regular profession began to see specific advantages in cooperating with homeopaths: regulars could solicit referrals from sectarian physicians and they could refer their own "troublesome" cases to them. Most importantly, this new strategy would improve the standing of regular physicians with the lay population—they could no longer be accused of adopting such a self-interested posture in the face of competition from other providers, an accusation that had hurt them in the past and had helped their competitors.

With the shift to this new strategy, the previous dynamic of growing sectarian strength through conflict began to break down. The distance between regular and homeopathic medicine began to decrease as homeopaths were increasingly granted hospital privileges and certain homeopathic principles and practices were incorporated into regular medical training (Kett 1968, 155). Moreover, as the distance between the regulars and their competitors decreased, the unique identity of homeopathic practices became increasingly obscured. Once again, the adoption of an accommodative approach by the regulars produced paradoxical results. Whereas homeopaths had gained converts while under attack by regular doctors, they began losing patients under the new conditions of improved relations with the regulars.

Greatly accelerating this tendency towards synthesis were the efforts by both the regular and homeopathic professions to incorporate positivist scientific principles and methods into their respective systems. Homeopaths shared in the widespread enthusiasm over the accomplishments of science and wished to place their own medical model on a firm scientific foundation. In this sense, they were in complete agreement with regular physicians who had also started to clamor for more science in medicine. The positivist model became a powerful synthesizing force as the two previously divergent medical approaches strived, with equal determination, to be more scientific.

The incorporation of science into their respective models altered the character of these models in different ways. The distance between allopathic (regular) medicine and the positivist scientific model was relatively short because both systems were rooted in a common reductionist framework. By comparison, the distance between the more holistic homeopathic perspective and positivist science was rather large because homeopathy had been deeply rooted in an antipositivist tradition. The effect of this movement to incorporate science into both systems, then, was to move the homeopathic model closer to the reductionist principles that had always been at the core of regular medicine. Maintaining a distinct identity in the face of the creeping influence of positivist science was also made more difficult by the loss of resources that homeopaths had gained from the conflict with the regulars. By contrast, the allopathic perspective embraced by regular practitioners was revitalized by the positivist model. Armed with the more systematic methods of this tradition and new knowledge from the basic biological sciences, regular practitioners were able to break new ground in the use of invasive, tissue-specific therapies.

In summary, the triumph of regular medicine over homeopathy was due to several factors, including the emergence of dissension within the homeopathic movement itself, the adoption of an accommodative strategy by the regulars, and the selective influence of the broader socio-economic order. This is only part of the story however. Other important actors besides homeopaths and regular physicians were involved in the struggle between advocates of reductionist medicine and their more holistically oriented rivals. Observing this struggle from the sidelines were key members of the corporate elite who could direct significant financial resources to either one party or the other. I refer to the managers of corporate philanthropies who had a direct interest in cultivating a social/cultural environment that would support the interests of the capitalist class.

The Rise of the Medical Scientific Model

A detailed account of the role of corporate philanthropies in shaping the development of medicine can be found in E. Richard Brown's (1979) volume entitled Rockefeller Medicine Men. Brown offers convincing evidence of a campaign by corporate elites to help promote the incorporation of positivist science into medicine. By the turn of the century, corporate leaders had discovered a new and powerful mechanism for shaping the direction of change within a number of social sectors. Through the strategic use of philanthropic funds, involving the use of foundation money to fund various organizations and demonstration projects, corporate leaders could promote policy strategies to insure that newly evolving social structures protect, rather than threaten, their interests. In dealing with the medical domain, foundation managers decided to commit significant financial resources to the advancement of medical science at the point when regular physicians abandoned their efforts to delegitimize the sectarian approaches. The incorporation of positivist science into medical thinking, which I described previously as a central synthesizing force in resolving the contradiction between the regulars and the sects, was not a natural or inevitable development driven by abstract social/cultural forces. This structural change was brought about through the goal-oriented action of specific people, a key group being corporate foundation managers.

Perhaps the most important steps undertaken by corporate philanthropists to promote the incorporation of science into medicine were the various foundation initiatives relating to the reform of medical education. As Brown clearly demonstrates, the revolutionary changes occurring in medicine from

1890 to 1925 came through the efforts of a coalition group made up of elite practitioners, academic medical scientists, and philanthropists. Each party in the coalition had a direct stake in the promotion of scientific medicine. Elite practitioners understood that curricular changes in the direction of integrating more of the basic sciences into medical education would increase the costs and length of training and would, therefore, work as a selective factor to reduce the number of new entrants into the field. Academic physicians had an intrinsic interest in promoting a form of medicine that would lend legitimacy to their scientific research activities and saw the shift to scientific medicine as an opportunity for them to control entry into the profession. However, both of these parties fully understood that they could not bring about the desired changes by themselves—the capital needed to finance medical schools that taught medical science could not be raised through student tuition and faculty resources alone.

Entering the picture at this point were some farsighted foundation managers, individuals like Frederick Gates and John D. Rockefeller, Jr. of the principle Rockefeller philanthropic organizations, who had come to appreciate the significance of medical science to the interests of the corporate class. These individuals were easily persuaded by medical faculty to lend their considerable resources to the cause of scientific medicine:

"Gates saw clearly the potential value of academic medicine—doctors subordinated to the university, the university controlled by men and women of wealth, and academic physicians researching the causes of disease and eliminating those causes at their microbiological source. All these relationships and functions would assure that academic doctors, unlike their practitioners colleagues, would serve the needs set before them and not some competing professional interest" (Brown 1979, 175).

Equally important to corporate interests was the ideological value of medical science. Although Gates and other foundation managers were, no doubt, only dimly aware of the political implications of the medical scientific paradigm, this approach could serve corporate interests by reducing human problems to the level of body tissues and microbes. In doing so, the paradigm medicalized all social problems, "defining them out of political struggle and even religious morals, and giving them over to technical expertise and professional management" (1979, 129).

With the financial backing of corporate foundations, medical schools were reorganized as institutions of medical science where students could receive training in the basic sciences as well as the clinical sciences, where they could be socialized into the norms of medical scientific research (although it was understood that only a few would choose such a career), and where medical faculty would have the resources and support for research as well as teaching. The details of this reorganization of medical education and the further changes it engendered have been described elsewhere (Starr 1982) and are too complex to be extensively reviewed here. Briefly stated, the important stages and steps in the transformation of medical education included efforts to lend formal legitimation to the reorganization through the work of the AMA's Council on Medical Education (and also the Carnegie Foundation for the Advancement of Teaching), the issuance of the famous Flexner Report in 1910, the transformation of the AMA from an impotent professional organization to an effective political force, and the gradual shift from philanthropic promotion of medical education reform to state support for this movement.

The campaign to reform medical education also had far-reaching consequences for the medical profession and the developing health care system. With the reorganization of medical schools as institutions of medical science, the number of medical schools operating in the United States decreased while the costs and length of medical training increased. These changes in turn, resulted in several crucial developments emphasized by previous researchers: the decline in the supply of physicians with a parallel increase in the reward for physician's services, a change in the social composition of people entering the medical profession and an increase in the power of physicians to shape the character of the health care system. The change I wish to emphasize here, however, concerns the role of this reform movement in resolving the contradiction between holism and reductionism in medical thinking. The efforts of regular physicians (or some segments of this group) and corporate foundation managers to promote reform in medical education was a driving force behind the institutionalization of the reductionist-professional system as the dominant medical model of the twentieth century. As the reform movement proceeded, the more holistic concepts and practices of sectarian physicians were increasingly undermined while the reductionist approach of the regular physicians became more fully elaborated. This trend is revealed in the dynamic changes occurring at the level of macro social structures, i.e., a gradual historical shift to a medical scientific conception of health and illness among both practitioners and the lay public. Underlying this macro-level transformation were such concrete changes as the closing of many sectarian medical schools as well as proprietary schools that offered more holistic versions of regular medicine (Brown 1979, 154, 162). Hence, the emergence of the medical scientific paradigm out of the contradiction between regular medicine and the sectarian approaches can be understood in terms of specific changes in social (read material) conditions of the period.

In summary, the medical scientific model that emerged in the early twentieth century represents a diachronic Relation of the contradiction between the allopathic model and the opposing sectarian models (a contradiction that is itself a diachronic Relation). The medical scientific model was by no means a synthesis of the opposing systems, in the sense of the Hegelian dynamic of thesis/antithesis/synthesis. Rather, it emerged as a more elaborate and a more empirically and logically sound version of the allopathic medical model, employing the same reductionist presuppositions as the latter model and emphasizing its invasive principles. With the emergence of medical science, then, regular, allopathic medical principles finally triumphed over the holistic principles of sectarian medicine.

The decline of sectarian medicine did not mark the end of the opposition between reductionism and holism in medical thought, however. Before the medical scientific model would attain complete hegemony in the twentieth century, it would be challenged again by a holistic model of an entirely new form. The new conflict would involve the contradiction between the medical scientific model and the public health model.

The Public Health Model: A New Form of Holism

The relationship between clinical scientific medicine and the public health model is unlike any of the other relationships between competing medical models I have discussed thus far. The analysis up to this point has revealed a common dynamic underlying each of the contradictions examined. In each case, the existing medical model played a determinant role in the development of an alternative model (or set of alternative models) that opposed it. The professional model of the early nineteenth century possessed characteristics that directly reflected it's negative connection to the existing system of domestic medicine. Likewise, the sectarian perspectives of the next century congealed around the concepts and practices that were missing from the dominant system of allopathic medicine. In contrast, the public health model initially developed through the interplay of a number of social and political factors and not as a negation of any existing medical model. This does not mean that the public health perspective was unrelated to and uninfluenced by other medical models. Quite the contrary, public health and clinical medical science did come to oppose one another as separate poles of a contradiction and as such each model influenced the development of the other. However, this relationship did not form until well after the public health model had been formally established as a distinct approach to health.

If domestic medicine and the various medical sects can be classified as holistic systems by virtue of their commitment to the principles of self-care, the natural healing power of the body, and other micro-level holistic health concepts, the public health perspective can be labeled holistic because of its macro-level approach to health and illness. Consonant with the countersys-tem perspective, the public health model emphasizes the causal importance of certain metaorganic dimensions in the functioning of the human body; i.e., the social and ecological environmental factors that impinge on body function. This approach to health, which initially took form around the middle of the nineteenth century, developed out of a broader perspective dealing with problems of moral and social reform.

Partisans of this latter perspective viewed the increasing industrialization and urbanization of American society as a degrading influence on human beings and the social and ecological environments they occupy. These trends had not only contributed to a general decline in the moral quality of human life, they had also posed significant threats to the health of the population. The growth of industry, and the urban migration it had stimulated, was directly responsible for the accumulation of filth (human and otherwise) in the living environment of more and more people and had given rise to a new and more disturbing form of poverty. Advocates of this viewpoint believed that efforts to deal with human disease should focus on the social structure and ecological correlates of disease—the ultimate causes of human problems rather than the more immediate effects of these structural factors.

Following an independent course of development from the other medical models discussed, the public health model in no sense emerged as the negation of allopathic medicine or any other medical model. However, the model did come to assume a position of opposition to allopathic medicine and medical science, as well as to many of the social and economic parties ideologically tied to these latter medical perspectives. Moreover, as one pole of this new contradiction in medical thinking, the public health model was subjected to transforming influences that would fundamentally alter its structure.

One aspect of the contradiction between the regular/medical scientific model and public health was identical to the contradictions that had arisen in the era of medical sectarianism. As Paul Starr (1982) notes, regular physicians initially opposed the public health movement because they perceived that activities by public health advocates would directly threaten their economic interests, in the same way that sectarian practitioners had previously threatened them. With the emergence of public dispensaries, school health services, public health departments, and community health centers, physicians began to complain that a segment of the market for health services received essentially free care even though this population could well afford to pay private physicians for their services. The primary concern then was competition in the area of diagnosis and treatment under the guise of public health. If public health practitioners could respect the medical profession's jurisdiction in this area, doctors had little quarrel with them. In fact, physicians could even lend their support to public health activities under certain conditions: "just as doctors did not want hospitals or dispensaries to steal patients from them, so they did not want public agencies to interfere in their business. While they favored public health activities that were complementary to private practice, they opposed those that were competitive" (1982, 185).

The opposition to public health from medical professionals who wished to maintain their monopoly over medical diagnosis and treatment was much less important in the developing course of events than opposition from other sources. Unlike the challenge posed by sectarian medicine, the public health movement, in the earliest stages of its development, constituted a broad-based threat to the social status quo. Public health advocates not only engaged in activities that threatened the economic interests of physicians, they also embraced an ideology that directly challenged the American economic system as a whole. In accordance with the ideological emphasis of our medical countersystem, the public health perspective of the late nineteenth century placed a significant part of the blame for poor health on the existence of poverty and substandard living conditions. Moreover, government was called upon to take responsibility, to intervene, and to remedy these problems. Indeed, the earliest definition of the public health mandate was,

> (s)o broad—and downright subversive—a conception, (it was) an invitation to conflict. Public health (could) not make all these activities its own without, sooner or later, violating private beliefs of private property or the prerogatives of other institutions. Much of the history of public health is a record of struggles over the limits of its mandate (Starr 1928, 180).

As Starr suggests, medical professionals were not the only antagonists of public health. Joining with physicians in an effort to restrict the boundaries of this new approach to health care were religious and other groups that were interested in minimizing government intervention in social life, specific business groups seeking to protect their economic interests, and members of the corporate class who feared the implicit criticism of capitalism contained in this perspective. Groups that had occupied a sideline position in past conflicts between competing medical models were directly involved in this conflict. The opposition of these latter groups perhaps more than opposition from the medical profession shaped the outcome of the struggle.

Further consideration of the conflict between public health advocates and the various groups allied with the medical profession supplies a missing piece of the puzzle we have been constructing in this chapter. As previously noted, a crucial factor in the triumph of regular medicine over sectarian medicine was the decision by corporate philanthropists to commit significant financial resources to medical schools that embraced the medical scientific model. While ample empirical support exists for this argument, no one has adequately explained why foundation managers were inclined to support medical science over the sectarian models. Some have suggested that corporate elites came to appreciate the ideological value of the reductionist approach to illness offered by medical science (Brown 1979): but a question remains—precisely how did they develop such a sophisticated understanding of the ideological functions of medical knowledge? The answer to this question lies in a consideration of the role of the public health model in making explicit the political/ideological dimension of medical thought.

Political activism figured most prominently within the public health perspective at precisely the same time that the contradiction between regular and sectarian medicine had become most intense. In the later decades of the nineteenth century, public health was still in its first stage of development, when the primary concern was dealing with the environmental causes of disease (Winslow 1923, 57–58). Consequently, outside observers of the struggles within the medical domain were not only confronted with the polarity between regular and sectarian medicine but also between regular medicine and public health. The specific contrasts offered by each of these two contradictions were unique. When regular medicine was contrasted with the sectarian perspectives, the former system emerged as an invasive, heroic approach directly opposed to the noninvasive, naturalist emphasis of sectarian practices. No overt political distinction seemed to be involved in this comparison. However, when regular medicine was contrasted with the public health model, the political distinction was clear-cut. With its macro-level focus, the public health perspective contained an explicit political message: the true sources of disease can be found in those social and economic factors that have given rise to urban filth and poverty, and these problems could be solved only through the adoption of a progressive social change agenda. This comparison helped to reveal the hidden political dimension of regular medicine. Confronted with the social change agenda of the public health model, corporate elites could now clearly see that it was in their interest to support a medical approach that reduced focus of medical diagnosis and treatment to the most microscopic level possible—in their view, the further medical discourse moved from macro-level discussion of health and illness, the better.

The contrast provided by the public health approach very likely played an important role in the decision by corporate philanthropists to champion the cause of regular medicine and its direct descendent, medical science. Thus, we have in this case an example of the common-sense use of the countersystem logic: the comparison between regular medicine and public health served to instruct corporate observers on the political implications of medical thought and practice. Before the emergence of the public health model, outside observers of the medical sector were unlikely to have appreciated the political implications of the practice of medicine. The conflict between one medical model and another was viewed as a struggle to be resolved through the public assessment of the efficacy of the competing systems. However, the contrast with the public health model made explicit what had previously been an implicit feature of medical practice. Astute observers could now see that holistic medical approaches were inherently threatening to the social status quo while reductionist medical practice posed no threat to established interests (cf. Lyng 1988). Corporate elites therefore came to understand their interests in supporting the most reductionist medical system, regular medicine cum medical science, against any of the competing alternatives, either sectarian systems or public health.

In the end, the contradiction between regular medicine (and its nonmedical supporters) and the public health model was resolved by the same forces that mediated the challenge by sectarian medicine. First, the medical profession's fears about competition from public dispensaries disappeared after the reform of medical education. The mobilization of social and economic forces to place medical training on a medical scientific basis led to the establishment of research facilities and teaching hospitals as integral parts of medical education. At this point, the public dispensaries ceased to offer any advantages to physicians who might donate their time to dispensary work. Before medical educational reform, the dispensaries were staffed by physicians who used them for teaching and research purposes and for developing professional connections. As these functions were gradually taken over by the new institutions for medical scientific training and research, the dispensaries lost the free services of physicians and soon began to disappear.

The fate of the public dispensaries was part of a more general pattern of change involving a redefinition of the function of all public health agencies. With the decision by corporate elites to commit significant financial and political resources to the cause of clinical medical science, professional medicine gained widespread legitimacy as the front-line defense against disease. Accompanying this increasingly popular viewpoint was the belief that all nonclinical health care organizations should function to complement rather than compete with private practice. Agencies such as school health services, community health centers, and public health departments moved more and more in the direction of aiding the business of private practitioners.

While these agencies could legitimately provide diagnostic services, it came to be accepted that all treatment must be provided by private physicians (Starr, 1982).

While the opposition of a coalition of elite practitioners, academic physicians and key individuals within the capitalist class was a crucial factor in the demise of the early public health model, a second factor also played an important role resolving the contradiction between clinical medical science and the radical public health approach. As noted previously, a crucial force in the decline of sectarian medicine was the growing legitimacy of positivist science around the turn of the century. This same dynamic contributed to the transformation of the public health model and its demise as viable alternative to clinical medical science.

Medical historians generally agree that the public health movement passed through three separate stages, each of which was defined by a unique perspectival orientation. As we have seen, the first stage of the movement was characterized by the advocacy of an environmental approach to disease causation and treatment and a progressive social change agenda. This model began to break down, however, as new advances in the basic biological sciences led to the accumulation of knowledge about previously unexplored dimensions of reality. Not surprisingly, these new dimensions—the new "spaces" of medical perception (Foucault, 1973)—belonged to the micro end of the continuum. Biology's use of the positivist method led researchers to look for the answers to many of the problems that had concerned them in the realm of microorganisms. One of the most promising areas of research involved efforts to apply the new science of bacteriology to problems of human disease.

The second stage of the public health movement thus involved a radical shift away from holism of the environmental model and toward the reductionism dictated by a bacteriological approach to disease. The shift from environmentalism to individualism carried with it a change from a critical social change orientation to the conservative stance of a perspective that ignores the causal influence of macro-level structures in generating human problems. After 1890, public health advocates were no longer chiefly concerned with the environmental and social disruptions caused by an urban/industrial society but with developing new ways of controlling the attack of germs on the human body, involving such techniques as quarantine and disinfection.

Finally, the third stage of the movement, heralded as the "new public health," pushed even more in the direction of individualistic strategies for dealing with disease. This perspective was unique in advocating education in personal hygiene and medical examinations as the most appropriate way to keep the population healthy. With the emergence of this latter stage (which C.-E. A. Winslow dates around 1910), the critical and progressive political themes that had been such a prominent feature of early public health were completely purged from the model. Most importantly, this political transformation was accomplished without any discussion of political matters by anyone involved with public health:

> Although authorities such as (Charles) Chapin presented the new public health as a response to the bacteriological findings, it had another function. Narrowing the objectives of public health made it more politically acceptable. As in other fields, the growth of professionalism saw a movement away from the broad advocacy of social reform toward more narrow judgments that could be defined as the exercise of neutral authority (Starr 1982, 191).

In summary, this last contradiction between reductionism and holism in medical thought emerged through a different process than did the contradictions that preceded it but was finally resolved in much the same way as the others had been. The public health model initially followed an independent course of development that did not include the dialectical process of progenitors identifying what was missing in the dominant clinical perspective. Once the model took shape though as a formidable challenge to regular medicine (and as a challenge to existing social and economic arrangements), its subsequent development was influenced by the same forces that mediated the opposition between regular and sectarian medicine. On the one hand, the coalition of interests that had formed around the promotion of the medical scientific model and medical educational reform took actions to eliminate resources that had helped to maintain both sectarian medicine and public health. The threat posed by the public health model was a crucial factor in mobilizing this coalition of interests, which included academic regular physicians, elite regular practitioners, the managers of corporate foundations, and certain political elites.

On the other hand, the growing hegemony of positivist science played a crucial role in transforming the public health perspective, in the same way that it had transformed many of the sectarian approaches. The steady accumulation of scientific knowledge opened up new spaces within which to locate the causes of disease. Consonant with the reductionist precepts of positivist science, the incorporation of these new spaces into the public health model shifted the focus from the social and ecological environment to the level of microorganisms. The public health model reduced to this dimension no longer constituted a challenge to clinical medicine or the prevailing social order.The model now merely complemented the work of regular physicians rather than threatening it.

THE HISTORICAL EVOLUTION OF MEDICAL PRACTICE

The last set of diachronic Relations I wish to discuss in this chapter are those associated with the actual behavior patterns of medical practitioners rather than the knowledge system or systems they employ. In the previous section, I described various stages in the historical evolution of medical knowledge, which consisted of a series of dialectically related medical models. As I noted, the medical models under discussion here are ideal/typical models, primarily medical knowledge systems that define a general approach to medical practice in theoretical terms. From the 1920s to the present, the formal training of physicians has been structured by the medical scientific model, but this does not mean that physicians receiving this training have always conducted their clinical practices in strict accordance with the formal model. As I suggested in an earlier chapter, the degree of correspondence between the formal medical model that prevails at a particular point in time and the actual practices of physicians is always a historically specific phenomenon. This last section focuses attention on the historically evolving character of the discrepancy between knowledge and practice within the medical scientific model. The discrepancy between medical scientific theory and actual practice of medical professionals has been a crucial force shaping the character of the health care system in the twentieth century.

In developing this thesis, my primary concern is to provide a new understanding of a historical pattern designated in the previous chapter as a central feature of the modern health care system, one that has garnered significant attention from past analysts of the medical sector. This pattern involves the medical profession's control over the means of health production and its power to shape the character of the system as a whole. The argument also applies to the most recent developments within the medical sector involving the decline of professional control and influence and the rise of corporate power. As we will see, both of these patterns are manifestations of a historically evolving relationship in which the medical profession and the corporate groups share an identity of interests in some respects while fundamentally opposing one another in other respects. The central point in this section is to describe the structural forces that have shaped the conflict between these two groups in the last century.

A review of the existing political economic analyses of the historical transformation of American medicine reveals three basic frameworks. First, the approach exemplified by the work of Kenneth Arrow (1963) represents an application of neo-classical economic theory to the medical domain. This approach cannot be properly classified as a form of historical analysis because it relies primarily on an abstract analysis of the structural characteristics that shape medical practice rather than theoretically organizing historical data. However, Arrow's model does identify the structural forces that, in theory, would account for the historical development of a system characterized by professional dominance.

The principle analytical strategy of Arrow's study is to indicate how the operation of the free market is distorted within the medical domain. In this view, the provision of medical services is unlike most other economic sectors because health care consumers do not have the ability to accurately assess their medical needs or the value of the treatment they receive. The central feature of the illness experience for patients is their uncertainty about the possible outcomes of the experience and the efficacy of the treatment they receive. The dependency of patients on their physicians is therefore much greater than the dependency of buyers on sellers in any other economic sector.

The unique characteristics of modern medical practice are seen as deriving from this unusual relationship between medical providers and consumers. The ethical restrictions on physician behavior embodied in professional codes and norms, extensive and costly medical training, licensing laws, and similar structures all evolved to protect patients against medical incompetence and moral misconduct. In short, these features can be understood as the consequences of imperfections in the medical market. Similarly, the medical profession's power and influence within the medical sector is viewed as an anomalous pattern that can be traced to the patients' dependency on their physicians. Such dependency is a departure from the ideal market, which, by definition, can involve no dependency relationships between buyers and sellers. Professional control over the means of health production is simply historical consequence of imperfect market conditions.

Opposing the neoclassical model is the approach articulated by Marxist analysts of American medicine. Eschewing the abstract, nonempirical approach of the free market analysts, Marxists have focused on historical data relating to the broad structural forces that helped to bring about professional monopoly within the medical sector. Richard Brown (1979), for example, places primary emphasis on the relationship between medical science, the medical profession and key members of the capitalist class. In Brown's view, micro-level relations between patients and practitioners should not be treated as the causes of macro-level characteristics of the health care system but rather as the consequences of these macro structures. Patient dependency on professional providers is a product of the profession's monopoly over diagnosis and treatment rather than a cause of it. If we wish to identify the factors that have given rise to professional monopoly, we must look to other macro-level relations.

This perspective suggests that the crucial macro-level relation involved in the historical evolution of professional monopoly was the support provided to the professional, medical scientific model by sources within the corporate domain. In a broader application of the argument I presented in an earlier section, Brown posits that certain key managers of corporate foundations (primarily the Rockefeller and Carnegie foundations) joined forces with elite practitioners and academic physicians to promote medical educational reform, which they understood would advance the medical scientific model as well as professional control over diagnosis and treatment. This coalition was forged by the recognition that medical scientific hegemony and professional monopoly would serve the interests of all three parties. Hence, the Marxist perspective differs from other approaches by emphasizing the identity of interests between the capitalist class and the medical profession while dismissing conflict or opposition between these two parties as a factor in the development of the health care system.

What is not fully explained by this model is why capitalists would wish to lend their support to a system of professional control over the means of health production. The specific capitalist interest served by promoting the medical scientific paradigm is easily identified: by defining health and illness in reductionist terms, medical science functions to direct attention away from the socioeconomic determinants of biological function. However, the medical scientific perspective could be employed just as easily by health care workers controlled by corporate management as it could by professional practitioners who control the conditions of their own work. With the steady expansion of capitalist control over economic production in the twentieth century, workers in most craft and professional occupations have been transformed into wage laborers. In the same way that capitalist interests were advanced by establishing control over these workers, it has always been in their interest to control the labor of medical practitioners as well. Thus, Brown's emphasis on the common interests between capitalists and the medical profession diverts attention from this important source of conflict between the two groups. A crucial chapter in the story is missing from Brown's analysis: an account of the way in which this inherent contradiction between the corporate and professional models has been mediated.

A third perspective can be identified that represents, in one sense, the antithesis of the preceding approach. Where Brown emphasizes the identity of interests between capitalists and the medical profession and downplays corporate-professional conflict, Paul Starr (1982) makes the opposition between these two groups a central concern of his analysis and largely dismisses the role of corporate support in the rise of professional dominance. For Starr, the struggle between corporate groups and the medical profession for control over the provision of health care services has been a central feature of the medical sector for most of the twentieth century. He sees the evolution of American medicine in this century as involving, most simply, a shift from professional dominance to a more recent tilting of advantage to corporate forces.

In Starr's account, the medical profession has been forced to compete with many groups for control over the health care system and/or the provision of medical services. Alternative practitioners, complexes of medical schools and hospitals, financing and regulatory agencies, health insurance companies, prepaid health plans, and other health care corporations have long challenged the medical profession for dominance within the health care sector, but the profession has possessed one critical resource in this conflict. In contrast to every other party involved in the struggle, physicians have been able to develop and maintain "cultural authority." Starr defines this term as "the probability that particular definitions of reality and judgments of meaning and value will prevail as valid and true" or, in the case of the medical profession, "the authority to interpret signs and symptoms, to diagnose health or illness, to name diseases, and to offer prognosis," which shapes patients' understanding of their own experience and creates the conditions under which the physician's advice seems appropriate (1982, 14).

Starr posits that cultural authority is the antecedent of "social authority." Once physicians were able to legitimately define the experience and needs of their patients, the latter became dependent upon physicians in a way that violates the rules of an ideal market: "In the ideal market, no buyer depends upon any seller, but patients are often dependent on their personal physicians, and they have become more so as the disparity in knowledge between them has grown. The sick cannot easily disengage themselves from relations with their doctors, nor even know when it is in their interests to do so" (1982, 24). The usual dependence of patients upon their practitioners has meant that no challenging group wishing to gain control over the provision of services could attract clients away from professional providers.

Following the premise that the cultural authority of physicians and the resulting dependency of patients on their physicians were the key factors in the struggle for dominance in the medical sector, Starr endeavors to identify the historical forces that transformed medicine into an authoritative profession. Here he focuses on a number of factors ranging from the organizational efforts of the profession to more effectively pursue its collective interests to the broader social structural changes that increased demand for professional services and lowered the real costs of these services (urbanization and rationalization of American society, the growth of transportation and communication technology, etc.) A central theme in this analysis is the historical shift within the profession from a competitive to a corporate orientation involving the movement toward greater colleague dependence and less client control over the work of physicians. Once again, Starr does not view support from the corporate domain as an important structural factor contributing to the growth of professional sovereignty. An assumption maintained throughout his study is that the relationship between the medical profession and the corporate order has consistently remained antagonistic rather than mutually supportive.

The principle problem with Starr's analysis concerns his proposition that the medical profession's cultural authority is the basis of its control over the provision of medical services. Insofar as the medical profession was able to persuade the public that its medical perspective and skills were legitimate and effective, it gained control over the market for the provision of health care. Starr allows that there was a significant discrepancy between reality and the ideology promoted by the medical profession because many of their claims to competent authority "were not yet objectively true" when the public came to accept them (1982, 15). Nevertheless, the driving force behind the transformation of American medicine was the manipulation of public opinion by the medical profession. The key causal relationship in the analysis is the relation between cultural authority and social authority, with the former taken as subject and latter as predicate.

Unfortunately, Starr's basic premise is inconsistent with the rest of his analysis. In his effort to identify the historical forces that have contributed to the growing authority of the medical profession, Starr emphasizes such things as the increase in colleague dependence due to the growth of hospitals and the need for referrals, the structural developments that reduced the costs of services, and the growing differentiation of American society with an attendant decline in self-reliance (1982, 18). However, these changes bear no logical relationship to the increasing cultural authority of the profession and, therefore, could have no direct causal connection to the increasing legitimacy of the profession's definitions of medical reality. Starr proposes that the lay public's beliefs about the value of professional medicine account for their patronage of regular doctors, but he leaves unexplained how the profession's cultural authority was established in the first place.

Another problem with Starr's idealist interpretation of the history of medicine is his disregard for the way in which ideological struggles are influenced by the broader structures of power and domination within American society. He assumes that the parameters of the conflict between different interest groups are defined by the needs of the health consuming public alone. The public is simply "persuaded" that one point of view or another is legitimate within a context of freely exchanged ideas about the nature of health and illness or health care policy. In adopting this view, he completely ignores the way in which groups whose power is structurally determined come to mediate the conflict between various interests groups and the perspectives they promote. Some researchers (cf. Navarro 1984) have produced evidence to indicate that the persuasiveness of a particular interest group does not ultimately determine which perspectives become dominant in American society; rather, the crucial factor is the use of coercion and repression by ruling groups in setting the parameters of the debate.

None of these perspectives on the history of American medicine, taken alone, can adequately account for the principle developments in the evolution of the health care system. What is required at this point is an alternative explanation that incorporates the central insights from all three perspectives into a systematic and comprehensive account. The framework I have developed in this volume yields such an account.

One important step in this direction involves reversing the subject and predicate of Starr's central causal proposition. It makes much more sense to designate the increase in the social authority of physicians as the source of their growing cultural authority than it does to argue the opposite. The historical factors that Starr emphasizes *do* bear a logical connection to the rise of the profession's social authority, and they appear, in fact, to be causally related to the growth of the profession's monopoly over the provision of medical services. What remains to be explained, however, is what other factors contributed to the social authority of regular physicians and how all of these factors relate to the profession's control over the means of health production or, in Starr's terminology, the rise of the profession's cultural authority. In identifying the factors contributing to increasing professional authority, we must also remain cognizant of the determinant influence of structurally based power relations with modern United States society.

In an earlier section, I described the conflict between various practitioner groups at the turn of the century and the role of the positivist scientific paradigm in shaping the course of this conflict. As noted, most of the practitioner groups sought to incorporate science into their respective medical models, but allopathic medicine was particularly well-suited for integration within the positivist scientific paradigm because it was rooted in many of the same basic assumptions as positivist science. Consequently, the chief adherents to allopathic medicine—regular physicians—had the upper hand in the effort to claim medical science as their own. At the same time that scientific principles served to elaborate reductionist themes within allopathic medicine, efforts to apply these principles to the nonallopathic models undermined the holistic themes that distinguished many of these models. Gradually the alternative models began to lose their unique identity, and allopathic medicine qua medical science remained as the only surviving system.

One should not assume, however, that there was complete consensus among regular physicians about the value of placing their therapeutic model on a scientific basis. I previously described three separate factions within the regular profession, which were defined by different work experiences and economic interests and possessed different orientations towards the issue of science in medicine. Two of these three groups, academic physicians and elite practitioners, were committed to the medical scientific model, not chiefly for theoretical or therapeutic reasons but for the purpose of advancing or protecting their interests. For academic physicians, embracing the scientific model would broaden the knowledge base of medicine, increase the number of courses needed to be taught within the standard medical school curriculum, and enhance the research component of academic work—all of which would increase the importance of the academic physician's role within the profession. For elite practitioners, bringing science into medicine offered the possibility of reducing the number of physicians and raising social status of the practitioner population by lengthening and increasing the cost of training, changes that would clearly protect and enhance their own privilege.

In forming a coalition to promote the development of medical science, academic physicians and elite practitioners stood opposed to the larger faction within the regular profession, those physicians who served the vast majority of the population but who scarcely managed to secure a livable salary doing so. For the latter group, there was little to be gained by placing medicine on a scientific foundation. Within the competitive environment of medical practice in the early twentieth century, most regular physicians were especially committed to providing the kind of medical attention their patients wanted. Generally speaking, what patients wanted was a therapeutic approach that dealt with illness by attending to the many different dimensions of their life—biological, psychological, social, and spiritual. The success of this more holistic approach had been demonstrated by the popularity of homeopathy and related perspectives, those multidimensional perspectives emphasizing sympathetic attention to patient complaints. The mainstream of regular physicians resisted the movement by other factions in the profession to bring science into medicine because they perceived that the scientific model would move medical practice away from the very things that had traditionally helped them to keep their patients.

Within the system of regular medical practice, then, an important contradiction began to take form in the early decades of this century. One pole of this contradiction involved the movement to formally place medicine on a positivist scientific foundation, a movement that was pushed by academic physicians and elite practitioners. This movement was focused only on formal changes, involving such things as integrating science in medical school curricula and encouraging the medical school faculty to engage in medical research, because the possibilities of bringing about significant changes in the actual therapeutic procedures used by the existing population of practicing physicians were almost nonexistent. The actual behavior of practicing physicians reflected the opposing force within the medical profession—an overt commitment by physicians outside of the circle of academic and elite practitioners to resist any changes in a practice system, which they regarded as therapeutically effective and crucial for maintaining access to the client population. In the view of this group, science would undermine the basic principles that guided their medical practices and therefore ultimately reduce the quality of care they could offer their patients.

By the turn of the century, the basic outlines of a crucial contradiction within the medical profession had begun to crystallize. As I emphasized earlier in this volume, the way in which a contradiction develops, when (and if) it gets resolved in one way or another, is greatly influenced by the broader structural context in which it emerges. This principle was especially important in the development of the contradiction under discussion here. While the faction promoting the incorporation of science in medicine was numerically small as compared to those who opposed this agenda, two factors worked in favor of the former group, ultimately preventing the resolution of the conflict in favor of the numerically stronger group of practicing physicians. One development internal to the profession, involved a political struggle within certain professional organizations. From 1900 to the 1920s, academic physicians occupied key positions within the AMA and therefore possessed specific political resources for advancing their agenda. Even more important than this was an external influence that worked in their favor—the support of certain corporate elites. The thing that tipped the balance in favor of the "science faction" within the medical profession was their success in convincing corporate philanthropies to fund the reorganization of medical schools.

While corporate support of the medical scientific model was significant, this support remained focused on the specific task of reforming medical education, which meant that the transformation of medicine by the pro-science coalition would take place only at the level of formal medical theory. After the Flexner revolution of the 1920s, medical science became the official theoretical model embraced by the profession—new generations of physicians were all being formally trained in the principles of positivist science embodied in the basic medical and biological sciences. For several decades following the Flexner revolution, however, this formal medical model was largely irrelevant to the actual clinical practices of working physicians. Most practicing physicians had *not* received formal training in medical science, having acquired their medical credentials in the pre-Flexner era. Moreover, younger physicians just leaving medical school typically developed their therapeutic skills under the tutelage of older physicians who knew little of medical science and were doubtful of its efficacy. An important change in the political structure of the AMA also helped to bolster the antiscience forces within the profession. By the 1920s academic medical scientists had been removed from leadership positions within the AMA, and the more conservative practitioner interests began to dominate the organization (Brown 1979). With this change in leadership, a certain degree of retrenchment occurred, and the old system gained greater legitimacy.

A critically important transformation began to occur at this point: the conflict between the pro- and anti-science factions of the early decades of this century evolved in subsequent decades into a contradiction between medical theory and medical practice. This opposition between theory and practice was a crucial factor shaping the character of the evolving medical system. In the fifty or more years following the reformation of medical education, the opposition between medical theory and practice helped to create the unique conditions that allowed for the emergence of medical professional sovereignty. By the same token, the disappearance of this opposition in more recent decades has altered these unique conditions and therefore we have witnessed a significant decline in professional sovereignty. Let us now examine more closely the socio-economic consequences of the theory versus practice contradiction.

We can begin by considering the way in which medicine's theoretical commitment to science effected the market for the professional services of regular physicians. As I argued above, the movement toward the positivist scientific model in medicine served primarily an ideological function—not only for the medical profession but for the other major nonmedical supporter of this movement, the corporate class. For the medical profession, the claim that regular medicine was a scientifically based discipline allowed this group to wrap itself in the cloak of scientific progress. Evidence of the tremendous potential of scientific approaches for solving practical problems was everywhere in the early twentieth century and any practitioner group that could claim to offer such an approach to medical therapy could certainly attract the following of clients. No group had a stronger grip on this claim than regular physicians. By the 1920s, science was firmly entrenched within the medical school curriculum, and scientific research activity on the part of medical school faculty had become more commonplace. None of the sectarian groups could point to such developments in their own training institutions. Regular physicians had taken the lead in developing this crucial ideological resource.

By offering the public evidence of the scientific basis of regular medicine, which involved formal changes in the profession bearing little relation to actual character of clinical practice, regular physicians were able to increase demand for professional services in general and capture some of the market previously controlled by sectarian physicians. In most other accounts of the rise of professional sovereignty, the story ends here. The transformation of medicine into a science within a cultural environment in which all science was granted great legitimacy has been almost uniformly regarded as the ultimate source of social and cultural changes that eventually led to professional monopoly. This account suffers from several serious problems, the most obvious of which is its disregard of the clear discrepancy between theory and practice in medical work during this early period. The reformation of medical education could not have led to instantaneous changes in the practices of regular physicians. Even if most physicians had been committed to the medical scientific model, it would have taken several decades for the shift in medical theory to filter down to level of the actual clinical practice, and most physicians in this period were *not* particularly enthusiastic about scientific medicine. Orienting the traditional account to the actual historical facts, then, would require a new chapter in the story—one that deals with the response of clients to a system of practice in which the gap between medical ideology and the actual behavior of physicians was significant.

Another problem with the traditional account is that it implies a rather sudden shift taking place at the turn of the century is how the health consuming public perceived its needs. Historians of medicine generally agree that many of the sectarian medical systems gained a large following in the late nineteenth century because the therapeutic approaches they offered were closer to what patients wanted in a medical encounter. In contrast to the invasive character of regular medicine, sectarian systems such as homeopathy provided a more appealing naturalistic approach to healing. The emphasis on their patients reporting symptoms, the homeopathic drug use strategy that minimized unpleasant side effects, the rejection of the heroic medical philosophy, and the subsequent reduction in the iatrogenic effects of therapy all helped to draw patients to homeopathic physicians and other sectarians practicing similar naturalistic approaches.

The question that this raises is, Why would people suddenly find these characteristics unattractive as compared to an approach that simply elaborated the invasive principles of regular medicine through the use of positivist scientific methods and concepts? Contrary to what the traditional account implies, it seems much more likely that an initial attraction to a scientific medical approach would turn to aversion when clients confronted the unpleasant features of an invasive, reductionist form of therapy. This, of course, assumes that physicians actually used the scientific therapies that they claimed to offer. Rejecting this latter assumption may yield an account that is more consistent with the actual historical record.

The fact that people did not become alienated toward medical scientific practice but actually came to patronize regular physicians in increasing numbers suggests a lack of identity between medical ideology and actual medical practice. After the reform of medical education, the public did look more favorably upon the medical profession because they could see that medicine was moving in the same direction as other scientifically based applied disciplines. At the same time, when people visited their doctors, they were treated in essentially the same way as they had been treated in the past. Physicians did not approach their patients in the way dictated by the medical scientific model—that is, as "representative instances of a standard disease category." Rather, they viewed patients as biopsychosocial entities with personal histories, and their efforts to define and treat the patient's problem typically reflected this view. In contrast to the model that had come to structure medical theory, actual medical practice conformed more closely to what could be described as the "family practice" model, an approach incorporating many of the nonscientific elements that characterized domestic medicine and the sectarian systems.

In summary, this analysis reveals a powerful contradiction within the professional medical system that emerged from the reform period of the early twentieth century—a dynamic tension between the ideological/theoretical dimension of the system and the realm of actual medical practice. Although the profession had undertaken a campaign of educational reform to establish a formal commitment to the medical scientific model, the daily clinical practices of working physicians diverged significantly from this model. Moreover, the failure of practicing physicians to fully live up to the standards of the formal medical model was not due entirely to deficiencies in training; rather, it was largely the result of a conscious rejection of many of the basic scientific/reductionist premises of the model. In confronting this contradiction, one is naturally inclined to assume that such a fundamental inconsistency within the system could only serve to impede the development of professional medicine. In fact, just the opposite is true. Precisely because of this contradiction, the medical profession was able to rise to a position of dominance within the medical sector.

The opposition between medical theory and medical practice created a unique situation in which the profession was able to draw upon two very different resources in its campaign to win the allegiance of the client population. On the one hand, people were attracted to regular physicians because of the profession's formal commitment to the scientific model. On the other hand, the attention of practicing physicians to the psychosocial dimensions of their patients' lives and their close interpersonal connections to them made people unusually dependent upon their personal physicians. In one sense, patients in this era had the best of both worlds—by taking their problems to medical professionals they believed they were gaining access to the most progressive system of medical diagnosis and treatment ever known to humankind; at the same time, they were receiving the help of an individual who was capable of offering caring attention and a biopsychosocial analysis of their problems, an analysis that only a member of their interpersonal network could provide. Paradoxically, this combination of scientific ideology and antiscientific practice helped to create the strong relationship between medical professionals and patients.

The opposition between medical ideology and practice is the key to understanding those dynamic forces that shaped the historical development of the medical sector. Past analysts of the history of medicine have correctly emphasized patient dependency upon physicians as a distorting influence in the operation of the medical market, but unfortunately, these analysts have failed to identify the real source of patient dependency. While the belief in the power of medical science initially drew patients to medical professionals, widespread ignorance of medical scientific theory was not the thing that made patients dependent upon physicians once the patient-practitioner relationship was established. The buyers of various services are commonly ignorant of the knowledge required to provide those services (consider, for example, contemporary consumers of auto repair services), but this ignorance does not necessarily make buyers dependent upon the sellers of such services. What leads to dependency is the ability of the sellers to establish multidimensional historical and social-psychological connections to their clients, particularly connections that are directly relevant to the problems being addressed. The holistic character of the "family doctor" model functioned effectively to achieve this end.

Understanding the true source of patient dependency also offers a way to resolve an important point of disagreement among medical historians—the question of whether the relationship between the medical profession and the corporate order was mutually supportive or fundamentally antagonistic. In actual fact, this relationship contained elements of *both* mutual support and antagonism. The profession and corporate elites clearly had a common interest in promoting medical scientific ideology. We have seen the ways in which both parties benefited from the growing influence of the positivist scientific model in formal medical theory. The fact that corporate elites were willing to lend their support to the efforts by some factions of the medical profession to place medicine on a firm scientific foundation is not at all surprising. Along another dimension, however, the interests of medical professionals and the corporate world were fundamentally opposed. While the medical profession played an important role in protecting the power and economic privilege of the corporate class by disseminating the medical scientific definition of health and illness, it also opposed corporate interests by seeking to maintain exclusive control over the market for medical services. The line of conflict between the medical profession and corporate interests was defined by the battle for control of the medical market.

From the corporate perspective, the ideal health care system would not only incorporate the medical scientific model as the culturally hegemonic definition of health and illness but also would place all medical labor under the direct control of corporate management, including the labor of physicians. In order to achieve this ideal, corporate agents tried to make use of the same market mechanisms that had been effective in gaining control of other economic sectors. Through the use of capital-intensive production techniques, corporate organizations could offer products or services at lower cost and/or higher quality than their noncorporate competitors and eventually drive these competitors from the marketplace. In the domain of medical services, this process would involve the more specific task of attracting patients away from their private physicians by offering the lower cost services of a rationalized corporate health care organization. Corporate alternatives such as prepaid health care plans, company plans, and similar arrangements, were organized at various times in the early twentieth century to directly compete with private professional practice. While these corporate organizations offered the services of licensed physicians and largely succeeded in achieving the goals of lower price and greater accessibility, the corporate campaign to establish a foothold in the medical market was a failure (cf. Starr 1982, 198–232). Patients could not be attracted away from their private practitioners, even with the prospect of paying less for physician's services. The reason for this can be found in the unusual dependency of patients upon their family physicians.

Although corporate health care organizations had gone to great lengths to insure that the services they marketed were essentially the same as those offered by private physicians (except cheaper), one characteristic of private practice could not be duplicated. The rationalizing principles of the corporate model made it difficult to provide the type of holistic care that characterized the family practice approach of private medicine. Because holistic practice was largely inconsistent with the rational-efficient imperative of corporate medical organizations, no real contradiction existed between medical scientific theory and actual medical practice within these organizations. With physicians working under the direct control of corporate management, any resistance to treating patients in the way dictated by the medical scientific model could be eliminated. The conceptualization of patients as representative cases of disease categories accorded with a system of processing patients that could be organized in a highly efficient and cost-effective fashion. If physicians were inclined to stray from the medical scientific conceptualization by treating patients more holistically, this could be defined and sanctioned as inefficient productive activity that also violated the standards of good medical practice.

The absence of structural arrangements that would support a family practice model within corporate medicine meant that alternative health care enterprises could not offer services comparable to private practice, and they simply could not break the dependency of patients upon their private practitioners. The cost savings of corporate medical services was not a sufficient reason for clients to give up the personalized care of their family practitioners. In the view of both patients and private practitioners, this personalized, more holistic form of medical practice was synonymous with quality care. The health consuming public at this point in United States history was not willing to sacrifice what they viewed as quality care for cost savings.

We see then, that the relationship between the capitalist class and the medical profession has been complex, involving a simultaneous identity and opposition of interests. In the realm of medical perception—definitions of health and illness and all related medical theoretical concepts—the interests of both the capitalist class and the medical profession were tied to the promotion of the medical scientific paradigm. In the domain of medical practice, however, the interests of these two parties diverged, with each seeking to gain exclusive control over the provision of services. Interestingly, the nature of the *relationship* between medical theory and practice within both the private practitioner and corporate models ultimately determined the outcome of the conflict between the two parties.

Of course, the conflict between the profession and the various corporate groups seeking to gain entry to the medical market did not remain static but continued to change over time. As with all conflict between powerful contending interests, the socio-economic structures that form the context of the struggle constantly change, which alters the character and distribution of resources that can be used by the parties involved. In this particular struggle, what fundamentally altered the situation was the medical profession's gradual loss of its principle resource—the dependency of patients upon their private practitioners. Through the middle decades of the twentieth century, there was little outward evidence of any change in the structural foundations of professional sovereignty. During this period, the medical profession seemed to enjoy complete control over the means of health production and acted as the premier interest group in health care politics (cf. Starr 1982, 335–378). Despite the appearance of stasis, however, steady and almost imperceptible changes *were* taking place at the level of the "forces of medical production." The most important of these latter changes was the evolving character of the relationship between medical theory and medical practice, from a relationship of opposition toward one of identity. This change served to steadily erode the foundations of patient dependency on private practitioners, which, in turn, opened the door for corporate forces to enter the medical market.

As noted above the medical scientific model represented, at best, an ideal type when the formal campaign to reorganize medical education occurred at the beginning of this century. However, the factors that accounted for the discrepancy between the formal medical model and actual medical practice began to disappear in subsequent decades. First, an important demographic shift occurred: older physicians, many of whom had received their formal medical education in proprietary schools and had been influenced by the sectarian perspectives, began to leave the profession and were replaced by physicians who had acquired their training in the post-Flexner period. Although the younger physicians had been influenced in their practical, clinical training by their less scientifically oriented elders, the younger doctors had much less of an ideological commitment to the family practice model.

Second, as the pedagogical techniques for educating physicians became more sophisticated and as technical accomplishments and knowledge within the basic biological sciences accumulated, medical students gradually came to more fully internalize the medical scientific perspective in their formal medical training. Obviously, spectacular progress in the treatment of certain acute disorders served to convince more and more medical trainees of the basic efficacy of medical science, even for the treatment of the nonacute problems that would constitute the bulk of most doctors' practices. While the discovery of medical scientific techniques for treating relatively rare disorders have only minor impact on the general health of the population, they typically have a much greater impact on the legitimacy of the model as a whole.

A third factor contributing to the breakdown of the contradiction between theory and practice involves the specific economic interests of later generations of physicians. The corporate approach to organizing medical practice, which accepts the basic identity between the medical scientific paradigm and efficient medical production, was increasingly embraced by later generations of private practitioners who had become more concerned than their predecessors about increasing their earning capacity. The most direct way for a private practitioner to increase cash flow is to undertake measures to increase the volume of patient visits. An increase in volume, in turn, means that less time can be taken with each individual patient. For older physicians who were strongly committed to the family practice model, spending less time with patients violated the standards of "good medical practice" because it limited the physician's ability to collect information about the social, psychological and/or spiritual conditions of the patient's existence. For later generations of physicians, however, limiting the length of patient visits by restricting clinical assessment to the patient's biological condition only was perfectly consistent with medical scientific standards of competent medical practice. In the medical scientific view, the patient is a representative instance of a standard disease category—nothing more, nothing less. To spend extra time relating to patients as people, i.e., as complex social, psychological, historical entities, may constitute "good bedside manner" but it contributes nothing to resolving their health problems. In short, an approach to patient care in which physicians make maximum use of their time by narrowing attention to the data needed for diagnosing disease makes good sense from both an economic and professional point of view.

Finally, the growing identity between medical scientific theory and actual medical practice can also be related to some of the broad historical changes in United States society in the twentieth century, trends that are most commonly associated with the disappearance of the family physician. The concern within classical social theory with the historical movement from mechanical to organic solidarity (Durkheim), from *Gemeinschaft* to *Gesellschaft* (Tönnies), from a society based on primary relations to one in which secondary relations predominate, speaks to the kind of historical change that has contributed to a weakening of emotional and psychological ties between most societal members, including patients and practitioners. Increases in urbanization and social and geographic mobility in American society have diminished the possibilities for patients to establish long-term relationships with their doctors. More and more, patients and physicians face one another in the medical encounter as strangers. Because the likelihood of geographic or career moves by either party is fairly high, there is little possibility for establishing a close relationship. The only thing that would mitigate the anonymity of such relationships would be an extensive and time-consuming review of both the patient's and practitioner's psychosocial history as a prerequisite to every newly formed therapeutic relationship. Such a procedure is not therapeutically indicated by the medical scientific model, however.

These social, cultural, economic, and demographic factors set the direction of change for the evolving relationship between the ideal/formal model of medical practice and the actual clinical behavior of practicing physicians. In the span of the last seven or eight decades, the relationship between medical theory and practice has undergone a transformation from a contradiction to a virtual identity. We have witnessed in this century the gradual diminishing of the discrepancy between the dictates of the formal medical scientific model and the daily practice of working physicians. The most important consequence of this transformation is, of course, the impact it has had on the patient-practitioner relationship.

If the contradiction between medical theory and medical practice contributed in large part to the phenomenon of patient dependency in earlier years, the disappearance of this contradiction in the last several decades has accounted for a recent decline in patient dependency. Ever larger populations of patients and practitioners now confront one another in the medical encounter as anonymous individuals engaged in a strictly functional exchange relationship. Within this context, the norm of functional specificity (Parsons 1951, 435) is perfectly appropriate as a standard for the behavior of both patients and practitioners. Physicians do not need to know anything about the personal and social life of their patients in order to render competent professional service to them; nor do patients need to rely on personal information about physicians as a criterion for selecting who they will patronize. For patients who accept the profession's claim that it has insured the general competency of its members, one physician is as good as another for providing the service they need. All competent physicians should see the same things when they diagnose a patient's illness; a physician who knows one's personal history is no more likely to provide good medical care as one who knows nothing of this history.

This analysis of the decline of patient dependency is critical to any effort to fully understand the recent dramatic developments in the medical sector, involving the eclipse of professional sovereignty and the unprecedented success of recent corporate incursions into the medical market. Past analyses of these recent changes have emphasized a variety of social and economic factors, but all have, unfortunately, ignored the most important force behind the transformation. Just as patient dependency acted as a distorting influence on the medical market in an earlier period, the decline of patient dependency in recent years has moved the medical market in the direction of the ideal competitive model. Corporate experiments in the past failed because corporate health care organizations could not attract patients away from private practitioners. Conversely, corporate medical organizations are experiencing some success today because they have managed to attract patients away from private practitioners. Patients now rarely consider a doctor's understanding of their personal histories as crucial to the success of medical treatment, therefore, they pay little attention to interpersonal factors in selecting a physician, and the more standard criteria used to select goods and services prevail, i.e., such things as price and availability. When medical services are judged by this latter set of criteria, corporate services become much more attractive.

In summary, recent changes within the health care sector are best understood by focusing on the historical evolution of the forces of health production—the conceptual tools by which disease is recognized and the therapeutic behavior of those who possess these conceptual tools. Like the forces of production in other domains, medical productive forces have never remained static but have experienced ongoing change and development. This development has taken the form of diachronic Relations passing through phases of contradiction and identity in a never ending dialectical sequence. I have gone to some lengths to demonstrate how the nature of the medical forces of production, i.e., the predominance of either contradiction or identity in the relationship between medical theory and practice, comes to structure the "relations of production" in the medical sector, that is, the political-economic arrangements within the health care system. This is not to imply that the relationship between theory and practice is the *only* factor that contributed to the recent changes in the medical sector but rather to suggest that this relationship has played a central role in the transformation.

CHAPTER EIGHT

Emerging Trends: Back to the Future

The diachronic analysis of American medicine contained in the preceding chapter has taken us a great distance—from the system of medical practice that prevailed in the eighteenth and nineteenth centuries and the transformations wrought by the Flexner revolution to the fundamental changes that are currently taking place with the movement of corporate forces into the medical market. As I noted in discussing the theoretical/ methodological framework for this study, the diachronic analysis of a system involves both the study of the existing system's relation to its past structure *and* its relation to its future structure. I have addressed this latter task by constructing a utopian medical system to serve the interest of most members of American society. As a practical matter, this medical utopia will be brought about only by investing intellectual and political resources into a well organized movement for social change. In order to maximize the likelihood of this development, though, the utopian vision of the future of medicine must be reconciled with the various trends and tendencies that are currently transforming the system. We must consider at this point where the system seems to be heading, using the preceding analysis as a basis for identifying the parameters of these emerging trends. A comprehensive analysis of the future diachronic Relations of medical practice should involve not only a description of desired alternatives but also a sober assessment of how these alternatives relate to the transforming forces of the system.

At the end of the previous chapter, attention was focused on the forces that have contributed to the recent success of corporate initiatives for gaining access to the market for medical services. The problem of concern to recent observers of the corporate incursion into medicine is assessing the impact of this change on the future structure of the system. Those who have helped promote the movement of corporations into medicine believe that the forces of the "free market" will bring about positive changes in the system—high quality care at lower cost to the consumer. According to this perspective, the

221

recent decline in professional power and autonomy and the growing predominance of wage earner status among physicians can only benefit the system because most of the past problems with medical sector stem from the guild-like character of medical practice. The superiority of the corporate model has been demonstrated in every other sector of the U.S. economy so it makes good sense to extend the model to the medical sector.

In contrast to this view, some see the possibility of negative consequences arising from the growth of corporate medicine and the physician's transformation to a wage earner status. The argument here also rests upon a comparison between medicine and other sectors of the American economy. Neo-Marxists challenge the claim that the corporate model can insure the production of high quality goods and services at low cost and point to evidence that would suggest otherwise. Under conditions of corporate oligopoly, entire sectors of the economy are controlled by a handful of major corporations who make informal agreements to divide the market for their mutual benefit. In the absence of any real competition between producers, products become virtually indistinguishable from one another, and prices are kept artificially high. The people who actually produce goods and services (i.e., the workers) have little control over the quality of the things they produce or the conditions of work that directly impinge on their interests. From this point of view, the shifting of control within the medical sector from the medical profession to corporate forces cannot be seen as a positive development. Professional autonomy may be at the root of many of the problems that have plagued the system in the past, but this autonomy has, at least, protected the system from the rationalizing and exploitative tendencies of the corporate model.

As things currently stand, then, we find considerable confusion about how to evaluate emerging trends within the health care system. Some analysts, disturbed by the power and privilege of the medical profession in the past, may feel much more comfortable about a health care system under corporate rather than professional control. Other analysts, who have also been critical of professional monopoly, nevertheless may champion the cause of professional autonomy in the face of the rationalizing consequences of a system under corporate control. Adopting a position on this issue is made even more difficult by the fact that the transformation currently taking place has not presented alternatives clearly supported by existing political perspectives. For instance, liberal social scientists seem to be more troubled by the aristocratic nature of professional privilege than they are by corporate domination while Marxists see corporate control as the greatest threat to the system. For both groups, however, it is a close call. Only free market advocates are confronted with a clear-cut case: a system under corporate control is, to them, the best of all possibilities.

The present dialectical perspective provides a novel way of evaluating the recent changes in American medicine. One of the fundamental ideas guiding the analysis up to this point is the dialectical principle that every existing social system or subsystem contains within it the potential for transformation—the seeds of its own distruction, which also define the principle or principles by which the new system will be organized. We have seen how this dynamic has been revealed most recently in the medical sector. With the growing identity between the formal medical scientific model and the actual practices of physicians, the basis of professional control was increasingly undermined, and the stage was set for the emergence of control by corporate rationalizers. We can now refer to this same dialectical principle in speculating about the further transformation of the health care system, focusing more specifically on the new potential that exists in the corporate medical model. This approach allows us to identify both the positive and negative possibilities of the emerging system: the positive possibilities can be achieved through the collective effort of the patient population to develop the potential of the corporate model in a direction that maximizes patient interests; the negative possibilities are represented by the likely outcome of change in the system that is *not* directed by the collective effort of the patient population (and therefore controlled by groups that already possess great power).

I will begin by identifying the potential for progressive change (i.e., change in the direction of the countersystem model) that exists within the emerging corporate model. From the vantage point of the countersystem perspective, the system currently taking form under growing influence of corporate-bureaucratic groups possesses several positive potentials. First, corporate domination has in the recent past and will continue in the future to erode the general authority of physicians. One aspect of this decline in medical professional authority is a growing restriction of the profession's right to dictate the parameters of medical diagnosis and treatment. Just as the growth of professional authority occurred hand in hand with the growing legitimation of the medical scientific definitions of health and illness, the decline of professional authority may serve to diminish the legitimacy of these definitions. This creates the potential for the emergence of a system similar in structure to the health care system of the nineteenth century—a multiperspectival, multitherapeutic system in which nonallopathic physicians who offer efficacious therapy can develop a following within the patient population. This more holistic system would not represent a return to nineteenth century medicine because it would incorporate the important advances made in both allopathic and nonallopathic medicine during the last century. In the new system, patients would be allowed to escape their current reliance on a narrowly defined approach to diagnosing and treating their own problems. It would also create the structural potential for a change in the distribution of power between patients and practitioners. In addition to enhancing competition among practitioners, the greater perspectival heterogeneity of the practitioner group would undermine the ability of this group to collectively organize for the pursuit of its own narrow interests.

The opening of the practitioner role to nonallopathic physicians may also be encouraged by organizational changes presently taking place under the aegis of corporate control. In an effort to deal with the more specific problem of controlling the cost of health care (primarily costs incurred by employers and the government), policy initiatives by political actors committed to the corporate rationalization agenda have promoted the concept of health maintenance organizations as a delivery system that, in theory, reverses the logic of utilization embraced by medical organizations in the past. Whereas existing organizations have a market incentive to increase the utilization of their services, HMOs can operate profitably only by reducing their costs, which means they must not only strive to control the use of their services but also to organize the delivery of these services in a rational, efficient manner. Although there is currently much discussion about whether or not HMOs actually operate in accordance with these formal principles, evidence indicates that they have established a new distribution of manpower within their own operating domain. HMOs have increasingly relied on physician's assistants and nurse practitioners as substitutes for physicians in the provision of primary care. This practice brings significant cost savings with apparently few negative consequences in the terms of patient complaints about the quality of service.

The use of physician's assistants in place of M.D.s is a long cry from the multiperspectival ideal of the countersystem (after all, physicians assistants and nurse practitioners are trained in the same general perspective that physicians employ), but it demonstrates the potential that would exist for the HMO concept under proper interest structure conditions. In an organizational structure in which practitioner influence is effectively balanced by administrative control, the lower labor costs and potential therapeutic benefits of using alternative practitioners as substitutes for allopathic physicians can be realized. A crucial consideration, of course, is the problem of determining which particular interests will guide the administrative agenda. Under present conditions, the administrative agenda of most HMOs reflect corporate interests, which means that nonallopathic practitioners are not likely to be used in the provider role. As I argued in earlier chapters, corporate interests are firmly wedded to the medical scientific paradigm. While for-profit health care organizations may occasionally attempt to exploit the market for alternative approaches, corporate agents will continue to promote the biomedical approach and HMOs under their influence will restrict the practitioner role to those trained in the medical scientific paradigm. The interest structure of HMOs will be discussed in more detail below.

Another dimension of the HMO concept is relevant to the countersystem medical model. The formal principle that governs the operation of HMOs is the linking of profit-making potential to the restricted and rational use of services. The promotion of preventative health measures by HMOs certainly accords with this logic: these organizations have an interest in preventing the onset of serious illnesses that can consume vast amounts of organizational resources and, subsequently, profits. Embodied within this organizational structure, then, is a formal principle that supports many aspects of the countersystem approach although existing HMOs have generally failed to support anything other than curative medical practice.

In the present view, the failure of HMOs operating today to function as preventative health organizations or to transcend traditional forms of medical practice is due to the absence of a medical ideology that would allow them to realize their full potential. The countersystem perspective constitutes this missing ideological dimension. The HMO concept and the countersystem perspective are mutually supportive structures that, if merged, could produce a particularly effective health promotion institution. In addition to the aforementioned cost savings and therapeutic benefits involved in using alternative practitioners, an aggressive program for the development of self-healing capabilities in the patient population would be in the economic interests of the organization. Patients who possess the knowledge and ability to deal with their own health problems and who are normatively committed to this course of action would make minimal demands on the resources of their HMOs, which, in turn, would enhance the profitability of the organization. Moreover, encouraging people to adopt an ongoing campaign of health production, as called for by the countersystem approach, would actualize the preventative health agenda that HMOs, in their own economic interest, should seek to promote.

These ideals reflect only a small part of the potential that exists in the merging of the countersystem model with the HMO organizational form. If one adopts the holistic view of the determinants of health and illness as called for by the countersystem perspective, one could envision HMO operations being extended into many other domains that impact on the health of patient enrollees and, subsequently, the profitability of the organization. For example, recognition of the important role of nutritional factors in health would justify efforts by HMO administrators to influence the food consumption patterns of their enrollees by marketing food products in direct competition with corporate grocery store chains. In addition to producing another source of revenue, this expansion into food distribution would allow the HMO to structure the dietary practices of its enrollees in a way that reflects the organization's interest in keeping them healthy. Similarly, an understanding of the important relationship between physical exercise and health might justify the expansion of the HMO into the "fitness center" market. In doing so, the organization could direct the focus of physical exercise programs away from the narcissistic "hard body" emphasis that predominates in most fitness centers today to a more healthful agenda. To encourage enrollees to use the food and exercise services controlled by the HMO, a payment scheme could be devised in which individuals who invest their money in these services receive credits that can be applied to the costs of their HMO premiums.

The possibilities I have described here reflect a *potential* within the HMO structure that is logically consistent with the formal principle upon which it is organized. As I noted above, whether or not this potential is actually realized depends on many factors, the most important being the interest orientation of those who possess the power to shape the formal agenda of the organization. This point can be fully appreciated by considering another potential that exists in the HMO concept—the expansion of its sphere of operations into the political domain, involving efforts to deal with the social-economic determinants of health. Clearly, HMOs have an interest in promoting a political agenda for improving the quality of the ecological environment and for bringing about changes in lifestyle that enhance the general health of the population. In accordance with the data reviewed earlier in this volume dealing with the impact of ecological and social factors on human health, a population occupying an ecological environment relatively free of toxins and pollutants and a social environment that insures an equitable distribution of economic resources and offers freedom from threats to social-psychological balance and well-being (stress, etc.) would be a healthier population and therefore make fewer demands on the health resources of health care organizations. Once again, under these circumstances HMOs would have increased opportunities for turning a profit.

Only a political agenda of a decidedly "radical" character could be expected to produce the improvements in public health that would ultimately benefit HMOs. Advocating an agenda to create and maintain a healthful ecological and social environment would put such advocates in direct conflict with industries that pollute the air, water, and soil, that market health threatening products (alcohol, tobacco, etc.), and that organize production in a way that undermines the health of workers. If we focus more specifically on the relationship between social class and rates of mortality and morbidity, the radical nature of an "environmental" approach to health promotion becomes even more obvious. The indirect correlation between economic status and rates of mortality and morbidity (the higher one's financial status, the lower one's risks of illness or premature death) is a clear indictment of capitalism from a health care perspective. One could argue that if the maldistribution of wealth is an inevitable feature of capitalism, then the maldistribution of illness is also endemic to the system. Consequently, HMOs that take seriously the environmental perspective on health must stand opposed to the interests of some of the most privileged groups in America.

Another important potential therefore exists within the HMO concept— the possibility that HMOs could serve as an organizational base for a radical social movement to promote the structural changes needed to improve the health of the population. Unfortunately, the possibility for realizing this potential, along with other potentials I have identified, seems remote if not impossible in the current climate of health care politics. The fact that HMOs have functioned principally as a conservative force in the health care system thus far does not engender optimism about their viability as a tool for progressive change. However, it is important to look more carefully at the specific factors that define the operating agenda of HMOs, which ultimately determine whether incipient potentials are realized or thwarted. The key factor here is the interest orientation that lies behind the administrative control of HMOs.

Under conditions of corporate control over the administrative structure of HMOs, these organizations have failed to pursue the progressive agenda that their organizing logic seems to imply. As noted earlier, the HMO concept was originally introduced two decades ago (it was first championed by the Nixon administration) as a possible free market solution to America's health care problems. Advocates of this strategy held that introducing the profit motive into the health care industry at the organizational level would result in the growth of high quality, low cost services. Clearly, from the perspective of a corporately controlled HMO administration, there is no merit in opposing the actions of corporate organizations in other economic sectors: criticism of other profit oriented industries for acting in ways that threaten the health of the population may lead to a more general suspicion of the profit motive as a positive force in society, particularly within the health care system.

The more fundamental insight underlying this argument is, of course, the Marxian proposition that those who control the means of production will organize production in a way that maximizes their own interests. This insight helps us to sort through the current debate about the likely character of an HMO-centered health care system. Some have complained that HMOs today seem to be moving medical care in the direction of lower rather than higher quality services, with efforts to reduce services at the expense of adequate patient care. The proposition that HMOs would place cost-cutting goals above all other possible goals makes perfect sense when one considers the predominance of investor ownership among these organizations. If the principle concern of HMO management becomes the task of maintaining the organization's attractiveness to investors, insuring the short-term profitability of the operation must take priority over all other goals. In addition, others have pointed out in a different context (cf. Starr 1982) that for-profit health care organizations do not have to be in the numerical majority in order to dictate the operating philosophy of all competing organizations, profit-making *and* nonprofit enterprises alike. Nonprofit organizations must compete with their for-profit counterparts for a share of the market, which means that the nonprofits must offer many of the same services and adopt the same fiscal policy as the for-profits if they are going to insure their survival.

The narrow economic concerns of HMOs currently operating under investor ownership suggest that the progressive potential residing in the HMO concept for achieving many of the countersystem ideals can only be realized under conditions of patient-dominated HMO management. In a system based on patient ownership of HMOs, through cooperative or similar arrangements, patients would exercise direct control over one important component of the health production process and could, therefore, organize this process in a way that maximizes their common interests. Only under such an arrangement could the common ground between the HMO concept and the countersystem medical perspective be explored. Unlike corporate interests, patient interests are *not* firmly wedded to the medical scientific model, which means that the logical dictates for HMOs to promote self-care and the use of alternative practitioners could be realized. By the same token, no contradiction exists between the holistic/environmental health emphasis of the countersystem model and the patient-controlled HMO. For HMOs to serve as organizational bases for a political campaign against the socio-economic threats to health would involve interest group conflict, which is built into the very fabric of American society — essentially the conflict between the working and the capitalist classes.

The emergence of the HMO as a vehicle for health care delivery is just one small part of the many changes brought about by the corporate incursion into the health care industry. Other changes have involved such things as the growth of corporate hospital and nursing home chains, the emergence of new outpatient clinical services, and the integration of a variety of health-related services (insurance, primary care, etc.) under single-company administrative control. The cumulative effect of these changes has been to centralize and rationalize the health care system. Health care organizations have become more horizontally integrated with the decline of freestanding institutions and the rise in multi-institutional systems. Vertical integration has also increased with the shift from single-level-of-care organizations to organizations that offer multiple levels of care.

Once again, the ultimate effects of these changes will depend on the interest orientation of those who exercise administrative control over the entities that make up the emerging system. The continued dominance of capitalist interests will have a number of possible consequences. If the health care sector succumbs to the same tendencies of other sectors dominated by corporate forces, we could expect a growing concentration of ownership in this sector and a movement toward monopoly control of the medical marketplace. In addition to the loss of local control over health care delivery organizations, this corporate centralization would lead to a movement of capital away from the localities in which it is generated as national and multinational corporations pursue development opportunities that offer the highest possible return on their investment. One could also expect a loss of services in localities where corporate operations are not profitable and among nonprofitable populations (the poor, the elderly, etc.). Finally, the example of other corporately controlled sectors suggests that health care services will be increasingly standardized as managers pursue mass production and mass marketing strategies to increase their profitability (cf. Starr 1982).

These outcomes can be avoided and the progressive possibilities contained within the emerging system pursued if the administrators of the various entities within this system come to embrace the interest orientation of the patient population. The most obvious potential offered by the newly emerging system is the possibility for a much more efficient distribution of health care resources—manpower, technology, etc. With the increasing centralization of administrative control, the costly duplication of services that has characterized the highly decentralized system of the past can be eliminated. As noted in an earlier chapter, health care reformers have long clamored for the rationalization of the health care system in the United States, but they envisioned this taking place under state control rather than corporate control. The process of rationalization is presently under way, but the issue yet to be resolved is the problem of determining what sorts of changes will accompany this rationalizing trend. This is ultimately what is at stake in the struggle for administrative control of the newly emerging system.

Although one can easily envision the progressive potential of the HMO concept being fully realized under a system of administrative control reflecting patient interests, it is more difficult to specify the precise mechanisms of control that would allow a centralized and rationalized health care system to achieve countersystem ideals, *even* a system that is dominated by patient interests. In other words, a shift from corporate control of the system to state control in the interests of the patient public (which is the most likely mechanism of patient control) would not necessarily lead to all or most of the positive changes that we might envision for this system. The example of nationalized health care systems in other countries suggests that the bureaucratizing tendencies that typically accompany state control may well work against the progressive changes called for by the countersystem model. Nationalized health care systems appear to be similar to corporately controlled systems in their resistance to the principles of self-care, multiperspectivism, and political activism. Moreover, the gains in efficiency that accompany the centralization of the system could possibly be lost to the bureaucratic inefficiency of a state-controlled institution. The dilemma we face here is, of course, one of the central dilemmas of modern times: in those societies that have moved in the direction of state-run economies as an alternative to capitalism, the system rarely works in favor of the class interests it is designed to promote. Again, the thing that underlies this dilemma is the problem of bureaucratic domination, an issue that has become the subject of much discussion inside and outside of the academic world.

In the face of this difficult problem, one has to be impressed with the immediate potential for progressive change that exists within the HMO structure. A health care system organized around patient-controlled HMOs that are vertically integrated (performing multiple functions as described previously) would offer perhaps the greatest hope for the realization of countersystem principles. Such a system would avoid the negative consequences of corporate domination because patients rather than private investors would own and control the principle organizational means of production through coopt arrangements, patient/worker ownership, and similar structures. This model would also represent an alternative to the centralized and highly bureaucratized system that would likely emerge under state control. The competitive principles championed by free market advocates could operate in an HMO-centered system because individual organizations would have the flexibility to define the type and quality of their services however they wish and compete with one another for enrollees. This system of health production would represent a counterpart to the "industrial democracy" or "worker ownership" models of industrial production proposed in recent years (Vanek 1975; Whyte 1983; Bernstein 1980; Zwerdling 1980; Bradley and Gelb 1983).

The problems of defining alternative arrangements for ownership and control of health care organizations, specifying the structure of relations between the various components of the health care system as a whole, dealing with the dilemmas of centralized versus decentralized and bureaucratized versus market-oriented strategies are obviously all difficult matters for which there are no clear-cut answers. One thing is clear, however: the general direction of change in the health care system will be determined by the interest group that comes to dominate in the struggle for control over the means of administration in health care organizations. The future structure of the system will reflect the interests of the party or parties that exercise control over the key elements of the health production process. I have shown how this has been so in the past; it will unquestionably be so in the future.

WHO WILL CONTROL THE HEALTH CARE SYSTEM OF THE FUTURE?

What remains to be discussed regarding the future structure of health care are the various possibilities that exist for either maintaining or transforming the present distribution of power between competing interests. From the historical vantage point of the 1980s, three general trends can be identified that could potentially impact on the distribution of power in the system and, therefore, define the future course of development in the medical sector. These trends involve (1) the movement toward a further consolidation of control by corporate forces; (2) the movement within the medical profession toward alternative models of theory and practice that may allow it to reclaim its authority; and (3) the emergence of a popular movement within the patient population to redefine health production and gain control of it. I will briefly describe each of these developing trends.

One scenario for the future of health care in America, one that, by many accounts, is most likely to be played out, involves the further growth of corporate dominance within the medical sector. The example of other sectors of the United States economy suggests that once corporate organizations gain a foothold within a particular market, complete control of the market by an ever shrinking number of corporate giants is the most probable longterm outcome. Guild-like enterprises or other noncorporate groups ("mom and pop" enterprises) simply cannot compete with the large organizations that benefit from economy-of-scale operations and sophisticated, well-financed marketing strategies. Small operations that *can* survive in the market because they offer superior products or services are often eliminated as a source of competition through corporate buyouts. In general, large corporate enterprises have access to the capital resources that can allow them to weather any real challenge to their hegemony—as, for example, in the case of protracted "price wars," which are usually won by the organization that can operate at a loss for the longest period of time.

Thus, the parties whose interests are opposed to corporate interests, i.e., the patient and the health care worker (including the physician), both of whom supply crucial inputs into the health production process, confront a monolithic force in the form of the capital resources of their corporate adversaries. The power wielded by patients, which resides in their ability to purchase services from the supplier who best meets their needs, can be easily controlled through marketing strategies that shape the needs structure of the consuming public. Just as the public has been convinced that it needs the type of nourishment provided by fast food corporations, it can also be convinced that the standardized, prepackaged, impersonal medical services of a corporate provider are sufficient to meet its needs.

Similarly, the well-documented history of labor/management relations demonstrates the effectiveness of corporate strategies for dealing with the challenge to corporate interests posed by those who supply labor to the productive process. With the emergence of a corporate oligopoly within the medical sector, corporate administrators possess a powerful advantage in their negotiations with physicians and other health care workers. The informal agreements characteristic of monopoly capitalism allows medical corporations to pursue their collective interest in keeping the cost of medical labor as low as possible and undermining the power of this interest group. In the case of both the patient population and the population of health care workers, the possibilities for mounting a significant challenge to the growing ascendancy of corporate interests seem limited.

While this scenario may be the most likely course of development for American medicine, the picture has been somewhat clouded by other developments with important implications for health care in the United States. One of these developments is associated with the principle theoretical problem I have addressed in the study. Consonant with the sociology of knowledge focus of the analysis, I have demonstrated that the character of medical knowledge in every historical period reflects the social context in which it emerges; more specifically, medical knowledge systems function as ideologies that support competing interests within the medical sector at a given point in time. This has been the case in the past and will continue to be the case in the future. In accordance with this insight, one now finds evidence of a possible "paradigm shift" in the realm of medical knowledge (or, rather, medical *ideology*) that relates directly to the medical profession's growing awareness of the incompatibility of professional and corporate interests and its desire to reassert its power and authority in the medical sector. Not surprisingly, this paradigm shift involves the same polar dynamic that has figured so prominently in the evolution of medical knowledge in the past—the movement between the reductionist and holist poles in medical thinking.

This transformation has taken the form of two movements, which derive from different sources but which seem to be moving in the same general direction. The first of these movements involves the effort to promote the biopsychosocial medical model, which was described in chapter 4. As I noted earlier, a new faction within the medical profession consisting primarily of physicians with formal training in psychiatry, has recently sought to promote an approach to medical diagnosis and treatment with a broader focus, extending beyond the physiological and biochemical dimensions to include also psychological and interpersonal parameters. Articulated most clearly in the work of George Engel, this approach is firmly rooted in the positivist scientific tradition, relies very heavily on the "system" metaphor, and has defined the "more emergent," metaorganic dimensions of the human whole strictly in terms of existing scientific disciplines—biology, psychology, and sociology.

The second movement consists of a different group of mostly practicing physicians who have drawn on some of the modalities and ideas advocated by the broader holistic health movement—the source of most of the elements that make up the countersystem model described in chapter 4. While this group shares some of the same concerns of physicians who advocate the biopsychosocial model, they appear to be much less committed to the positivist scientific tradition, more open to the metaphysical and nontraditional categories used by the holistic perspective in dividing up the human Gestalt (i.e., "energy field," "spirit," etc.), and more willing to make use of nontraditional therapies. In general, this relatively small group of physicians seems inclined to look beyond institutionalized scientific traditions (social or biological) for ideas and therapies that they can employ in their practices (cf. Goldstein, et al. 1987).

The emergence of both of these factions within the medical professional contradicts the dominant trend in medical thinking and practice described in earlier chapters. While the practice of most physicians is consistent with the basic tenets of the formal medical scientific model (more consistent than it has been at any time in this century), the members of these two factions have been openly critical of the reductionist character of medical science and have endeavored to establish actual therapeutic alternatives for patients dissatisfied with the traditional medical practice. However, a close examination of the alternative models advocated by these two factions reveals that neither seeks to advance the countersystem model I have constructed in this study.

Although they embrace certain elements of this model, there is no apparent interest in the alternative medical division of labor called for by the countersystem. The logical affinity between the holistic view of health reality and the multiperspectival/multipractitioner division of labor (a division of labor open to practitioners trained in a variety of perspectives) has not figured into either group's vision of the future of medical practice. The position that both groups have adopted on this issue reflects their interests as medical professionals.

This can be seen most clearly in some of the literature dealing with the biopsychosocial model. George Engel's (1977 1980) descriptions of the biopsychosocial model not only identify general parameters for the proper space of medical thinking and practice, they also define the kind of practitioner role that would accord with this model. In this latter regard, Engel is clearly committed to medical professionals *maintaining* their control over medical knowledge as opposed to distributing medical knowledge across many different practitioner groups. This is revealed in some of his comments about the "biopsychosocially oriented physician":

> Some argue that the biopsychosocial model imposes impossible demands on the physician. This misses the point. The model does not add anything to what is not already involved in patient care. Rather, it provides a conceptual framework and a way of thinking that enables the physician to act rationally in areas now excluded from a rational approach. Further, it motivates the physician to become more informed and skillful in psychosocial areas, disciplines now seen as alien and remote even by those who intuitively recognize their importance. . . . The biopsychosocial physician is expected to have a working knowledge of the principles, language, and basic facts of each relevant discipline; he is not expected to be an expert in all (1980, 543).

In Engel's view, the biopsychosocial model should serve as a template for transforming the medical practice system at the micro-level but not at the macro-level. The preceding statement represents a call for *reform* of existing medical practice but certainly no fundamental overhaul of the system. The more holistic approach he advocates will simply build on "what is already there" in current medical practice, subjecting aspects of existing practice to rational, scientific organization and updating the skills that most physicians currently employ. Most importantly, his model does not threaten one of the chief pillars of the existing health care system—the medical profession's control over medical knowledge.

Although research on the practices and attitudes of physicians within the holistic health faction of the medical profession has been limited, it is very likely that these physicians share the views of biopsychosocially oriented physicians about how best to distribute medical knowledge. Both factions believe that individual physicians should broaden the range of their knowledge and therapeutic practices, but they reject the idea that multiperspectivism in medical practice must go hand in hand with a multipractitioner system. The crucial point here is that the common agenda being pushed by these two groups of physicians could ultimately serve to reestablish the structural basis of medical professional authority within the health care system.

As I argued in the preceding chapter, the *real* basis of professional authority in the middle decades of this century was the close ties between physicians and their patients, which were fostered primarily by the family practice model embraced by a large number of physicians in this era. Although the medical profession has attempted, in various ways, to revitalize the family practice model, these efforts have largely failed, an outcome that is easily accounted for by the perspective of the present analysis. We have seen that the family practice model emerged as a product of the unique historical conditions that existed in this period. Because these conditions no longer exist, it is not possible to sustain the medical practice model that emerged out of them. A realistic alternative, however, is to reinstate some of the basic principles of this model in an entirely new form that reflects the unique social structural conditions of the present era. The call for holism in medical professional theory and practice, as voiced by the two physician factions described, represents an effort to establish such a system and the close physician-patient ties that it engenders.

Any implication that the efforts by these two professional factions to incorporate holism in medical practice and thinking is driven by a conscious motivation to reestablish professional authority would be misleading. To attribute such a motivation to these efforts would suggest that the physician advocates of holistic medicine possess a sociologist's understanding of the significance of the family practice model in the history of medicine (some perhaps do possess this understanding but most probably don't). The motives behind this effort are more practice-oriented than political. Some physicians trained within the medical scientific model confront firsthand the limits of this reductionist approach when they practice medicine in accordance with its tenets. The experience of daily practice may lead to a growing appreciation of the importance of the dimensions excluded from the medical scientific model. Consequently, when these physicians are exposed to medical perspectives that incorporate the excluded dimensions in a formal and systematic fashion, some are inclined to see definite therapeutic benefits in these alternative approaches. They might also find some personal satisfaction in the stronger ties that develop between themselves and their patients because of their commitment to the more holistic approach. In any case, physicians who have moved in the direction of a holistic health or biopsychosocial model seem to be impressed primarily by the practical therapeutic benefits of this approach in contrast to seeing this alternative model as tool for improving the standing of the medical profession as a whole.

In this sense, the current interest among some physicians in holistic medicine is comparable to the movement of physicians in the early twentieth century toward the medical scientific model. In the latter case, the motivations of some practicing physicians for supporting the changes brought about by the Flexner revolution were rooted in the perception of definite therapeutic benefits accruing to the new approach. This is not to deny that individuals in key positions inside and outside of the medical profession were promoting the medical scientific model for purely political reasons (cf. Brown 1979). We have seen the important role played by this latter group in institutionalizing the medical scientific model. However, we must remain cognizant of the mix of motivations that brought about this change, and attribute the success of the Flexner movement to the existence of multiple motivations among those who supported it. Either one of these groups standing alone would have found it difficult to push the Flexner agenda to a successful outcome.

Just as a mix of motivations was required for the success of the "science in medicine" movement, the effort to promote "holism in medicine" will have to incorporate groups with a variety of goal orientations if this movement is to achieve success. What is currently missing among the physician factions interested in holistic medicine is a goal orientation focused on the political significance of this transformation. We have no evidence at this point that anyone within the medical profession views the movement toward a holistic model as an effective strategy for reasserting professional authority. Indeed, there is little to indicate that members of the medical profession have even reached any consensus about the causes of recent changes in the health care system. In the absence of any recognition of the biopsychosocial medical model's potential as an ideology for advancing the interests of the medical profession, the chances of a wholesale shift to a holistic medical paradigm within professional medicine are greatly reduced. The failure of the holism in medicine movement could have significant consequences: with the loss of this potential for reestablishing close patient-practitioner ties, the medical profession's ability to reassert its authority in the face of growing corporate power will also be considerably diminished.

Finally, a third incipient movement within American society that could have important implications for the future of medicine can be identified. While the future of American medicine may be determined by the struggle between corporate and professional interests, a third interest group should not be counted out as a potentially influential force in the battle for control of the health care system. This latter group is, of course, the patient population.

Existing research dealing with the political economy of health care has tended to ignore collective action by groups representing patient interests as playing any potential role in defining the future of American medicine. This is not surprising considering the dearth of collective action on the part of the patient population during most of this century. In recent years, however, a number of developments within this population have increased the chances for the emergence of a broad-based movement to completely reorganize the health production process. As with the movement among physicians just discussed, this incipient movement among patients could easily lose steam or be entirely coopted by other interests in the medical sector, but it could also blossom into social movement that poses a significant challenge to the power of the interests currently dominating the medical sector.

The resource base for a health-oriented movement within the patient population has developed along two separate lines, one trend involving an explicit effort to organize collectively to transform health-producing behavior, the other trend consisting of more diverse changes within the cultural domain. The first trend has emerged under the banner of the holistic health movement whose perspective has figured so prominently in the present study. The second trend, which may have been stimulated to some degree by the holistic health movement, has been designated in the popular and academic literature as the "new health consciousness" (cf. Crawford 1984). Both of these indicate that some potentially important changes may be taking place in the health-related thinking and behavior of a significant portion of the patient population. The question to be addressed is whether these developments hold any potential for a revolutionary transformation of health care in America.

Although I have devoted significant space to discussing the ideological system embraced by the holistic health movement, little attention has been directed, thus far, to analyzing the movement itself. This reflects, in part, the fact that holistic health activities have not involved many of the features that have characterized more traditional social movements (i.e., a well-organized leadership cadre, an identifiable membership, and established lines of communication between members) and, therefore, may not even be properly classified as a social movement. My research indicates that the activities first identified with the holistic health movement took place in the early 1970s primarily in the West Coast areas of the United States. As an offshoot of the "human potential movement," the earliest efforts involved the dissemination of literature relating to alternative physical and mental health modalities. These early efforts led to the establishment of various holistic health associations throughout the country and a number of regional and national conferences held from the mid- to the late-1970s. As these sorts of activities have declined somewhat in more recent years, the movement goals and ideology have been taken over by more institutionalized entities—holistic health clinics and similar organizations that operate in most parts of the country.

The growth of interest in health promotion and fitness within the American population as a whole has been one the major cultural developments of the late twentieth century (cf. *Time* 1981). Robert Crawford's (1984) description of this trend captures its broad appeal and diversity:

> Health promotion and fitness have now acquired the momentum of a fad. Bodies are in motion on the jogging paths and in health clubs, with Jane Fonda, Diana Nyad, and Richard Simmons, with Jazzerciese, Jamnastics, aerobic this or that, Kinetics, Nautalis, even Believercise, a born-again version of the same. Anti-smoking has become a national crusade; nutrition the subject of endless conversation. Themes become entangled: body shape, fitness, strength, endurance, natural living, health, beauty, youth, longevity, disease prevention, wellness, and of course, sex appeal. So do the targets of concern: inside and outside, cardiovascular conditioning and waistline, physical status and social status.
>
> The commercialization of health and fitness is truly astounding. Advertising has attached every conceivable product to the changing physical fashion. A cascade of specialty magazines and books flood the market. Almost every major national magazine and network have run features on one or another aspect of the health and fitness revolution. In short,"health" and "fitness" are being manufactured. The complex ideologies of health are picked up, magnified, and given commodity form by the image makers (1984, 76).

What many critics of American medicine have failed to realize is that the current fad of health promotion and fitness has given rise to resources that are ripe for mobilization by a collective representing patient interests. To be sure, the various alternative concepts and practices for health promotion found within the population today are very diverse and, taken as a whole, evince a low degree of logical integration. However, the central assumptions that underlie the new health consciousness appear to be consistent with those of the utopian countersystem described earlier—such notions as personal responsibility for health, the lifestyle approach to health, and multiperspectivism. The countersystem I have constructed in this volume could be effectively employed to forge the disparate elements of current thinking about health promotion into a cohesive movement ideology. Most importantly, the countersystem would provide a crucial dimension of such an ideology, a dimension that is currently missing in the new health consciousness. This dimension involves the understanding of health and illness as essentially *political* issues, as problems that must be dealt with not only on an individual level but through the reconstruction of the socio-economic order as well.

I am fully aware that the present emphasis on the revolutionary potential of the current new health consciousness is at odds with the views of most leftist commentators on health care in America. Indicative of the latter group's position is Richard Brown's discussion of the holistic health movement and other self-help health care orientations (1879, 235–238). Brown argues that perspectives that emphasize personal responsibility for health constitute "blaming the victim" ideologies, which, like similar perspectives dealing with other social problems, direct attention away from the structural determinants of the problem by assigning responsibility for human misery to individuals themselves. I believe that this is a correct interpretation of the "personal responsibility for health" concept, but it applies to only one version of this notion. Only a nonsociological, nonactivist perspective on personal responsibility for health is subject to this criticism. When the notion of "personal responsibility for social problems" is placed within a sociological and praxis-oriented context, this approach can no longer be designated as a blaming the victim perspective. Personal responsibility within this latter context does not disassociate social problems from their structural determinants; it simply underscores the responsibility that people must bear for deciding to either acquiesce to social conditions that oppress them or organize collectively to change those social conditions. People are indeed to blame for the experience of poor health if they understand their condition to be socially determined and yet do nothing to change the society they live in. This sociologically informed version of "personal responsibility for health" is embraced by the countersystem perspective.

A related point has to do with strategic considerations that arise in any praxis-oriented social scientific enterprise. As I stated at the beginning of this volume, the principle goal of the countersystem method is to place social scientific analysis in the service of progressive social change. In a strictly academic exercise, we may find some amusement in revealing the conservative impulses that lie behind approaches that appear, on the surface, to be progressive in thrust. A praxis approach, however, focuses on the progressive potential that exists in any social form and seeks to identify the circumstances under which this potential can be realized. In pursuing this goal, it is important to remain cognizant of the conditions that can lead to a cooptation of the potential for meaningful social change, but this does not involve a casual disregard for potentially valuable movement resources.

In the present case, it seems prudent to look at a phenomenon like the new health consciousness as a resource to be shaped and mobilized for the purpose of advancing the interests of the patient population within the health care system. It is unclear at this point what particular interests will end up being served by this new health care ideology, but it makes sense to explore, in a positive way, how the perspective can be employed in the struggle to empower the patient population. This approach places primary emphasis on the problem of interpretation. As Robert Crawford (1984, 96) notes, "Stating the political connection . . . may contribute to the eventuality (of empowerment). Interpretation is itself a political act that occurs in an everyday context."

CHAPTER NINE

Epilogue

I have endeavored in this volume to describe a theoretical and methodological framework for sociological analysis that possesses great potential for dealing with many of the central problems faced by the social sciences today. To demonstrate this potential, I have employed the approach in the analysis of a major institutional sector of modern post-industrial society—the set of interrelated structures designated by the term "the medical-industrial complex." I now wish to offer some final observations about both theoretical and empirical matters of concern in this study.

First, the analytical power of the countersystem approach is revealed in the insights that have emerged in the preceding analysis of medical practice. This analysis demonstrates how cultural structures such as applied knowledge systems function as inputs within certain kinds of productive processes. Using the holistic health countersystem as an alternative reference point allows us to view the interrelated actions of patients and practitioners as a productive process that produces a specific form of value—the value of "health." In this realm of production, as in most other economic sectors, value is created by means that both reflect and define an opposition of interests among the parties involved in the productive process. The tools of production, whether they be technological or ideational in nature, are never politically neutral forces. The parties that control the means of production structure them so as to maintain their control and to advance their specific interests. While classical Marxian theory demonstrates this point within the realm of industrial production, the present study shows that this is also the case in a service industry like health care.

The analysis of medical practice undertaken here has implications for our understanding of other service occupations in which the possessors of "expert knowledge" can apply this knowledge to the resolution of personal or social problems. As I have noted elsewhere (Lyng, 1987), clinical medicine has served as an exemplar for many other occupations and

241

professions that employ applied behavioral science perspectives in their work. Consequently, most of these other applied disciplines embrace reductionist, micro-oriented models just as clinical medicine does. In doing so, they organize the process through which they render services in a way that maintains their control over these services and that contributes to the maintenance of the existing structure of privilege in the broader social order.

While reductionist applied perspectives have an "elective affinity" with the power structure of modern American society, holistic applied perspectives can exist only in a state of pronounced tension with this power structure. The inherently critical nature of holistic approaches typically puts practitioners who embrace them in direct conflict with those who most likely possess the resources to determine the success or failure of a profession. Taking these matters into account, then, we can easily understand why reductionist perspectives predominate within the consulting professions.

The power of the countersystem approach as a methodological tool for social scientific analysis is revealed not only by the present study but also by other studies which may not make explicit use of this method but which do employ it implicitly. For instance, two traditions within the medical sociology literature have relied on "analysis through contrast" to produce insights into the nature of medical practice. The most well known of these traditions is the model of professional medical practice articulated in its initial form by Talcott Parsons (1951:ch. 10). A careful reading of Parsons' early effort to identify the structural principles governing the organization of modern medical practice reveals his use of certain elements of the countersystem technique. By relying on a comparison between the professional model and the "free market," Parsons is able to identify the functions fulfilled by practice system organized around the application of expert knowledge by professional healers. In this analysis, Parsons essentially poses the question "why can't the market for medical professional services be organized in the same way that the free market is?" Hence, the insights he presents in this classic study emerge directly from the contrast established between the existing professional system and an analytically constructed system based on free market principles.

In choosing to compare professional practice with the free market, Parsons adopts the ideological stance of the medical profession itself, which has always sought to justify its special status in the division of labor by claiming that its work must be governed by higher standards than those that govern the marketplace (cf. Starr, 1982). Thus, the ideological content of Parsons' perspective reflects his choice of a countersystem. His analysis serves as social scientific legitimation for the sovereignty of the medical profession by relying on the same comparison that the profession has traditionally used to advance its interests.

One finds a similar connection between the countersystem adopted and ideological stance of a second tradition that makes implicit use of the countersystem method. This tradition, which has been advanced primarily by Marxist commentators on American medicine such as Brown (1979) and Navarro (1976), establishes a critical focus through the use of the "public health" model as its countersystem. As I noted earlier, even though the work of these scholars is not couched in the same theoretical/methodological terms I have employed in the present study, it meets the requirements of the countersystem approach. Unlike Parsons, who does not advocate the free market model as a practical alternative to the professional model, Brown and Navarro *do* see their public health countersystem as a practical alternative to the traditional medical model. More importantly, the macro-level focus of the public health model allows them to establish an analytical contrast with the micro-oriented (reductionist) biomedical model that yields a degree of insight unmatched by Parsons' framework. While Parsons merely systematizes and elaborates the viewpoint embraced by the medical profession itself, the Marxist analysts are able to trace the interrelations between the biomedical model and other social and political structures of modern American society.

My own reservations about the traditional Marxist analysis of the United States health care system, as noted above, have to do with the limitations of the public health model as a thorough-going analytical countersystem. Because this model focuses exclusively on the macro-level determinants of human health, it does not offer concepts that apply to the full range of interrelated structures that make up the human Gestalt, from those broad structures constituting the socio-cultural and ecological dimensions to the micro-structures within the psychological and physiological dimensions. Thus, I believe that what we can learn from the contrast between a countersystem and the existing system is limited in part by the scope of the comparison. This view dictated the choice of the holistic health model as the countersystem for my analysis of the United States health care system.

By synthesizing a medical countersystem that employs a sociological approach to conceptualizing medical reality (while also drawing on the perspective of a growing social movement within American society), I have endeavored to take advantage of a strategy first articulated by C. Wright Mills thirty years ago when he wrote of the "cultural uses of the sociological imagination" (1959:22). In Mills' view, the modern age increasingly demands that we deal with personal problems from a perspective that focuses on the connection between these problems and the historically evolving socio-cultural context in which they emerge. Defining individual medical "troubles" in terms of their relationship to various micro and macro social structures accomplishes this goal within the medical domain. Moreover, the broader scope of this new medical model allows us to address issues that have been ignored by the traditional Marxian account—such problems as patient control over the health production process, the objectification of illness, and related issues.

Despite the unique character of the medical countersystem synthesized in this study, the basic method by which insights were generated is similar to the method employed in the traditional Marxian analysis and, for that matter, the Parsonian analysis as well. In all three of these analyses, the effort to peer beneath the surface appearance of things started with the identification of an alternative analytical reference point—one that challenges our taken-for-granted assumptions about the phenomena being examined. Without this new reference point, we are relegated to viewing the structure in terms of conceptual categories that are shaped by the organizing principles of the structure itself. Under these latter circumstances, the most that we can hope for is an expression of the "truths" of common sense knowledge obscured to some degree by the mystifying language of social science. Many social scientific disciplines have been appropriately criticized in the past for not offering much more than this. In my view, the countersystem approach represents an alternative to this type of research.

While I have oriented the discussion of the countersystem method to my own field of medical sociology, the ideas expressed here are also applicable to other fields of study within the social sciences. Indeed, it is my hope that this method and the broader praxis dialectical framework to which it is tied will guide research in other empirical domains. I suspect that a close examination of past research in many different fields of social scientific study will reveal the same pattern I have discovered within the field of medical sociology: the reliance on the method of "analysis through contrast" either implicitly or, in some cases, in a more explicit fashion in many of the most insightful analyses within these fields. To maximize the possibilities for further progress in the social sciences, we must formalize this technique so that various issues not presently addressed by those making use of the countersystem method (either explicitly or implicitly) can be brought to the fore and made the subject of discourse—such issues as the political/ethical principles that underlie one's choice of a "contrasting case" or countersystem, the question of whether the countersystem is of sufficient scope to do the job for which it is designed, and a whole range of other theoretical and practical problems involved in countersystem analysis.

The greatest potential for the praxis dialectical perspective, of course, lies in employing the countersystem method for the analysis of entire institutional complexes—those constituting specific nation-states or designated by such terms as "post-industrial society." Such an undertaking is not unprecedented. One example of this type of analysis was discussed in an earlier section in which I attempted to show how classical Marxian theory can be construed as a form of countersystem analysis. Marx undertook the monumental task of analyzing an emerging socio-economic system in terms of both its diachronic (past and future) and synchronic Relations viewed in the broadest perspective possible. The success of this effort can be measured most directly by considering the intellectual and practical/political impact of Marx's work in the hundred years since his death. While this work has been extremely influential in the past and will no doubt continue to spawn valuable work in the future, contemporary critical theorists confront a troublesome fact: we live in a very different world today than the world that Marx inhabited. And although Marx was able to discern the organizing principles of a social order just beginning to take shape in his day, the emerging social order of our own time may be structured by other principles yet to be identified in any systematic way.

I will not attempt to describe here what principles may be involved in the emerging "post-industrial" social order of the present era but I can offer some reasoned speculations about the problem of identifying an appropriate countersystem for this task. First, it is clear that the problems we face today are of a much broader scope than the problems that concerned Marx. This is not to suggest that Marx's social problems perspective is no longer relevant to the contemporary situation: grinding poverty and the exploitation of workers continue to be critical problems faced by contemporary capitalism (conceived either in terms of national capitalist economies or the "world system"). Beyond these persistent problems, however, we face additional difficulties of global proportions that are unique to the modern era. Foremost among these is the problem of environmental degradation, of threats to the capacity of the planet to continue supporting life. While Marx's problematic focused primarily on the issue of human *species development* (i.e., full externalization of human "species-being"), we have been forced in the modern era to confront the new problem of *species survival* (of human beings as well as all other animal species).

This new problem must be a prominent consideration for any effort to synthesize a countersystem for the post-industrial era. Marx's "capitalist/communist" contrast does not sufficiently address this problem because both of these models incorporate the principle of mass production and distribution of commodities, a feature that appears to be a root cause of environmental degradation. The countersystem required for future critical theory must offer an alternative to the logic of industrialism that undergirds capitalist and socialist societies alike in the modern age. In a time in which we are witnessing what may be the greatest mass extinction of existing species in the history of life on earth, the need for a countersystem that addresses this problem is not only obvious but also urgent.

The capitalist/communist contrast also fails to shed much light on one of the central features of the post-industrial order—the set of micro and macro structural arrangements associated with the "bureaucratic imperative." Despite the variations in structural arrangements for ownership of the means of production in developed societies, all of these societies employ the bureaucratic model in organizing the means of administration within both the industrial and service sectors. The corporate bureaucracies that dominate capitalist world possess many of the same characteristics as the state bureaucracies governing socialist societies. In confronting this fact, critical theorists must ponder the possibilities for an alternative to the bureaucratic model, an alternative that would not only be viable in practical/political terms but one that would also provide a new reference point for the critical analysis of bureaucratic society. At present, it is difficult to conceive of such an alternative but I am confident that critical theorists possess the imagination to eventually solve this problem once consensus is achieved about the need to proceed in this direction.

The features I have mentioned here represent only two of several possible problems that countersystem theorists may wish to address. No doubt, many equally important issues should be taken into account in the effort to synthesize a utopian system for the future. To repeat, I cannot claim to offer here even the broadest outlines of the model that is needed for the countersystem analysis of contemporary post-industrial society. But I do believe that the time has come to begin articulating such a model. This task will likely require the collective efforts of people from many different disciplines and intellectual traditions and will probably involve considerable disagreement about what the future of post-industrial society should look like. But I think that consensus can easily be achieved among critically minded observers of modern society that we must begin a dialogue on this subject. Critical theory must move beyond its traditional ties to the utopian visions of nineteenth century thinkers. The seriousness of the problems we now face demands that we begin testing the limits of human imagination in order to solve them.

Notes

NOTES TO CHAPTER ONE

1. Following the convention established by Bertell Ollman (1976), I have chosen to capitalize "relation" (henceforth Relation) to designate one of the two separate meanings that this term carries in the present analysis. When the term "relation" (uncapitalized) is used, it will carry the more common meaning of a connection between factors, the relationship as distinct from the factors themselves. In contrast, the concept of "Relation" will refer to factors, units, structures, etc. conceived in holistic terms, as facets of a whole that cannot be clearly demarcated from other facets that make up the whole (cf. Ollman, 1976, 15–16).

NOTES TO CHAPTER FOUR

1. Craig, *Holistic Living News* (HLN), vol. 2(1):2.

2. Tiller, *Journal of Holistic Health* (JHH), vol. 3: 44.

3. Tiller, JHH, vol. 3:44–50.

4. Breaux, *Holistic Health Handbook* (HHH): 260.

5. Breaux, HHH: 260–261.

7. Lee, JHH, vol. 3: 64.

8. Travis, HHH: 94.

9. Lasater, HHH: 44.

10. Chang, HHH: 45.

11. Tribe, HHH: 80.

12. Khan, HHH: 271; Lasater, HHH:36

13. Chang, HHH: 45.

247

14. Lasater, HHH: 43–44.

15. Behramji, HLN, vol. 2(1): Lasater, HHH: 36.

16. Benedict, HHH: 85.

17. Fryling, HHH: 227.

18. Pannelier, JHH, vol. 3: 116.

19. Polidera, JHH, vol. 3: 79.

20. Chang, HHH: 47.

21. Polidora, JHH, vol. 3: 79.

22. Chang, HHH: 49.

23. Hoff, HHH: 206.

24. Lasater, HHH: 39.

25. Lasater, HHH: 42.

26. Polidora, JHH, vol. 3: 81.

27. Polidora, JHH, vol. 3: 78.

28. Levin, Lowell, Alfred H. Katz and Eric Holst, 1976, p. 31.

29. Tribe, HHH: 80.

30. Tiller, JHH, vol. 3: 46–47.

31. Lasater, HHH: 43; Knutsen, HHH: 255; Morris, HHH: 242; Fryling, HHH: 227; Leeds, HHH: 168; Spear, JHH, vol. 3: 99.

32. Khan, HHH: 271.

33. Cf. Moore and Moore, 1983, for additional data related to these ideas.

34. Breaux, HHH: 264.

35. Pannetier, JHH, vol. 3: 118.

36. Breaux, HHH: 260.

37. Pierce, HHH: 199.

38. Hoff, HHH: 209.

39. Grow, HHH: 151.

40. Leeds, HHH: 166.

41. Elke and Risman, HHH: 175.

42. Scully, HHH: 203.

43. Hoff, HHH: 209.

44. Fryling, HHH: 227

45. Siegal, HHH: 239.

46. Morris, HHH: 241.

47. Speeth, HHH: 248.

48. Rainbow-Wind, HHH: 361.

49. Picker, HHH: 368.

50. Picker, HHH: 369.

51. Pannetier, JHH, vol. 3: 116.

52. Lasater, HHH: 39.

53. Lasater, HHH: 37.

54. Leeds, HHH: 166.

55. Scully, HHH: 201.

56. Fryling, HHH: 227.

57. Speeth, HHH: 249.

58. Polidora, JHH, vol. 3: 79.

59. Fryling, HHH: 228.

60. Gawain, HHH: 374.

61. Speeth, HHH: 250.

62. Pannetier, JHH, vol. 3: 116; Tribe, HHH: 80.

63. Polidora, JHH, vol. 3: 75.

64. Knutsen, HHH: 225–256.

65. Brint, HHH: 161.

66. Brint, HHH: 161.

67. Hoff, HHH: 208.

68. Lee, JHH, vol. 3: 63.

69. Ibid.

70. Siegal, HHH: 234.

71. Solomon, JHH, vol. 3: 96.

72. Fryling, HHH: 227.

73. Leeds, HHH: 168.

74. Picker, HHH: 370.

75. Rainbow-Wind, HHH: 359.

76. Picker, HHH: 370.

77. Knutsen, HHH: 255.

78. Chang, HHH: 47.

79. Benedict, HHH: 84.

80. Brint, HHH: 163; Khan, HHH: 271.

81. Tiller, JHH, vol. 3: 49.

82. Tiller, JHH, vol. 3: 47.

83. Breaux, HHH: 264.

84. Vithoulkas, HHH: 89.

85. Hoff, HHH: 206.

86. Vithoulkas, HHH: 93.

87. Selye, Hans. 1976.

88. Lee, JHH, vol. 3: 62.

89. Breaux, HHH: 264.

90. Peck, HHH: 268.

91. Pannetier, JHH, vol. 3: 116.

92. Vithoulkas, HHH: 91; Hoff, HHH: 206; Rainbow-Wind, HHH: 360–361; Lee, JHH, vol. 3: 64.

93. Cf. McKinley and McKinley, 1977; Powles, 1973; Rydell, 1976; Eyer, 1984.

94. Tribe, HHH: 80.

95. Breaux, HHH: 260.

96. Breaux, HHH: 264.

97. Ardell, HHH: 407.

98. Peck, HHH: 267.

99. Benedict, HHH: 84; Vithoulkas, HHH: 92–93.

100. Ibid.

101. Hoff, HHH: 209; Pierce, HHH: 200.

102. Vithoulkas, HHH: 91.

103. Vithoulkas, HHH: 90.

104. Ibid.

105. Tiller, JHH, vol. 3: 46–47.

106. Tubesing, JHH, vol. 3: 72.

107. Chang, HHH: 51.

108. Brint, HHH: 157.

109. Brint, HHH: 159.

110. Leeds, HHH: 165.

111. Pannetier, JHH, vol. 3: 117.

112. Polidora, JHH, vol. 3: 77.

113. Brint, HHH: 163.

114. Kubler-Ross, HHH: 349.

115. Picker, HHH: 367.

116. Miles, HHH: 23.

117. Picker, HHH: 366.

118. Tribe, HHH: 80.

119. Vithoulkas, HHH: 91.

120. Lee, JHH, vol. 3: 64.

121. Pannetier, JHH, vol. 3: 118.

122. Lee, JHH, vol. 3: 64.

123. Tribe, HHH: 80.

124. Gawain, HHH: 375.

125. Lasater, HHH: 37.

126. Richter, HLN 2(1): 8–9.

127. Leeds, HHH: 168; Fryling, HHH: 227.

128. Peck, HHH: 267; Tubesing, JHH, vol. 3: 67, 73, 74.

129. Tribe, HHH: 80; Vithoulkas,HHH: 91.

130. Lee, JHH, vol. 3: 65.

131. Troyer, HLN, vol. 2(1), p. 6.

132. Chang, HHH: 45–46.

133. Binik, HHH: 105.

134. Rainbow-Wind, HHH: 361.

135. Vithoulkas, HHH: 89.

136. Chang, HHH: 52.

137. Ansher, HLN, vol. 2(1): 10; Pannetier, JHH, vol. 3: 168; Tribe, HHH: 80.

138. Greer, JHH, vol. 3: 99.

139. Lee, JHH, vol. 3: 64.

140. Hoff, HHH: 206; Lee, JHH, vol. 3: 64.

141. Hayes-Bautista, HHH: 402.

142. Tribe, HHH: 81; Travis, HHH: 98; Spear, JHH, vol. 3: 99; Ardett, HHH: 409; Levins, 1976: 63; Tubesing, JHH, vol. 3: 73.

143. Levin, et al., 1976: 43.

NOTES TO CHAPTER FIVE

1. Burns 1976: 202; Rosenkrantz, 1976:373.

2. Feinstein 1967: 24.

3. Feinstein 1967: 78.

4. Feinstein 1967: 137.

5. Feinstein 1967: 135.

6. Feinstein 1967: 78.

7. Murphy 1976: 112.

8. Adelman and Adelman 1977: 61.

9. Feinstein 1967: 131.

10. Feinstein 1967: 131.

11. Foucault 1973: 90.

12. Feinstein 1967: 24.

13. Feinstein 1967: 78.

14. Feinstein 1967: 78.

15. Foucalt Ch. 7.

16. Spaeth and Barber 1980: 16.

17. Murphy 1976: 120.

18. Rosenkrantz 1976: 373.

19. Murphy 1976: 120, emphasis mine.

20. Forstrom 1977: 9.

21. Feinstein 1967: 330.

22. Toulmin 1976: 43.

23. Wartofsky 1976: 293.

24. Murphy 1976: 82–83.

25. Murphy 1976: 94–98.

26. Murphy 1976: 86.

27. Feinstein 1967: 4,5.

28. Feinstein 1967: 12.

29. Feinstein 1967: 8.

30. Murphy 1976: 101.

31. Murphy 1976: 103.

32. Murphy 1976: 109.

33. Toulmin 1976: 44.

34. Wartofsky 1976: 293.

35. Heelan 1977: 28,30.

36. Heelan 1977: 31.

37. Feinstein 1967: 131–132.

38. Murphy 1976: 50.

39. Foucault 1973: 155–156.

40. Rosenkrantz 1976: 375.

41. Feinstein 1967: 133–134.

42. Feinstein 1967: 25–26

References

Adelman, Howard and Allan Adelman (1977). "Explorations toward a logic of empirical discovery: A case study in clinical medicine." *Journal of Philosophy* 2(1): 54–70.

Albrow, Martin (1974). "Dialectical and categorical paradigms of a science of society." *Sociological Review* 22(May): 183–201.

Alford, Robert (1972). "The political economy of health care: dynamics without change." *Politics and Society* 2(2): 127–164.

_____. (1975). *Health Care Politics: Ideological and Interest Group Barriers to Reform.* Chicago: University of Chicago Press.

Althusser, Louis and Etienne Balibar (1970). *Reading Capital.* Translated by B. Brewster, London: NLB.

Antonovsky, Aaron (1972). "Social class, life expectancy and overall mortality." pp. 5–30 in E.G. Jaco (ed.) *Patients, Physicians and Illness.* New York: Free Press.

Applebaum, Richard P. (1978). "Marx's theory of the falling rate of profit: towards a dialectical analysis of structural social change." *American Sociological Review* 43(Feb.): 67–80.

Arrow, Kenneth (1963). "Uncertainty and the welfare economics of medical care." *American Economic Review* 53(Dec.): 941–69.

Alexander, J.C., B. Giesan, R. Munch, and N.J. Smelser, (1987). *The Micro-Macro Link.* Berkeley, CA: University of California Press.

Baillie, J. B. (1966). "Introduction," in *The Phenomenology of Mind* by G.W.F. Hegel, translated by J. B. Baillie. London: George Allen and Unwin Ltd.

Ball, Richard A. (1979). "The dialectical method its application to social theory." *Social Forces* 57(May): 785–798.

255

Batiuk, M. E. and H. L. Sacks, (1981). "George Herbert Mead and Karl Marx: exploring consciousness and community," *Symbolic Interaction* 4(2): 207–223.

Bauman, Edward, Armand Ian Brint, Lorin Piper and Pamela A. Wright, (eds.) (1978). *The Holistic Health Handbook*. Berkeley, California: And/Or Press.

Benson, J. Kenneth (1977). "Organizations: a dialectical view." *Administrative Science Quarterly* 22(March): 1–21.

Berger, Peter L. and Thomas Luckmann (1967). *The Social Construction of Reality*. Garden City, N.Y.: Anchor Books

Berlant, Jeffrey L. (1975). *Profession and Monopoly: A Study of Medicine in the United States and Great Britain*. Berkeley CA: University of California Press.

Bernstein, Paul (1980). *Workplace Democratization: Its Internal Dynamics*. New Brunswick, N.J.: Transaction Books.

Bertalanffy, L. (1968). *General Systems Theory*. New York: Braziler.

Blake, J. A. (1976). "Self and society in Mead and Marx." *Cornell Journal of Social Relations* 11(2): 129–138.

Blake, John B. (1977). "From Buchan to Fishbein: the literature of domestic medicine." pp. 11–30 in G.B. Risse, R.L. Numbers, J.W. Leavitt (eds.) *Medicine Without Doctors*. New York: Science History Publications.

Bradley, F. H. (1920). *Appearance and Reality*. London: Oxford University Press.

Bradley, Keith and Alan Gelb, (1983). *Worker Capitalism: The New Industrial Relations*. Cambridge, Mass: MIT Press.

Braverman, Harry (1974). *Labor and Monopoly Capital: The Degradation of Work in the Twentieth Century*. New York: Monthly Review Press.

Brown, E. Richard (1979). *Rockefeller Medicine Men: Medicine and Capitalism in America*. Berkeley, CA: University of California Press.

Burns, Chester R. (1976). "The nonnaturals: a paradox in the western concept of health." *Journal of Medicine and Philosophy*. 1(3): 202–211.

Carlson, Rick J. (1975). *The End of Medicine*. New York: Wiley.

Cassedy, James H. (1977). "Why self-help? Americans alone with their diseases, 1800–1850." pp. 31–48 in G.B. Risse, R. L. Numbers, J.W. Leavitt (eds.) *Medicine Without Doctors*. New York: Science History Publications.

Coleman, J.S. (1986). "Social theory, social research and a theory of action." *American Journal of Sociology* 91(6): 1309–1335.

Coulter, Harris L. (1977). *Divided Legacy: A History of Schism in Medical Thought (Vol. II)*. Washington, D.C.: Wehawken Book Co.

Crawford, Robert (1984). "A cultural account of 'health': control, release, and the social body." pp. 60–103 in J.B. McKinlay (ed.) *Issues in the Political Economy of Health Care*. New York: Travistock Publications.

Dietzgen, Joseph (1928). *The Positive Outcome of Philosophy*. Translated by W. W. Craik. Chicago: C. H. Kerr and Co.

Edwards, Richard (1979). *Contested Terrain: The Transformation of Work in the Twentieth Century*. New York: Basic Books.

Engel, George L. (1977). "The need for a new medical model: a challenge for biomedicine." *Science* 1976 (4286): 129–136.

————. (1980) "The clinical application of the biopsychosocial model." *American Journal of Psychiatry* 137(5): 535–544.

Engelhardt, H. Tristam, Jr. (1976). "Ideology and etiology." *Journal of Philosophy and Medicine* 1(3): 256–268.

Eyer, Joe (1984). "Capitalism, health and illness." pp. 23–59 in J.B. McKinlay (ed.) *Issues in the Political Economy of Health*. New York: Travistock Publications.

Feinstein, Alvan R. (1967). *Clinical Judgement*. Baltimore: Williams and Wilkins Co.

Feyerabend, Paul (1978). *Against Method: Outline of an Anarchistic Theory of Knowledge*. London: Verso.

Flax, Jane (1978). "Critical theory as a vocation." *Politics and Society*. 8(2): 201–223.

Forstrom, Lee A. (1977). "The scientific autonomy of clinical medicine." *Journal of Philosophy and Medicine* 2(1): 8–19.

Fox, Renee C. (1957). "Training for uncertainty." pp. 207–241 in R. Merton, G.C. Reader, P. Kendall (eds.) *The Student Physician: Introductory Studies in the Sociology of Medicine Education*. Cambridge, Mass: Harvard University Press.

Friedson, Eliot (1970). *The Profession of Medicine: A Study in the Sociology of Applied Knowledge*. New York: Dodd, Mead and Co.

Friedricks, Robert W. (1972). "Dialectical sociology: toward a resolution of the current 'crisis' in western sociology." *British Journal of Sociology* 23(Sept.): 263–274.

Foucault, Michel (1973). *The Birth of the Clinic: An Archaeology of Medical Perception*. Translated by S. Smith. New York: Pantheon.

Gasking, Douglas (1955). "Mathematics and the world." in Anthony Flew (ed.), *Logic and Language*. Garden City, N.Y.: Doubleday and Co.

Goff, T. W. (1980). *Marx and Mead: Contributions to a Sociology of Knowledge*. London: Routledge and Kegan Paul.

Goldstein, Michael S., Dennis T. Jaffe, Carol Sutherland, and Josie Wilson. 1987. "Holistic physicians: implications for the study of the medical profession." *Journal of Health and Social Behavior*. 28(2): 103–119.

Gouldner, Alvin (1970). *The Coming Crisis of Western Sociology*. New York Basic Books.

Hamilton, Peter (1974). *Knowledge and Social Structure: An Introduction to the Classical Argument in the Sociology of Knowledge*. London: Routledge and Kegan Paul.

Heelan, Patrick A. (1977). "The nature of clinical science." *Journal of Philosophy and Medicine* 2(1): 20–32.

Hegel, G.W.F. (1966). *The Phenomenology of Mind*. Translated by J.B. Baillie. London: George Allen and Unwin Ltd.

Heydebrand, Wolf (1973). *Hospital Bureaucracy: A Comparative Study of Organizations*. New York: Dunellen Publishing Co.

Holistic Living News, 2(1). August-September, 1979.

Illich, Ivan (1976). *Medical Nemesis: The Expropriation of Health*. New York: Pantheon.

James, Susan (1984). *The Content of Social Explanation*. Cambridge: Cambridge University Press.

Jenkins, C. David (1983). "Social environment and cancer mortality in men." *New England Journal of Medicine* 308: 395–398.

Joas, H. (1981). "George Herbert Mead and the 'division of labor': macrosociological implications of Mead's social psychology." *Symbolic Interaction* 4(2): 177–190.

Journal of Holistic Health, vols., 1, 2, 3, 4 (1976–1979). San Diego, California: Holistic Health Association.

Katz, Jay (1978). "Informed consent in therapeutic relationships: legal and ethical aspects." pp. 770–778. in Warren T. Reich. (ed.) *Encyclopedia of Bioethics*, New York: Free Press.

Kett, Joseph F. (1968 (1980)). *The Formation of the American Medical Profession: The Role of Institutions, 1780–1860.* Westport, Conn.: Greenwood Press.

King, Lester S. (1958). *The Medical World of the Eighteenth Century.* Chicago: University of Chicago Press.

Knorr-Cetina, K. and A. Cicourel, (eds.) (1981). *Advances in Social Theory and Methodology.* Boston: Routledge and Kegan Paul.

Krause, Elliot A. (1977). *Power and Illness: The Political Sociology of Health and Medical Care.* New York: Elsevier.

Levin, Lowell S., Alfred H. Katz and Eric Holst (1976). *Self-Care, Lay Initiatives in Health.* New York: Prodist.

Lichtman, R. (1970). "Symbolic interactionism and social reality: some Marxist queries." *Berkeley Journal of Sociology* 15: 75–94.

Light, Donald Jr. (1979). "Uncertainty and control in professional training." *Journal of Health and Social Behavior* 20: 310–322.

Lyng, Stephen (1988). "Holism and reductionism within applied behavioral science: the problem of clinical medicine." *Journal of Applied Behavioral Science* 24(1): 101–177.

Lyng, Stephen G. and Lester R. Kurtz, (1985). "Bureaucratic insurgency: the Vatican and the crisis of modernism." *Social Forces* 63(4): 901–922.

McKee, Dwight (1987). Interviewed in the *Schenectady Gazette,* 28, Jan. 1987 (Reported by Kathy Peterson).

McKeown, Thomas (1979). *The Role of Medicine: Dream, Mirage or Nemesis.* Princeton, N.J.: Princeton University Press.

McKinlay, J.B. and S. M. McKinlay, (1977). "The questionable contribution of medical measures to the decline of mortality in the United States in the twentieth century." *Millbank Memorial Fund Quarterly/Health and Society* (Summer): 405–28.

McLellan, David (1969). *The Young Hegelians and Karl Marx.* New York: Praeger.

Maines, D. R. (1982). "In search of mesostructure: studies in the negotiated order." *Urban Life* 11: 267–279.

Mannheim, Karl (1949). *Ideology and Utopia: An Introduction to the Sociology of Knowledge.* New York: Harcourt, Brace & Co.

———. (1952). *Essays on the Sociology of Knowledge.* London: Routledge and Kegan Paul Ltd.

Marcuse, Herbert. (1955). *Eros and Civilization.* Boston: Beacon Press.

Marx, Karl (1940). *A Contribution to the Critique of Political Economy.* Translated by N. I. Stone. Chicago: C. H. Kerr.

————. (1938). *Capital: A Critical Analysis of Capitalist Production.* Translated by Samuel Moore and Edward Aveling. London: George Allen and Unwin Ltd.

————. (1964). *The Economic and Philosophic Manuscripts of 1844.* Translated by Martin Milligan. New York: International Publishers.

Marx, K. and Engels, F. (1976). *The German Ideology.* Moscow: Progress Publishers.

Mechanic, David (1976). *The Growth of Bureaucratic Medicine.* New York: John Wiley.

Merton, Robert K. (1973). *The Sociology of Science: Theoretical and Empirical Investigations.* Chicago: University of Chicago Press.

Montagna, Paul D. (1977). *Occupations and Society: Towards a Sociology of the Labor Market.* New York: John Wiley and Sons.

Moore, M. C. and L. J. Moore. (1983). *The Complete Handbook of Holistic Health.* Englewood Cliffs, N.J.: Prentice-Hall.

Murphy, Edmond A. (1976). *The Logic of Medicine.* Baltimore: Johns Hopkins University Press.

Murphy, Robert F. (1971). *The Dialectic of Social Life.* New York: Basic Books.

National Center for Health Statistics. (1980). *Health United States, 1979.* Washington, D.C.: U.S. Government Printing Office.

Navarro, Vicente (1977). *Medicine Under Capitalism.* New York: Prodist.

————. (1984). "Medical history as justification rather than explanation:a critique of Starr's *The Social Transformation of American Medicine.*" *International Journal of Health Services.* 14(4): 511–528.

Ollman, Bertell (1976). *Alienation.* New York: Cambridge University Press.

Parsons, Talcott (1951). *The Social System.* Glencoe, Illinois: Free Press.

————. (1964). *Social Structure and Personality.* London: Free Press.

Pfeffer, Jeffrey. (1981). *Power in Organizations.* Boston: Pitman.

Phillips, D. C. (1976). *Holistic Thought in Social Science.* Stanford, California: Stanford University Press.

Poulantzas, N. (1975a). *Political Power and Social Classes.* Translated by T. O'Hagan. London: NLB.

———. (1975b). *Classes in Contemporary Capitalism.* Translated by D. Fernbeck. London: NLB.

Powles, J. (1973). "On the limitations of modern medicine." *Science, Medicine and Man.* 1: 2–3.

Rosenkrantz, Barbara Gutman (1976). "Causal thinking in Erewhon and elsewhere." *Journal of Philosophy and Medicine* 1(4): 372–384.

Rothstein, William G. (1972). *American Physicians in the Nineteenth Century: From Sects to Science.* Baltimore: The Johns Hopkins University Press.

Russell, Bertrand (1945). *A History of Western Philosophy.* New York: Simon and Schuster.

Rydell, Lars H. (1976). "Trends in infant mortality: medical advances or socio-economic changes." *Acta Sociologica* 19(2): 147–168.

Schneider, Louis (1971). "Dialectic in sociology." *American Sociological Review* 36(Aug.): 667–678.

Schutz, Alfred (1962, 1964). *Collected Papers, Vols. I&II.* The Hague: Nijhoff.

Schwalbe, M. L. (1986). *The Psychosocial Consequences of Natural and Alienated Labor.* Albany, New York: State University of New York Press.

Selye, Hans (1976). *The Stress of Life.* New York: McGraw-Hill.

Shyrock, Richard H. (1960). *Medicine and Society in America, 1660-1860.* New York: New York University Press.

Siegrist, Johannes (1984). "Threat to social stress and cardiovascular risk." *Psychotherapy and Psychosomatics* 42: 90–96.

Sigerist, Henry E. (1943). *Civilization and Disease.* Ithaca, N.Y.: Cornell University Press.

Simpson, George (1967). "Review of Peter L. Berger and Thomas Luckmann's *Social Construction of Reality.*" American Sociological Review 32(Feb.): 137.

Sjoberg, Gideon and Leonard Cain (1971). "Negative values, countersystem models, and the analysis of social systems," pp 212–229 in H. Turk and R. Simpson (eds.). *Institutions and Social Exchange: The Sociologies of Talcott Parsons and George H. Homans.* Indianapolis: Bobbs-Merrill

Smuts, Jan E. (1926). *Holism and Evolution.* New York: Macmillan Co.

Spaeth, George L. and G. Winston Barber (1980). "Homocystinuria and the passing of the one gene—one enzyme concept of disease." *Journal of Philosophy and Medicine* 5(1): 8–21.

Starr, Paul (1982). *The Social Transformation of American Medicine.* New York: Basic Books.

Struik, Dirk J. (1964). "Introduction," in *The Economic and Philosophic Manuscripts of 1844* by Karl Marx. Translated by Martin Milligan. New York: International Publishers.

Time Magazine (1981). "The fitness craze: America shapes up." 2(Nov.): 94–106.

Toulmin, Stephen (1976). "On the nature of the physician's understanding." *Journal of Medicine of Philosophy* 1(1): 32–50.

Turner, Ralph (1976). "The real self: from institution to impulse." *American Journal of Sociology* 81: 989–1016.

Twaddle, Andrew C. and Hessler, Richard H. (1987). *A Sociology of Health.* New York: MacMillan Publishing Co.

van den Berghe, Pierre L. (1963). "Dialectic and functionalism: toward a theoretical systhesis." *American Sociological Review* 28(5): 695–705.

Vanek, Jaroslav (1970). *The General Theory of Labor Managed Market Economies.* London: Cornell University Press.

Wartofsky, Marx (1976). "Editorial." *Journal of Philosophy and Medicine.* 1(4): 289–300.

Weber, Max (1965). "The social psychology of the world religions." pp. 267–301 in H. Gerth and C.W. Mills (eds. and trans.) *From Max Weber: Essays in Sociology.* New York: Oxford University Press.

Weiss, Paul (1967). "One plus one does not equal two." in *The Neurosciences: A Study Program.* G. C. Quarton, F. Melnechuk and F. O. Schmitt (eds.). New York: a Rockefeller University Press.

———. (1969). "The living system: determinism stratified." in A. Koestler and J.R. Smythies (eds.) *Beyond Reducationism.* New York: Macmillan Publishing Co.

Weiss, Robert J. (1980). "The biopsychosocial model and primary care." *Psychosomatic Medicine* 42(1): 123–130.

Winslow, C.-E. A. (1923). *The Evolution and Significance of the Modern Public Health Campaign*. New Haven, Conn.: Yale University Press.

Zaner, Richard M. (1976). "Toward a philosophy of medicine: editorial." *Journal of Medicine and Philosophy* 1(1): 3–5.

Zwerdling, Daniel (1980). *Workplace Democracy*. New York: Harper and Row.

Index

Albrow, M., 12, 25–26
Alford, R., 149–150, 153
Allopathic medicine, 176, 186–187,
    190–192, 196–197, 208–209, 224
Althusser, L., 19, 39
Anatomo-clinical theory, 2–4, 49,
    101–117, 120, 123–124
Appelbaum, R., 23–24
Arrow, K., 203–204

Ball, R., 13, 26, 52
Bertalanffy, L., 67
Biomedical model, 67–68, 84, 109,
    111–112, 225, 243
Biopsychosocial model, 67–68, 98,
    213–214, 233–236
Bradley, F., 18–20
Braverman, H., 128
Brown, E. R., 138, 143, 151, 153,
    193, 204–205, 239, 243
Buchan, W., 175
Bureaucratic model, 4, 140–153,
    157–158, 223, 230, 246; Weber's
    analysis of, 140, 147–149

Capitalism, 146–149, 152–153,
    166–167, 173
Chinese medicine, 83, 88–90
Clinical practice, 196, 200–203, 211,
    213, 217, 241–242
Common-sense knowledge, 24–25,

29–32, 37, 42, 68, 132, 164, 168,
    200, 244
Communism, 56–59, 64
Contradictions, 40–41
Corporate interests in medicine,
    150–160, 168, 193–194, 199–207,
    210–211, 214–232, 246
Countersystem analysis, 3, 4, 50–53,
    241–246
Crawford, R., 139, 238, 240
Cultural authority, concept of, 206–208
Curtis, A., 184

Demographic transition, 164, 217–219
Diachronic partiality, 32–33, 36, 41,
    53, 56, 71, 221
Diachronic Relations, 47, 100, 163,
    172, 196, 203, 220–221, 245
Diagnosis, control of, 61–63, 126
Dialectical development, 174, 177–179,
    188, 189, 202, 220
Dialectical paradigm, 1, 9, 14, 22–24,
    37, 40–42, 52–53, 64, 158, 163;
    formalist approach, 23–24; method of
    analysis, 9, 23, 27, 52; praxis
    approach, 24, 28–29, 31, 33, 99
Dietzgen, J., 17, 19–20
Disjointness, principle of, 110
Domain assumptions, 3, 64
Domestic medicine, 174–181, 186, 196,
    213
Durkheim, E., 218

265

Edwards, R., 147
Engel, G., 67–68, 233–234
Entelechial therapy, 80
Estrangement, 56
Exhaustiveness, principle of, 110

Feinstein, A., 110
Foucault, M., 107
Fox, R., 141
Friedson, E., 132–133, 151
Functional specificity, 142, 219
Functionalism, 23, 25–26

Gates, F., 194
Hahnemann, S., 185–188, 190
Hayes-Bautista, D., 94
Health, anatomo-clinical definition of,
    101–102; corporate definition of,
    139; countersystem definition of,
    64–76; ecological determinants of,
    67, 83–85, 92, 136, 169–172, 197,
    202, 226; historical improvement in,
    165–173;
metaorganic dimensions of, 85–88, 90,
    104–107, 145, 156–157, 165, 173,
    182, 197, 233
Health maintenance organizations,
    224–230
Health production process, 59–61,
    65–66, 88–89, 95–96, 101–102,
    120–135, 231–232; balancing
    activities in, 66, 73–76, 88–89, 101,
    114; growth activities in, 66, 76;
    maintenance activities in, 66, 76, 79,
    88–89
Heelan, P., 112
Hegel, G.W.F., 15–18, 21–22, 34, 40,
    56
Heroic medicine, 175–188, 196, 199,
    212
Histopathology, role of, 105, 107,
    112–114, 123, 155–156
Historical materialism, 172

Holism, 1, 14, 16–17, 23, 35–39, 68,
    94, 116, 128, 174, 177–179,
    182–183, 201, 214–216, 235, 242
Holism/reductionism polarity, in
    medicine, 174, 178, 183, 195–196,
    202, 233
Holistic health movement, 50–52,
    233–240
Holistic health paradigm, 55–98,
    111–112, 120–121, 125, 160, 187,
    190, 193, 225, 234, 236, 241, 243
Homeopathic medicine, 185–193, 209,
    212
Homeostatic mechanism, 73–76, 82–83,
    86–88, 106
Hospitals, bureaucratic organization of,
    144–146
Human gestalt, 65–66, 69–78, 81–86,
    108–109, 141–142

Individualism, 38–39, 201
Interest group relations, 130–133, 135,
    146, 153–154, 157–158, 203,
    207–208, 217, 224, 226, 228–232,
    241
Internal relations, theory of, 15–18,
    20–23, 71, 77, 166, 172
Intuitive knowledge, 79–80

James, S., 38–39

Levin, L., 76
Light, D., 142
Logico-deductive method, 9, 79–80,
    109

McKeown, T., 84, 164
Mannheim, K., 13, 49–50
Marx, K., 15, 17, 30, 34–35, 42,
    55–58, 64, 128, 140, 245
Marxism, 20, 23, 34–35, 39–41,

51–52, 55–59, 165–167, 204–205, 241–245

Medical knowledge dimension, 48–49, 58–59, 92–99, 119–124, 141–146, 232–235

Medical practice, relation to medical theory, 211–220

Medical scientific model, 99–100, 135–146, 154–157, 194–196, 212–219, 235–236

Mills, C.W., 243

Mind/body relation, 126, 187; dialectical approach to, 77–78, dualistic approach to, 69, 102, 125

Morbid anatomy, 119, 123–124, 136, 143

Multidimensionality, 66–67, 70–73, 76–77, 80, 93, 112, 156, 209, 214

Murphy, E., 108, 114

Naturopathic medicine, 81

New vigorous therapy, 185–187

Noninvasive therapy, 115–116

Ollman, B., 20, 42

Organic disfunction, countersystem approach to, 77, 81, 83, 85–92, 95; medical scientific approach to, 101, 104–112, 114, 116

Parsons, T., 121, 242–244

Particularism, 143–145

Patient/practitioner relationship, 53, 55; countersystem conception of, 95–97; future of, 235–236; historical development of, 204, 214, 218–219; ideal conception of, 58–64; traditional structure of, 154–158

Philosophical analysis, 49

Positivism, epistemological tradition of, 10–14, 22, 102; within social science, 24–25, 27, 30–34, 42–43,

68, 109, 125, 192–193, 201–202, 210–215, 233

Poulantzas, N., 39

Principle(s) of organization, concept of, 52–54; countersystem, 55–64; traditional medical model, 140, 142–149, 158–161

Professional authority, 208, 223, 235–236

Professional autonomy, 134–135, 143, 151, 158, 222

Professional organization, 132–134, 137–138

Pubic health model, 196–202, 243

Reciprocal causation, 11

Reichian therapy, 77–78, 82, 86, 88

Relations, analysis of, 25–27, 33, 36; countersystem, 62, 64, 77, 94–96; notion of, 20–22; social crystal, 37–43; traditional medical model, 119, 125, 140, 144, 146–148, 163–164

Rolfing, 77, 86

Rothstein, W., 176, 180, 185

Schneider, L., 25

Self-care, 60–61, 73, 75, 89–92, 96, 115–116, 124, 125, 134, 175–176, 179, 181, 196, 225, 228, 230, 239

Social authority, concept of, 206–207

Social crystal, metaphor of, 20, 37, 48, 62

Sociology of knowledge, 28, 30, 40, 48–49, 50–52, 93, 174, 232

Starr, P., 127, 138, 151, 154–155, 158, 175, 197–198, 205–208

Subject/object relationship, 25, 27–28, 77–78, 102

Supersession, 56–57

Surgery, 115–116, 121, 131

Synchronic partiality, 32–33, 35–36, 41, 71

Systems theory, 11, 15, 20, 68

Thomas, W.I., 126
Thomson, S., 180–182, 184–185
Thomsonian medicine, 180–191
Tiller, W., 69, 82, 87
Tonnies, F., 218
Toulmin, S., 48
Travis, J., 72

Uncertainty theme, 141–142, 144
Universalism, 142–143, 157
Utopias, countersystems as, 35–36, 246

Weber, M., 138, 148
Weiss, R., 67
Wholes within wholes, notion of,
    70–71, 81, 103
Winslow, C.-E. A., 202